THE ASTOUNDING

CREATED BY
ROBERT KIRKMAN & JASON HOWARD

image

ROBERT KIRKMAN
writer

JASON HOWARD
penciler
inker (chapters 8-10 & 12)
colorist (chapters 8-10)

CLIFF RATHBURN
inker (chapter 11)

RUS WOOTON
letterer

FCO & IVAN PLASCENCIA
colorists

INVINCIBLE #57
(CHAPTER 11, PART 1)

ROBERT KIRKMAN
writer

RYAN OTTLEY
penciler

CLIFF RATHBURN
inker

RUS WOOTON
letterer

FCO PLASCENCIA
colorist

IMAGE COMICS, INC.

Robert Kirkman - chief operating officer
Erik Larsen - chief financial officer
Todd McFarlane - president
Marc Silvestri - chief executive officer
Jim Valentino - vice-president

ericstephenson - publisher
Joe Keatinge - pr & marketing coordinator
Branwyn Bigglestone - accounts manager
Tyler Shainline - administrative assistant
Traci Hui - traffic manager
Allen Hui - production manager
Drew Gill - production artist
Jonathan Chan - production artist
Monica Howard - production artist

www.imagecomics.com

International Rights Representative:
Christine Jensen (christine@gfloystudio.com)

THE ASTOUNDING WOLF-MAN, VOL. 2
ISBN: 978-1-60706-007-9
First Printing

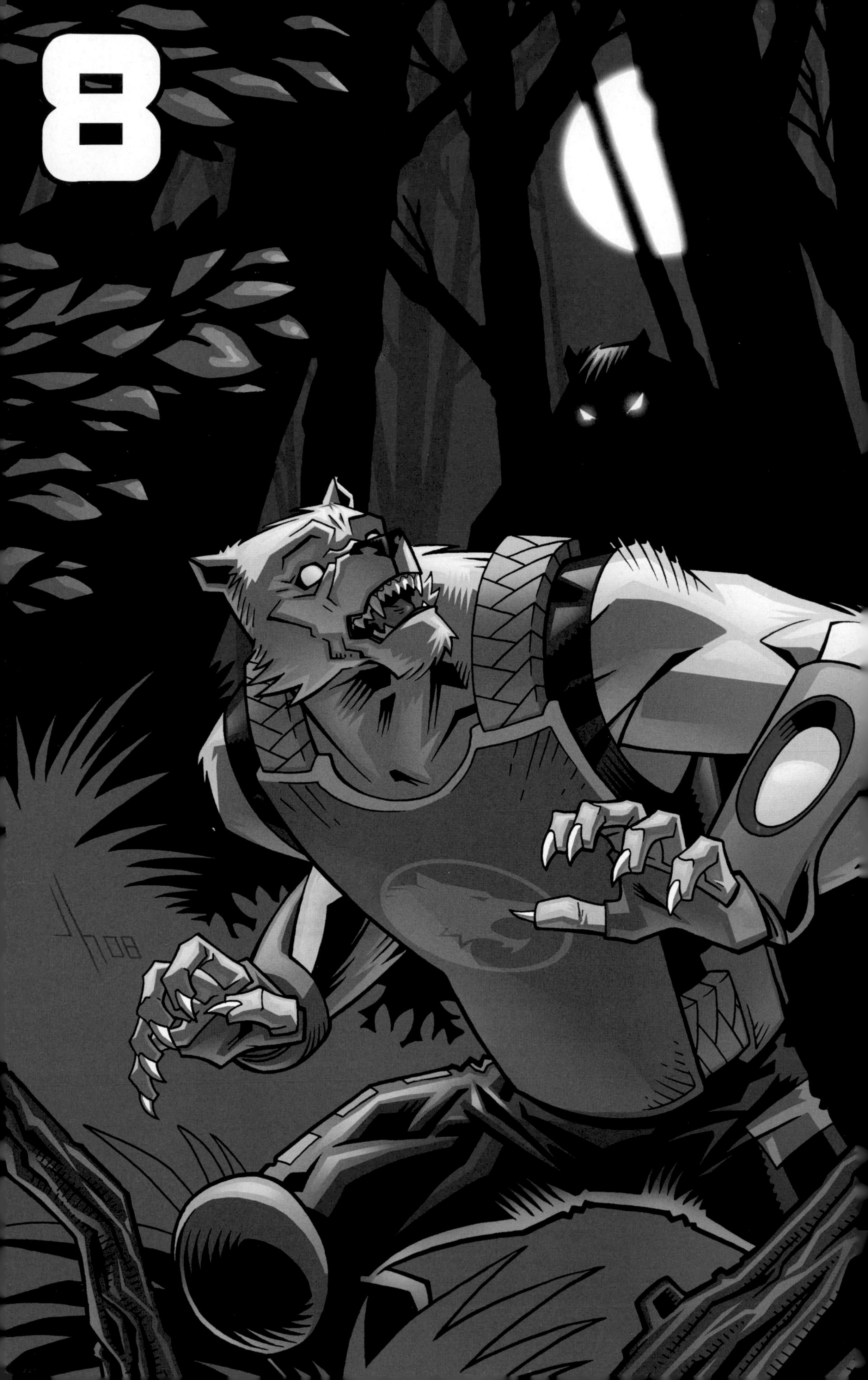
8

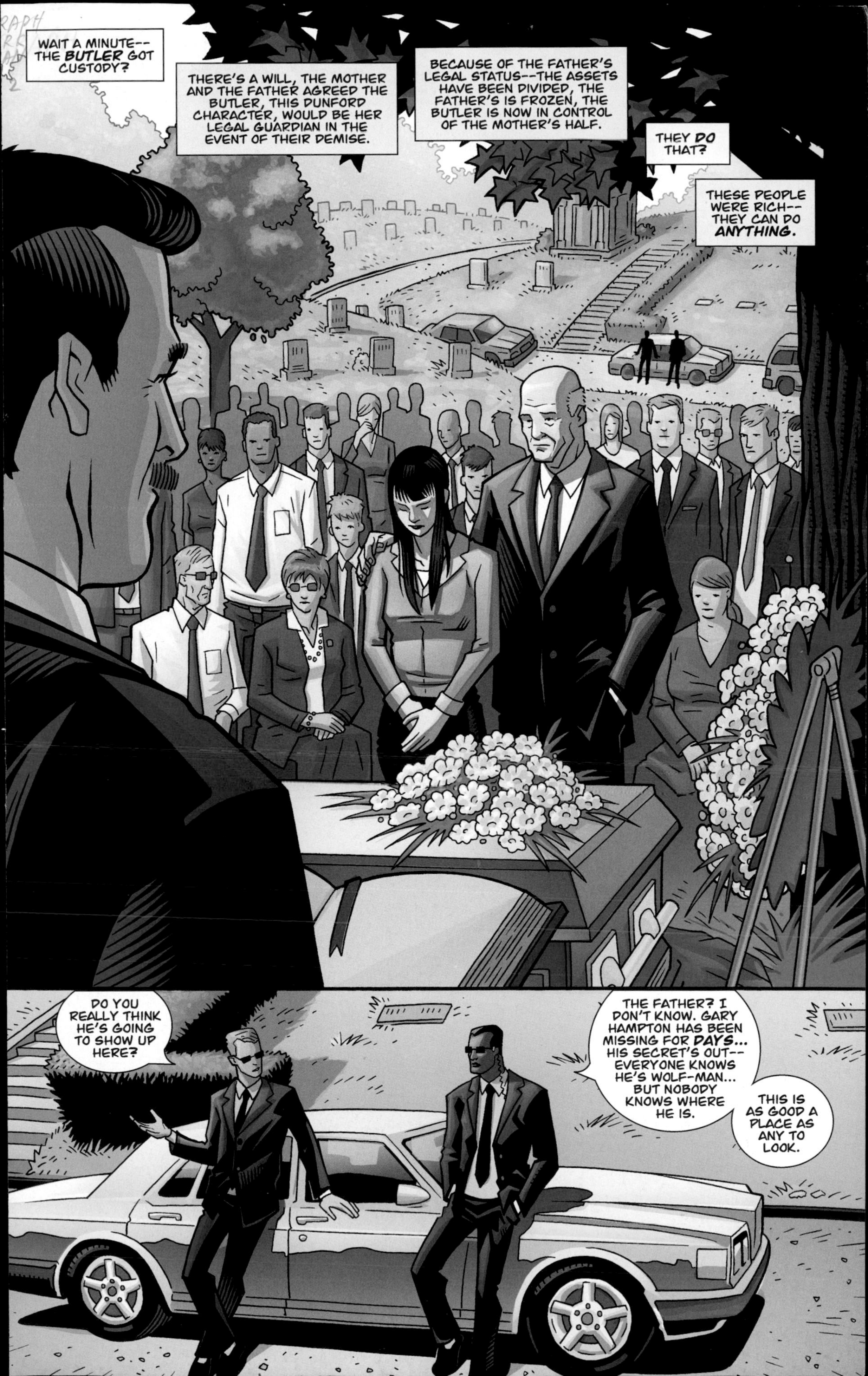
WAIT A MINUTE-- THE BUTLER GOT CUSTODY?
THERE'S A WILL, THE MOTHER AND THE FATHER AGREED THE BUTLER, THIS DUNFORD CHARACTER, WOULD BE HER LEGAL GUARDIAN IN THE EVENT OF THEIR DEMISE.
BECAUSE OF THE FATHER'S LEGAL STATUS--THE ASSETS HAVE BEEN DIVIDED, THE FATHER'S IS FROZEN, THE BUTLER IS NOW IN CONTROL OF THE MOTHER'S HALF.
THEY DO THAT?
THESE PEOPLE WERE RICH-- THEY CAN DO ANYTHING.
DO YOU REALLY THINK HE'S GOING TO SHOW UP HERE?
THE FATHER? I DON'T KNOW. GARY HAMPTON HAS BEEN MISSING FOR DAYS... HIS SECRET'S OUT-- EVERYONE KNOWS HE'S WOLF-MAN... BUT NOBODY KNOWS WHERE HE IS.
THIS IS AS GOOD A PLACE AS ANY TO LOOK.

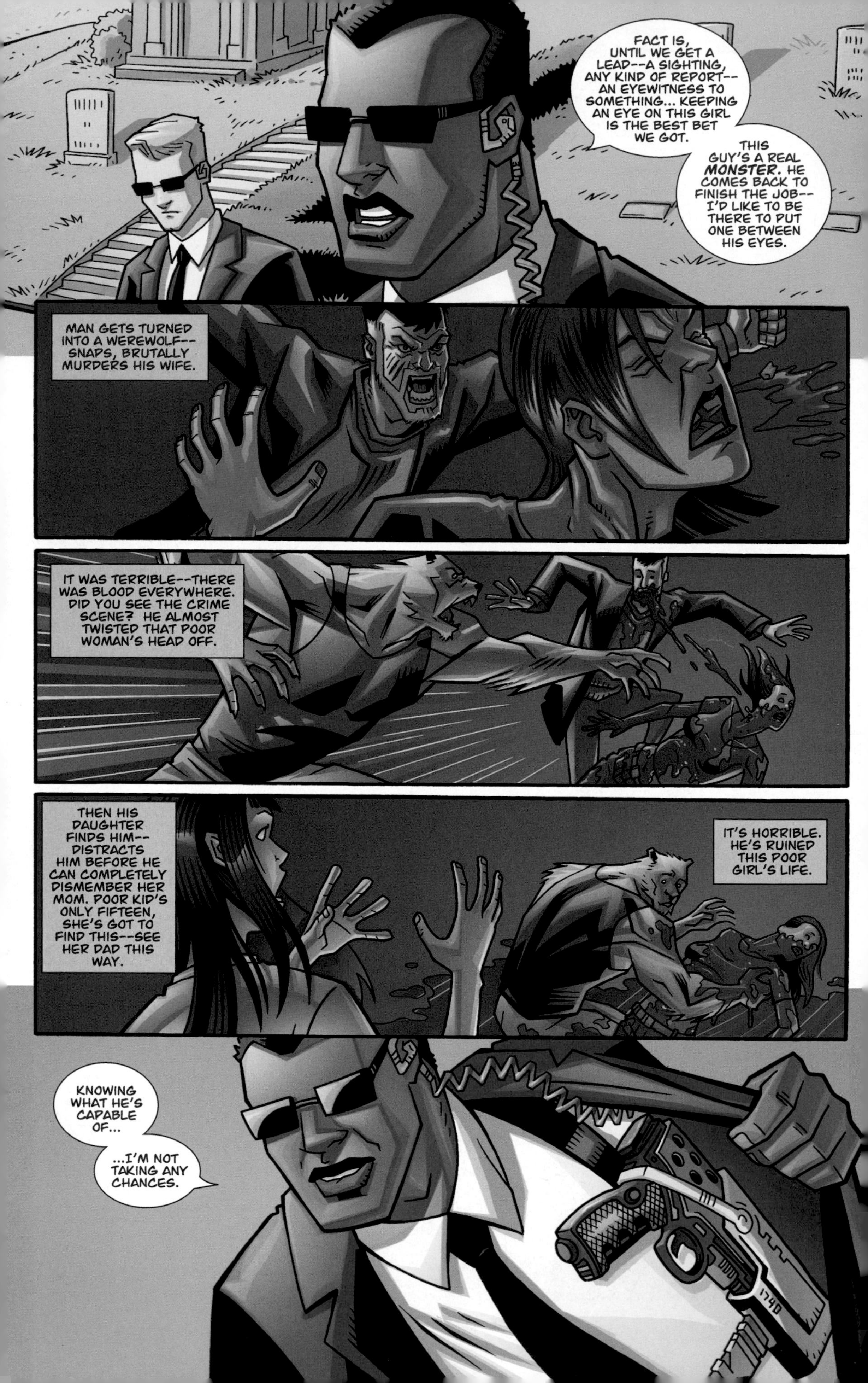

FACT IS, UNTIL WE GET A LEAD--A SIGHTING, ANY KIND OF REPORT--AN EYEWITNESS TO SOMETHING... KEEPING AN EYE ON THIS GIRL IS THE BEST BET WE GOT.
THIS GUY'S A REAL MONSTER. HE COMES BACK TO FINISH THE JOB--I'D LIKE TO BE THERE TO PUT ONE BETWEEN HIS EYES.
MAN GETS TURNED INTO A WEREWOLF--SNAPS, BRUTALLY MURDERS HIS WIFE.
IT WAS TERRIBLE--THERE WAS BLOOD EVERYWHERE. DID YOU SEE THE CRIME SCENE? HE ALMOST TWISTED THAT POOR WOMAN'S HEAD OFF.
THEN HIS DAUGHTER FINDS HIM--DISTRACTS HIM BEFORE HE CAN COMPLETELY DISMEMBER HER MOM. POOR KID'S ONLY FIFTEEN, SHE'S GOT TO FIND THIS--SEE HER DAD THIS WAY.
IT'S HORRIBLE. HE'S RUINED THIS POOR GIRL'S LIFE.
KNOWING WHAT HE'S CAPABLE OF...
...I'M NOT TAKING ANY CHANCES.

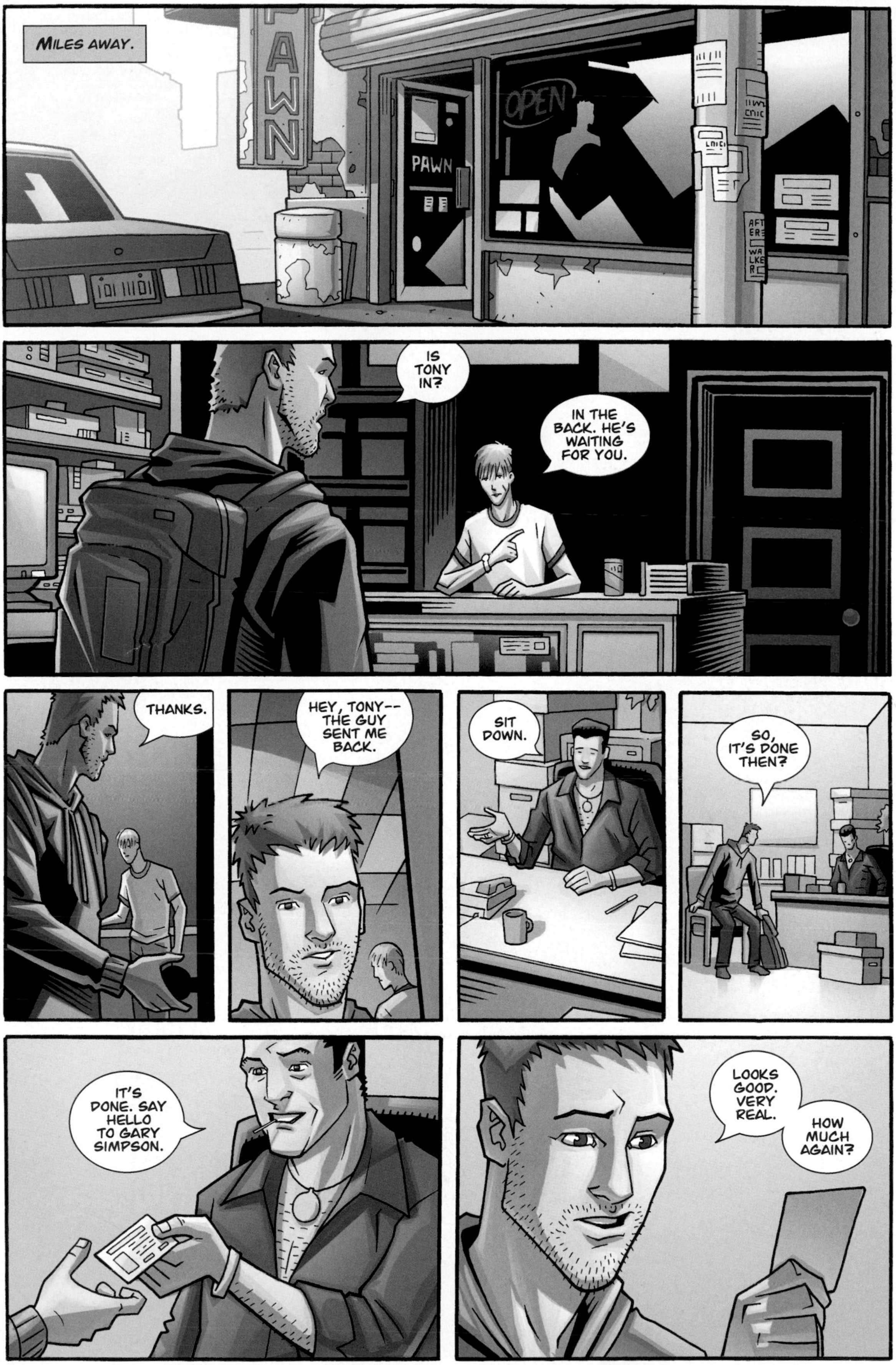
MILES AWAY.
PAWN
OPEN
PAWN
IS TONY IN?
IN THE BACK. HE'S WAITING FOR YOU.
THANKS.
HEY, TONY-- THE GUY SENT ME BACK.
SIT DOWN.
SO, IT'S DONE THEN?
IT'S DONE. SAY HELLO TO GARY SIMPSON.
LOOKS GOOD. VERY REAL.
HOW MUCH AGAIN?

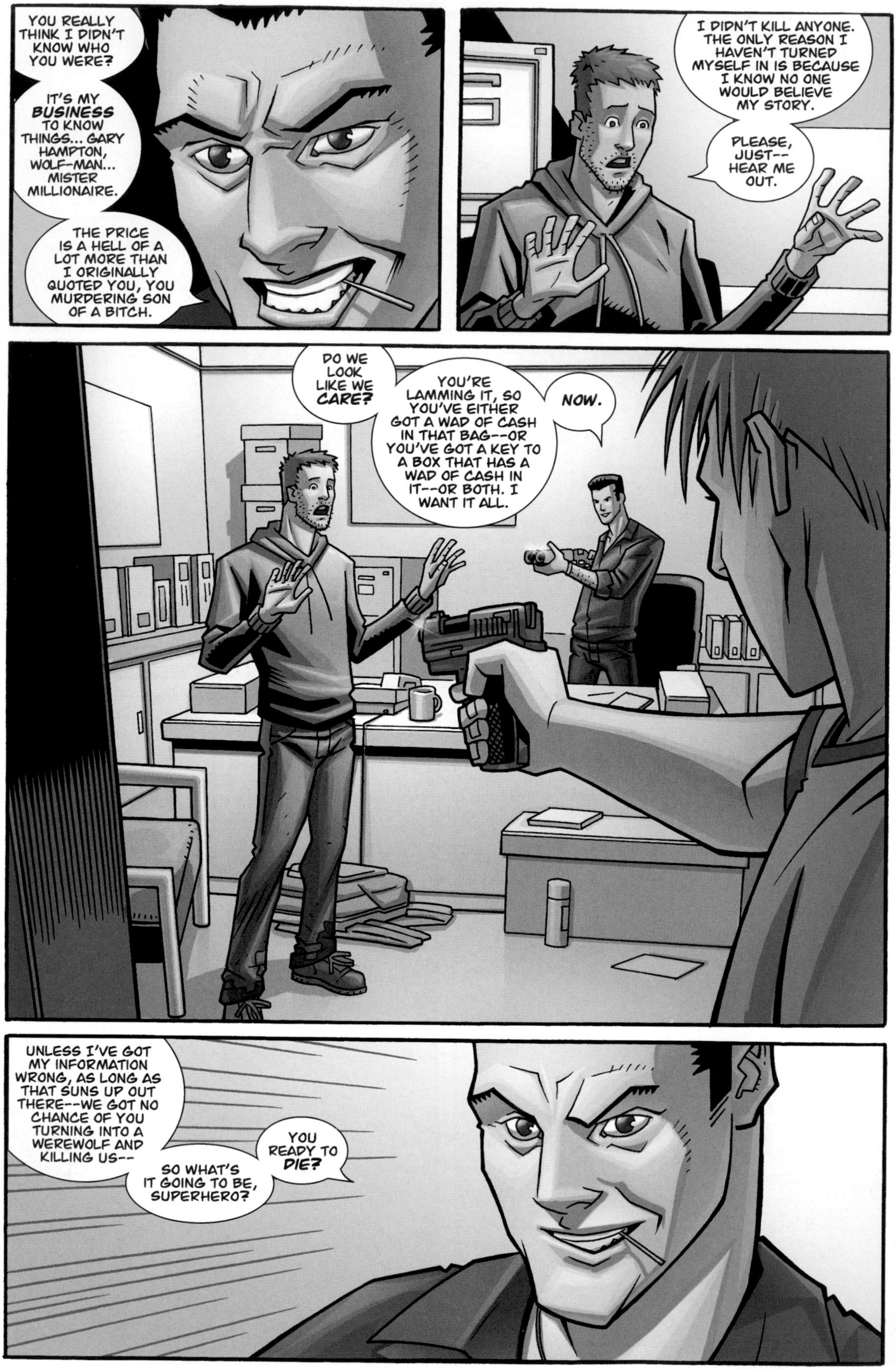
YOU REALLY THINK I DIDN'T KNOW WHO YOU WERE?
IT'S MY BUSINESS TO KNOW THINGS... GARY HAMPTON, WOLF-MAN... MISTER MILLIONAIRE.
THE PRICE IS A HELL OF A LOT MORE THAN I ORIGINALLY QUOTED YOU, YOU MURDERING SON OF A BITCH.
I DIDN'T KILL ANYONE. THE ONLY REASON I HAVEN'T TURNED MYSELF IN IS BECAUSE I KNOW NO ONE WOULD BELIEVE MY STORY.
PLEASE, JUST-- HEAR ME OUT.
DO WE LOOK LIKE WE CARE?
YOU'RE LAMMING IT, SO YOU'VE EITHER GOT A WAD OF CASH IN THAT BAG--OR YOU'VE GOT A KEY TO A BOX THAT HAS A WAD OF CASH IN IT--OR BOTH. I WANT IT ALL.
NOW.
UNLESS I'VE GOT MY INFORMATION WRONG, AS LONG AS THAT SUNS UP OUT THERE--WE GOT NO CHANCE OF YOU TURNING INTO A WEREWOLF AND KILLING US--
SO WHAT'S IT GOING TO BE, SUPERHERO?
YOU READY TO DIE?

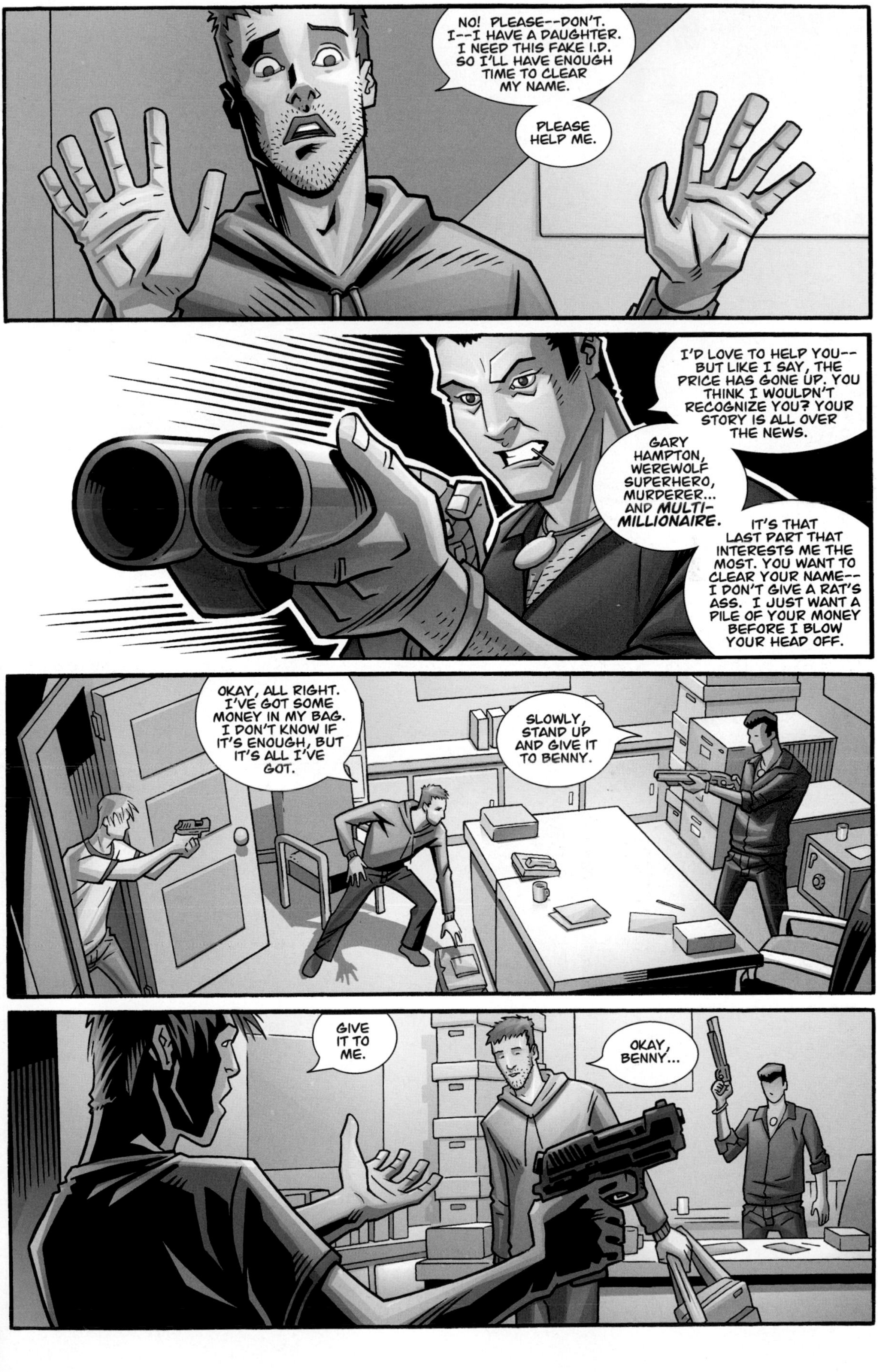
NO! PLEASE--DON'T. I--I HAVE A DAUGHTER. I NEED THIS FAKE I.D. SO I'LL HAVE ENOUGH TIME TO CLEAR MY NAME.
PLEASE HELP ME.
I'D LOVE TO HELP YOU-- BUT LIKE I SAY, THE PRICE HAS GONE UP. YOU THINK I WOULDN'T RECOGNIZE YOU? YOUR STORY IS ALL OVER THE NEWS.
GARY HAMPTON, WEREWOLF SUPERHERO, MURDERER... AND MULTI-MILLIONAIRE.
IT'S THAT LAST PART THAT INTERESTS ME THE MOST. YOU WANT TO CLEAR YOUR NAME-- I DON'T GIVE A RAT'S ASS. I JUST WANT A PILE OF YOUR MONEY BEFORE I BLOW YOUR HEAD OFF.
OKAY, ALL RIGHT. I'VE GOT SOME MONEY IN MY BAG. I DON'T KNOW IF IT'S ENOUGH, BUT IT'S ALL I'VE GOT.
SLOWLY, STAND UP AND GIVE IT TO BENNY.
GIVE IT TO ME.
OKAY, BENNY...

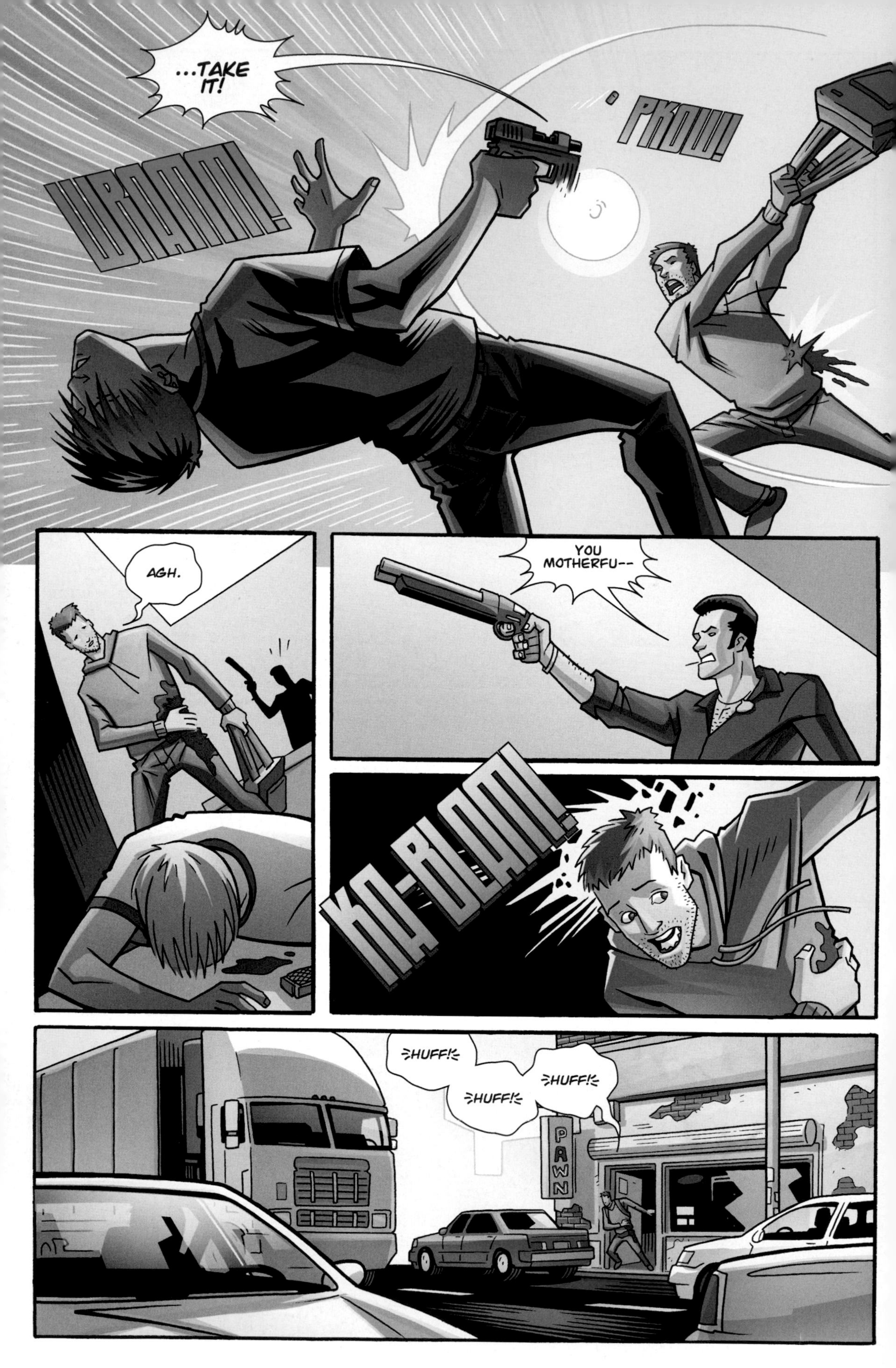
...TAKE IT!
PKOW!
AGH.
YOU MOTHERFU--
KA-BLAM!
HUFF!
HUFF!
HUFF!
PAWN

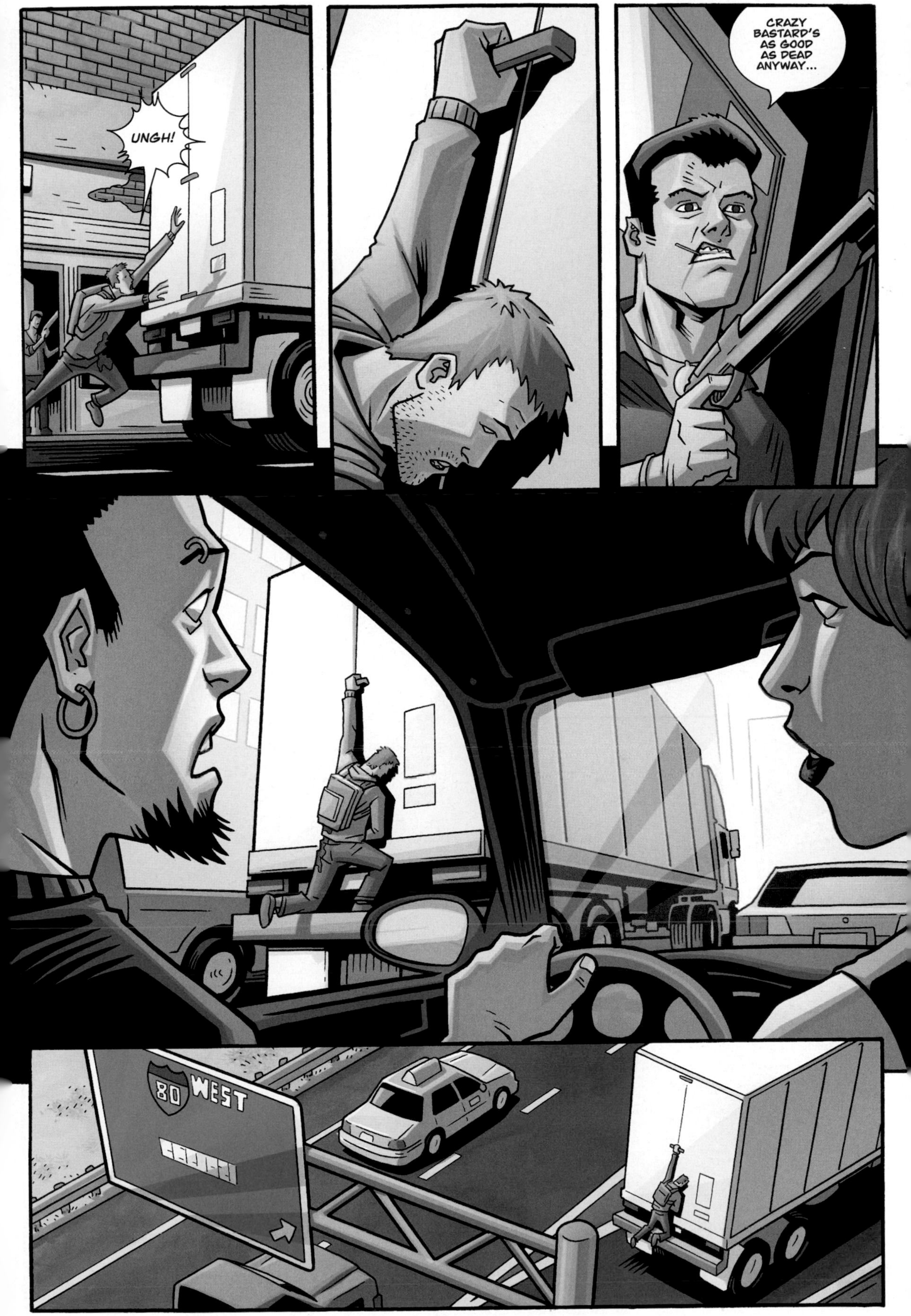
UNGH!
CRAZY BASTARD'S AS GOOD AS DEAD ANYWAY...
80
WEST

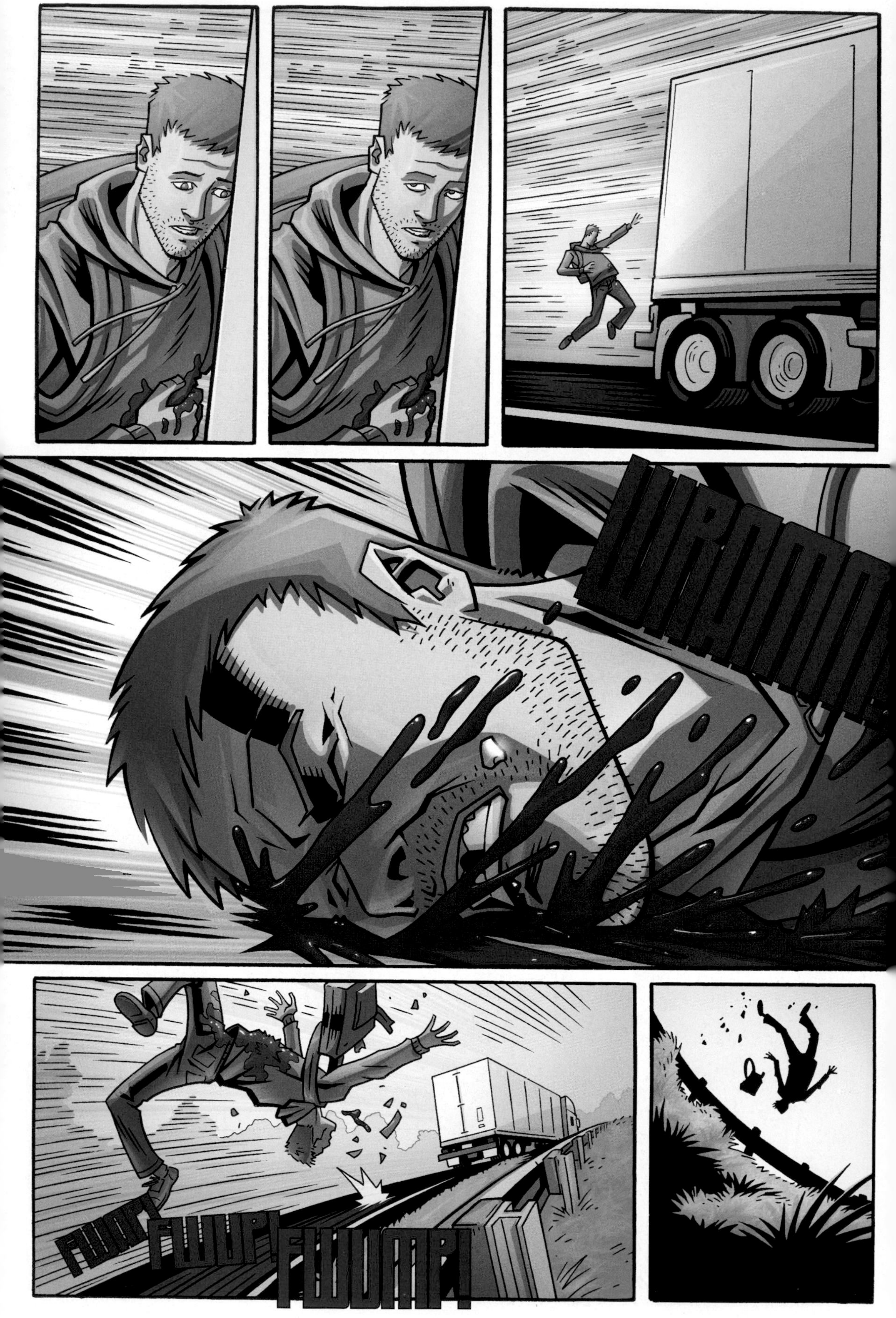
FWUP!
FWUMP!

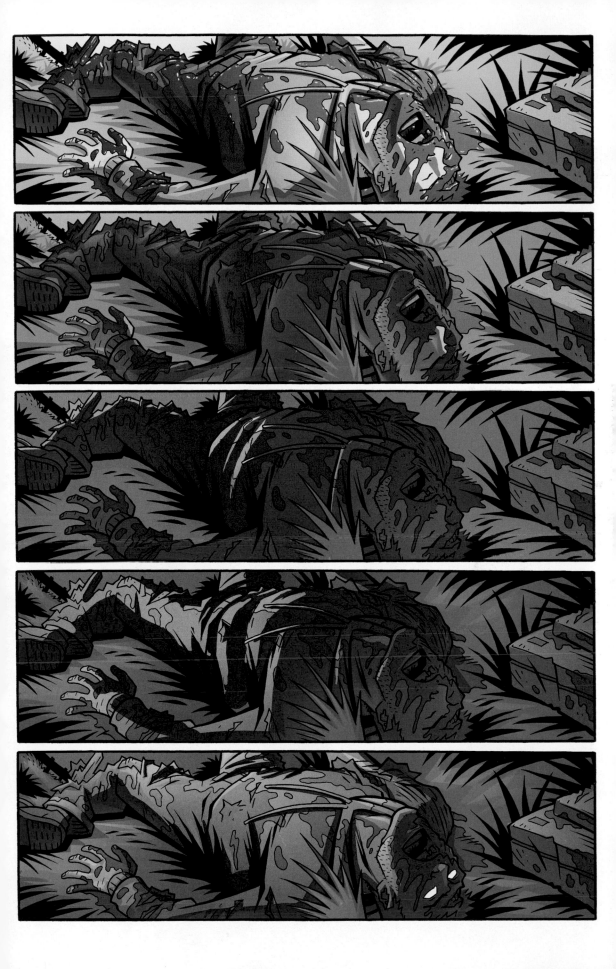

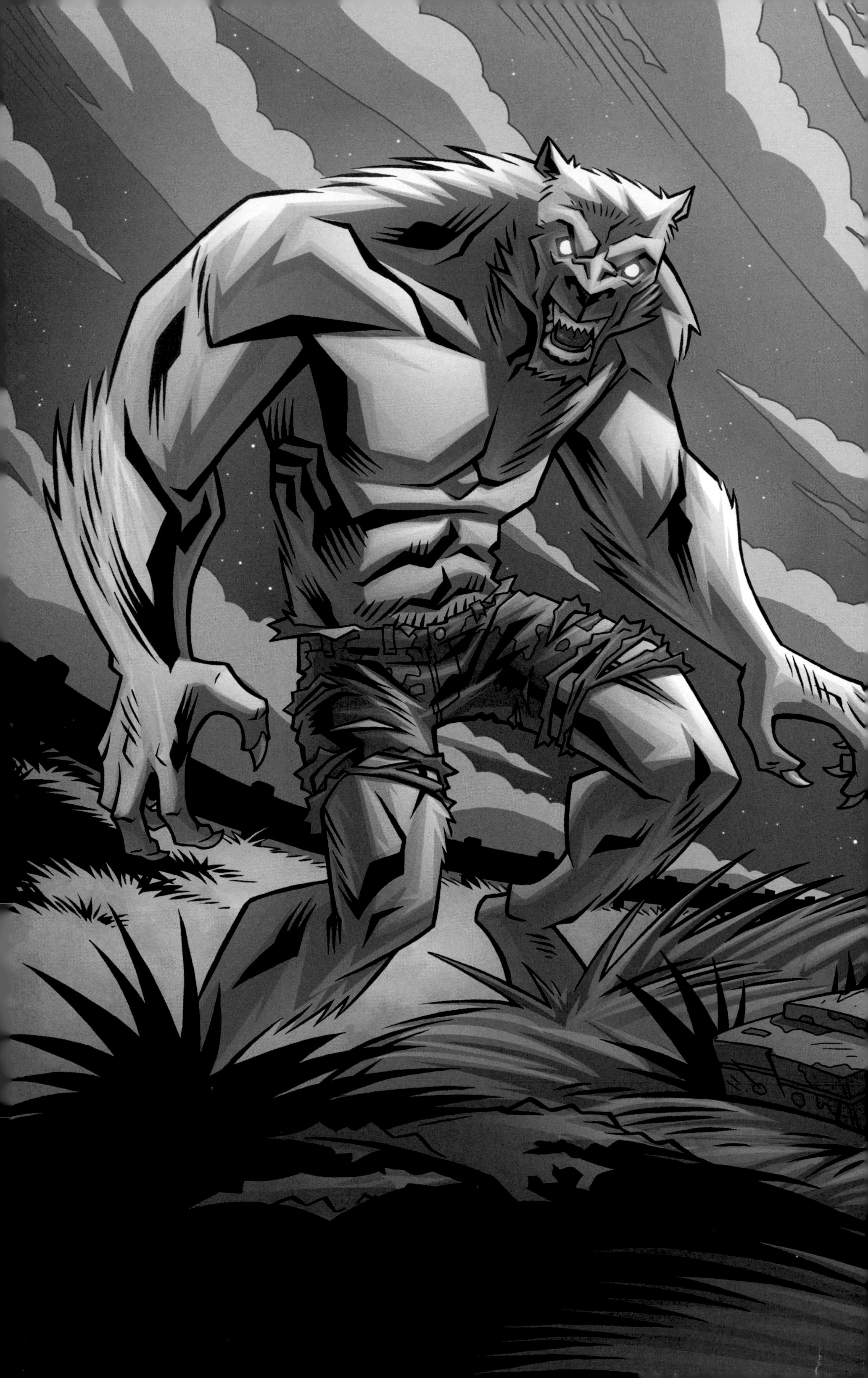

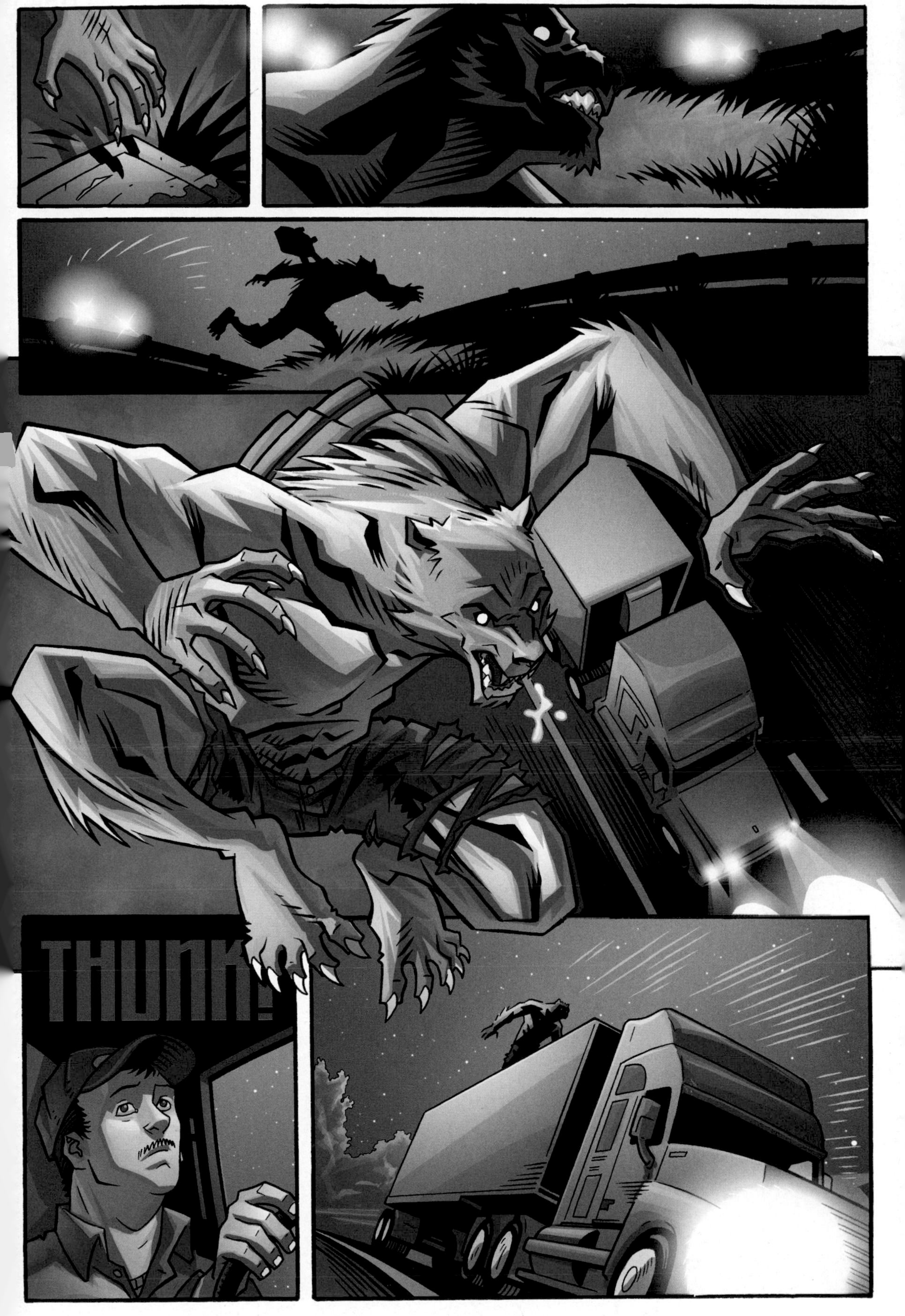
THUNK!

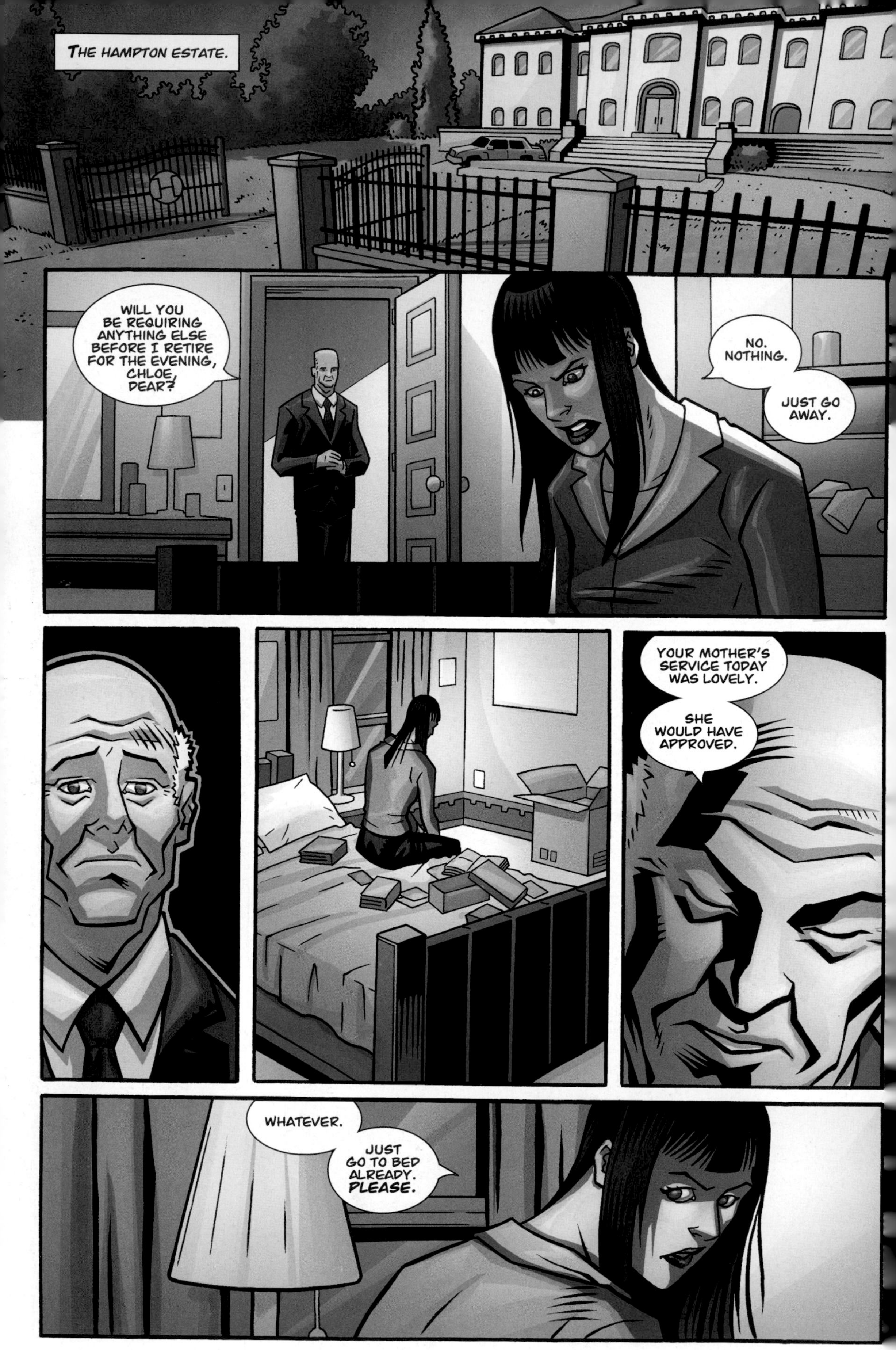

THE HAMPTON ESTATE.
WILL YOU BE REQUIRING ANYTHING ELSE BEFORE I RETIRE FOR THE EVENING, CHLOE, DEAR?
NO. NOTHING.
JUST GO AWAY.
YOUR MOTHER'S SERVICE TODAY WAS LOVELY.
SHE WOULD HAVE APPROVED.
WHATEVER.
JUST GO TO BED ALREADY. PLEASE.

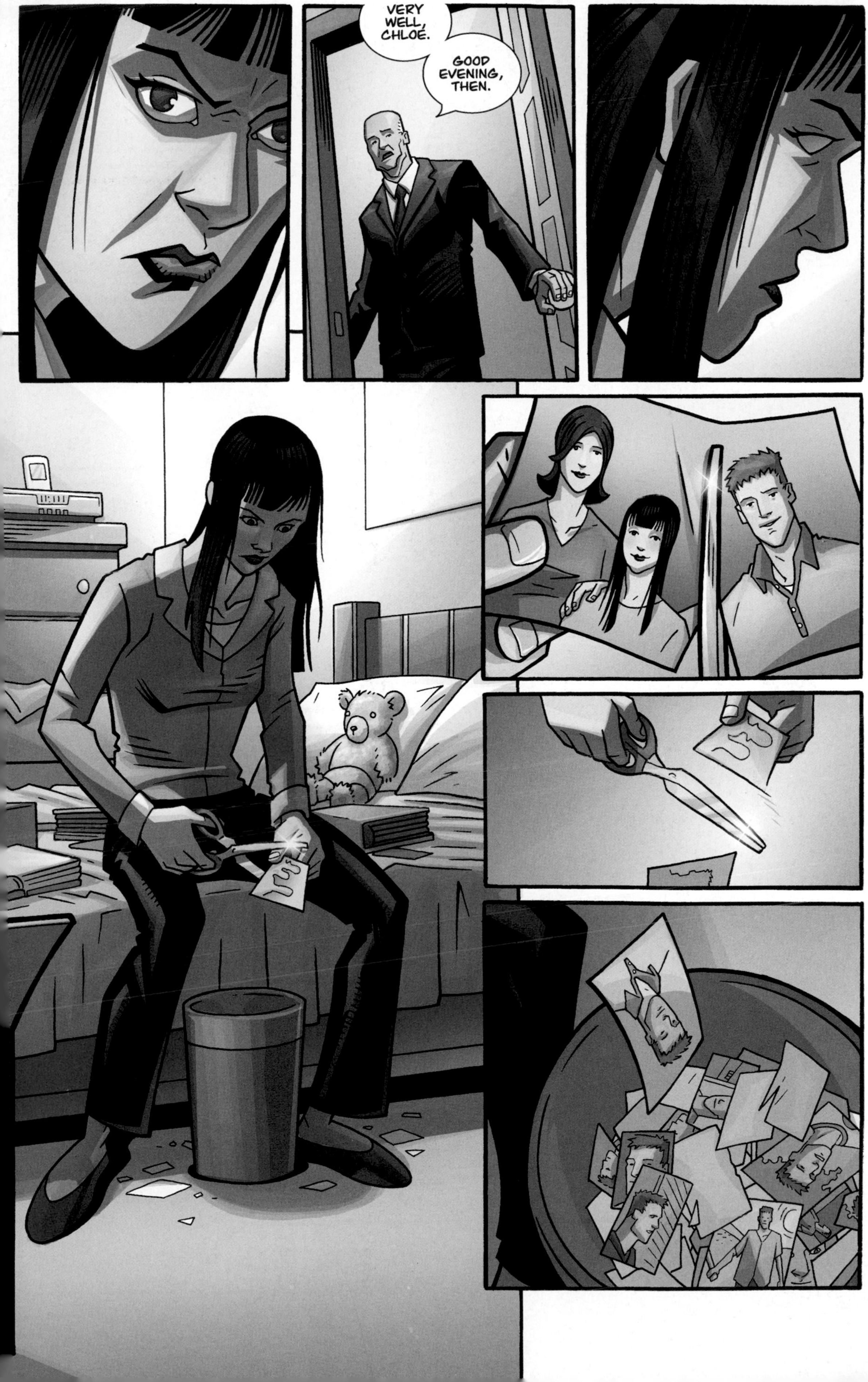
VERY WELL, CHLOE.
GOOD EVENING, THEN.

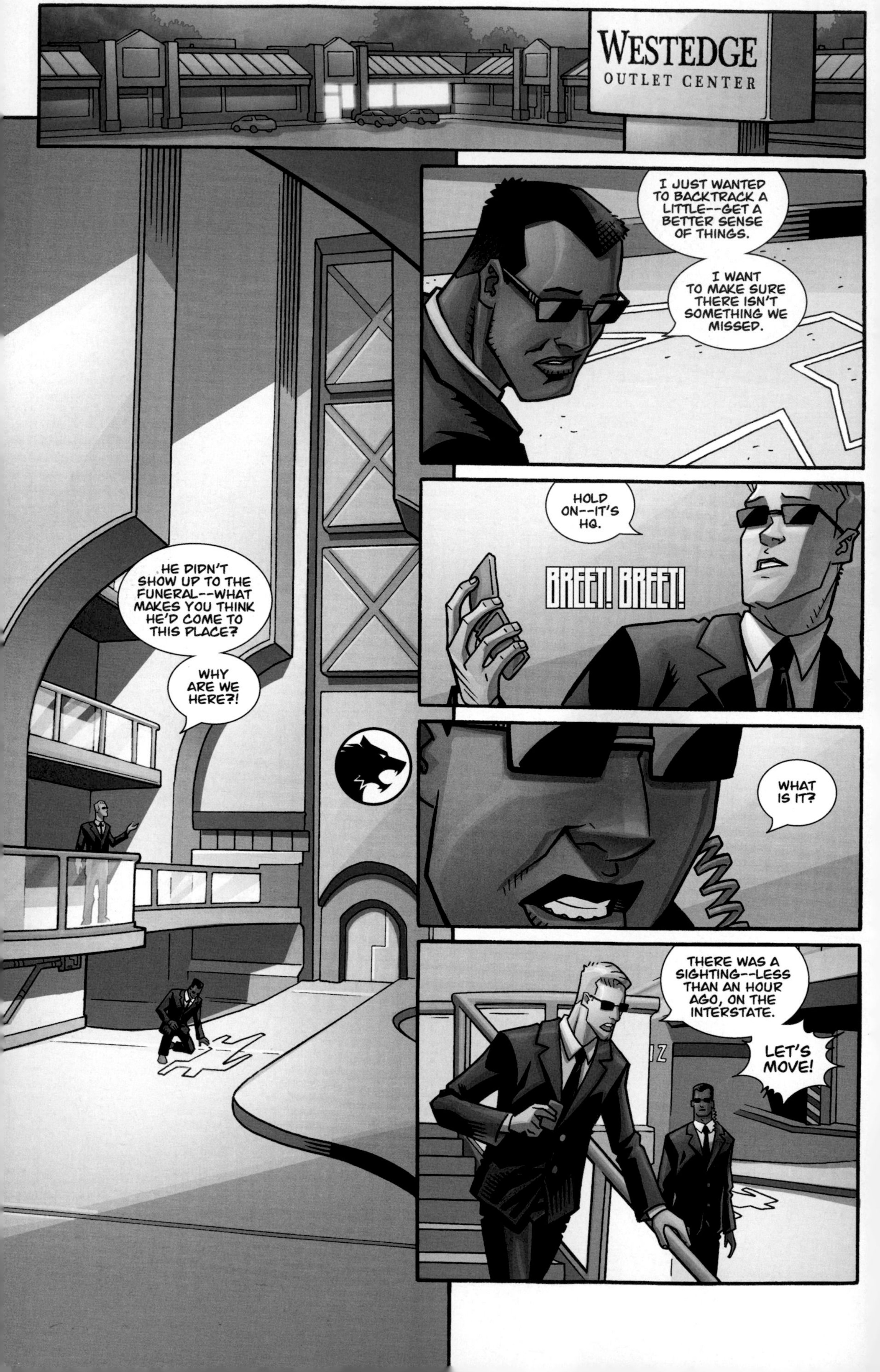
WESTEDGE
OUTLET CENTER
HE DIDN'T SHOW UP TO THE FUNERAL--WHAT MAKES YOU THINK HE'D COME TO THIS PLACE?
WHY ARE WE HERE?!
I JUST WANTED TO BACKTRACK A LITTLE--GET A BETTER SENSE OF THINGS.
I WANT TO MAKE SURE THERE ISN'T SOMETHING WE MISSED.
HOLD ON--IT'S HQ.
BREET! BREET!
WHAT IS IT?
THERE WAS A SIGHTING--LESS THAN AN HOUR AGO, ON THE INTERSTATE.
LET'S MOVE!

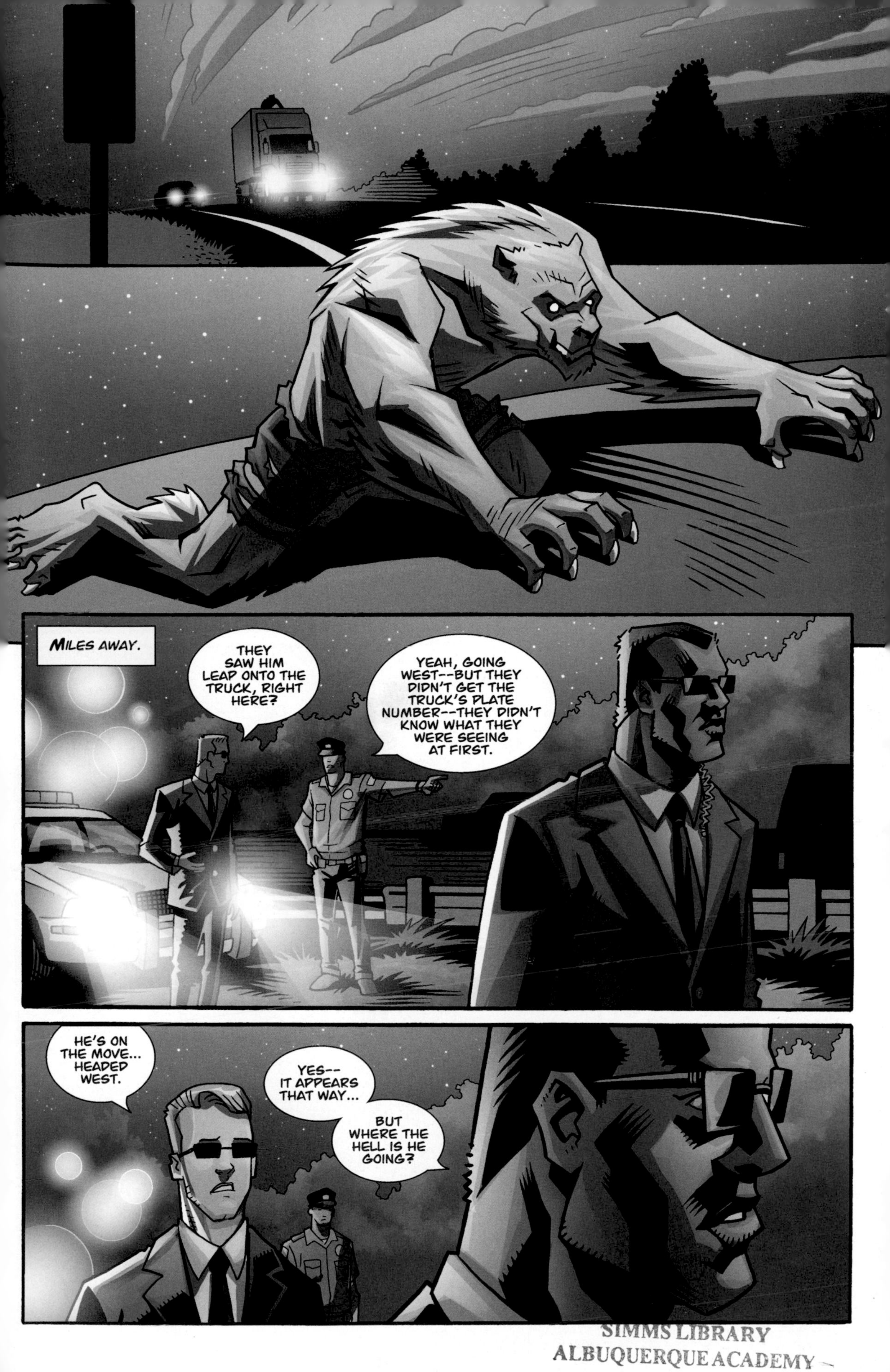
MILES AWAY.
THEY SAW HIM LEAP ONTO THE TRUCK, RIGHT HERE?
YEAH, GOING WEST--BUT THEY DIDN'T GET THE TRUCK'S PLATE NUMBER--THEY DIDN'T KNOW WHAT THEY WERE SEEING AT FIRST.
HE'S ON THE MOVE... HEADED WEST.
YES-- IT APPEARS THAT WAY...
BUT WHERE THE HELL IS HE GOING?

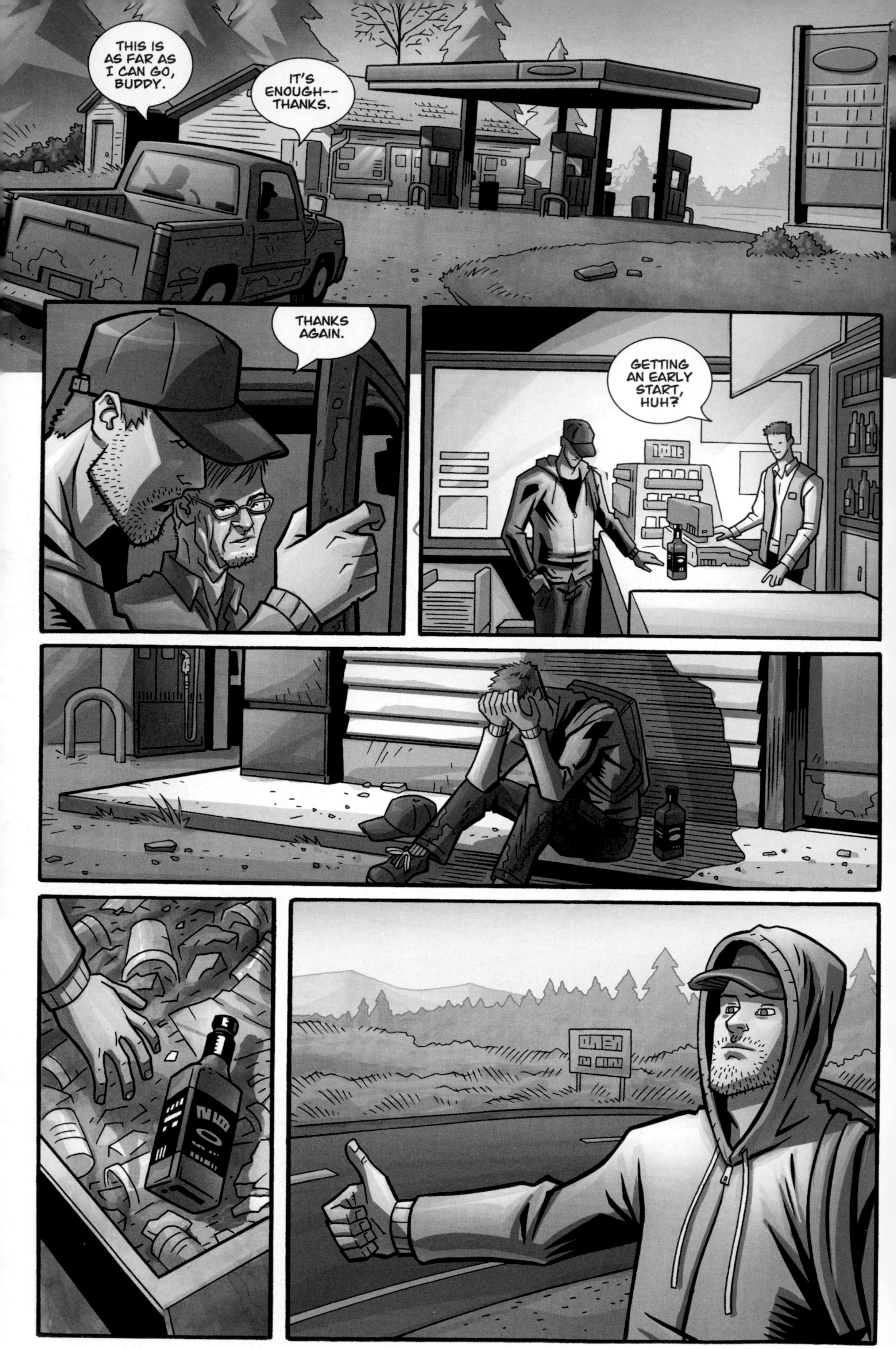
THIS IS AS FAR AS I CAN GO, BUDDY.
IT'S ENOUGH-- THANKS.
THANKS AGAIN.
GETTING AN EARLY START, HUH?

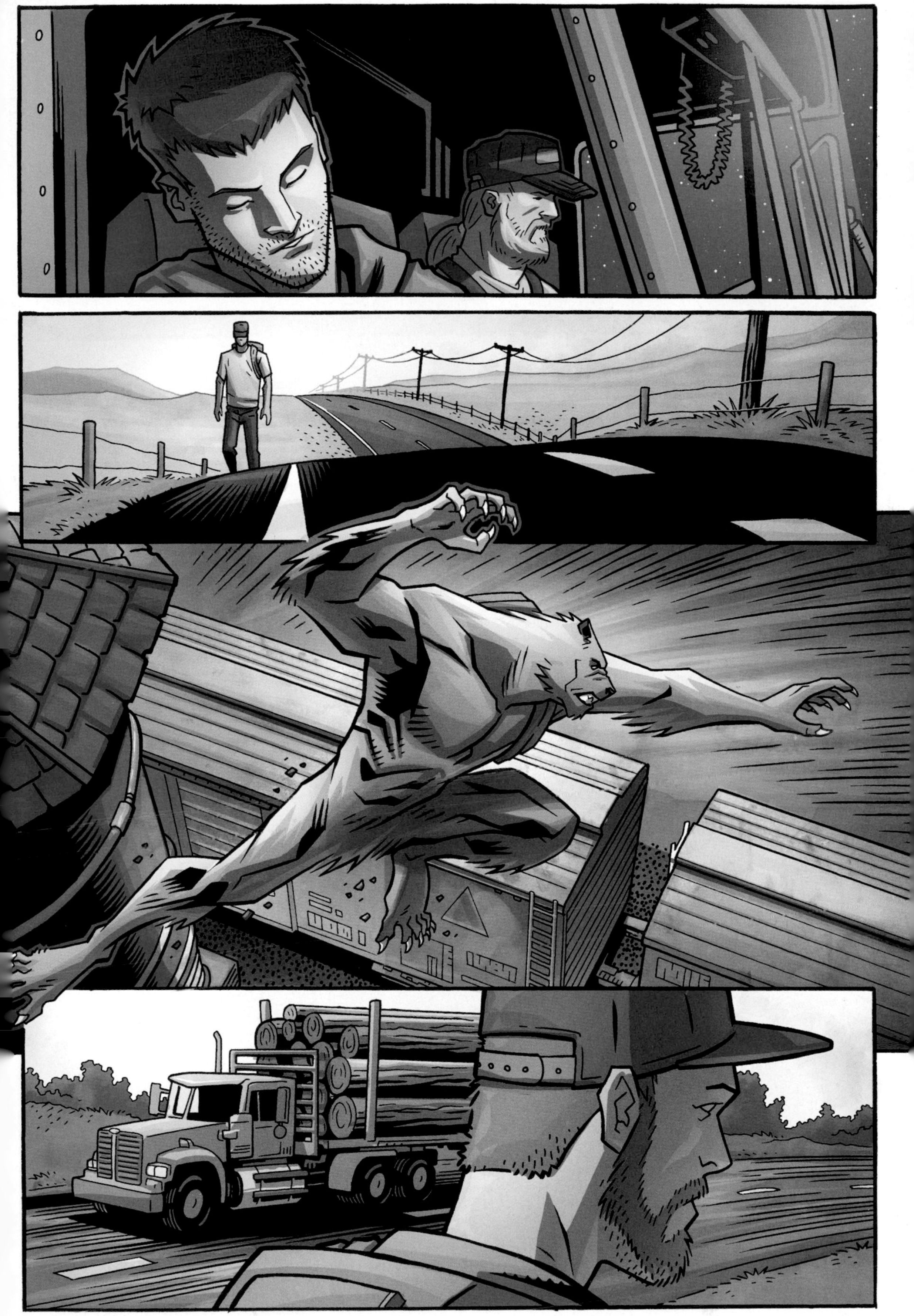

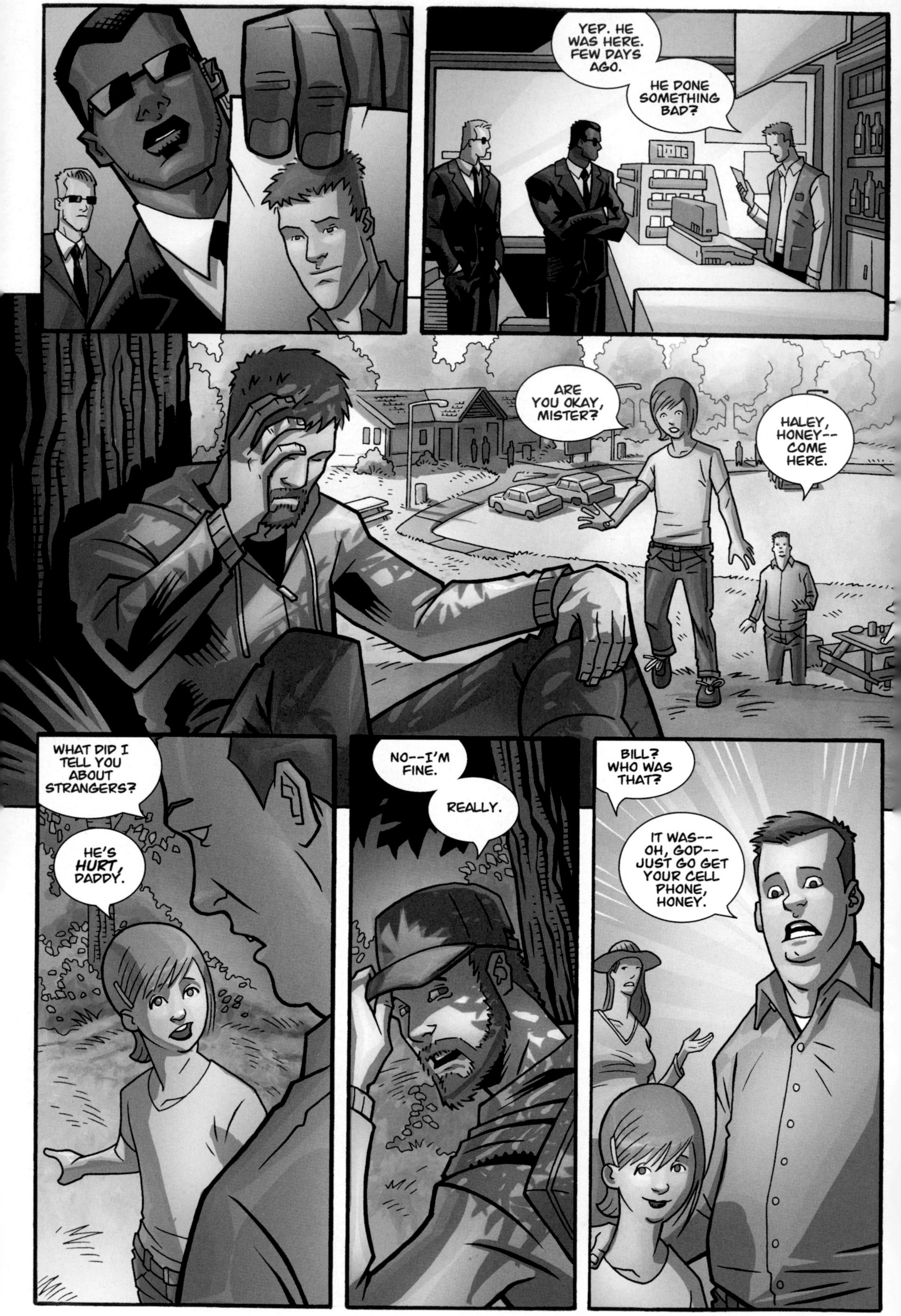
YEP. HE WAS HERE. FEW DAYS AGO.
HE DONE SOMETHING BAD?
ARE YOU OKAY, MISTER?
HALEY, HONEY-- COME HERE.
WHAT DID I TELL YOU ABOUT STRANGERS?
HE'S *HURT*, DADDY.
NO--I'M FINE.
REALLY.
BILL? WHO WAS THAT?
IT WAS-- OH, GOD-- JUST GO GET YOUR CELL PHONE, HONEY.

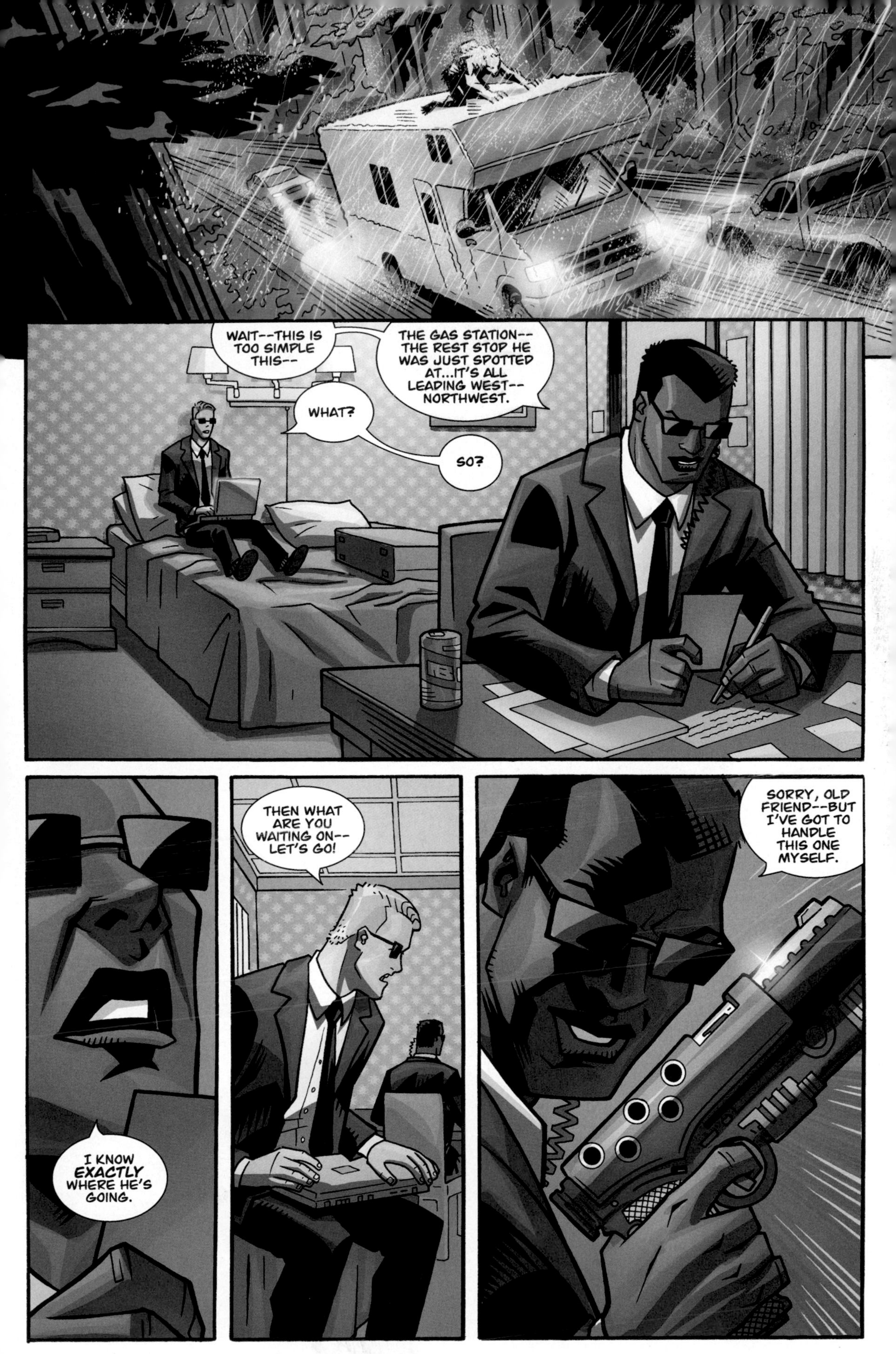
WAIT--THIS IS TOO SIMPLE THIS--
THE GAS STATION--THE REST STOP HE WAS JUST SPOTTED AT...IT'S ALL LEADING WEST--NORTHWEST.
WHAT?
SO?
I KNOW EXACTLY WHERE HE'S GOING.
THEN WHAT ARE YOU WAITING ON--LET'S GO!
SORRY, OLD FRIEND--BUT I'VE GOT TO HANDLE THIS ONE MYSELF.

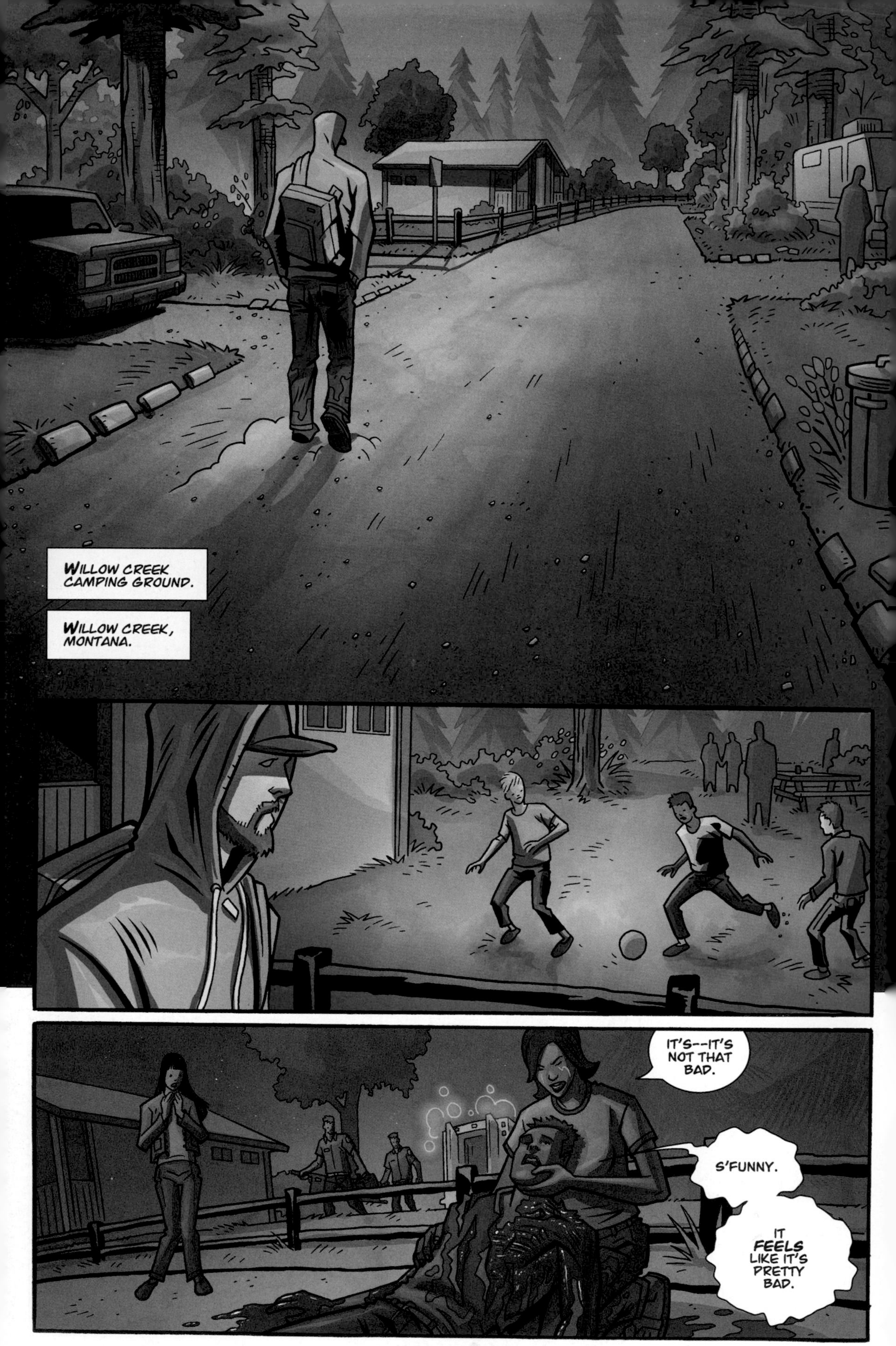
WILLOW CREEK CAMPING GROUND.
WILLOW CREEK, MONTANA.
IT'S--IT'S NOT THAT BAD.
S'FUNNY.
IT FEELS LIKE IT'S PRETTY BAD.

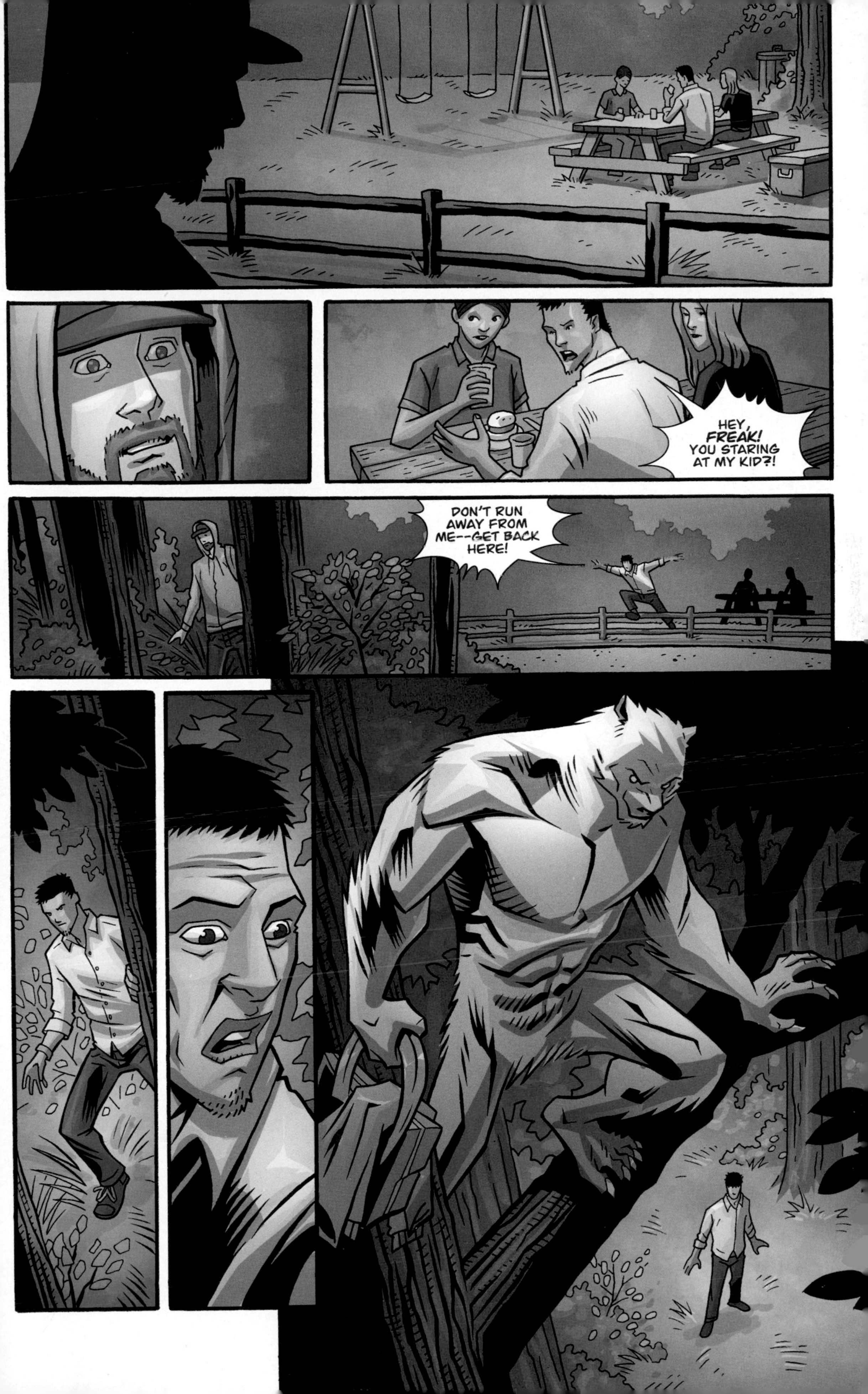
HEY, FREAK! YOU STARING AT MY KID?!
DON'T RUN AWAY FROM ME--GET BACK HERE!

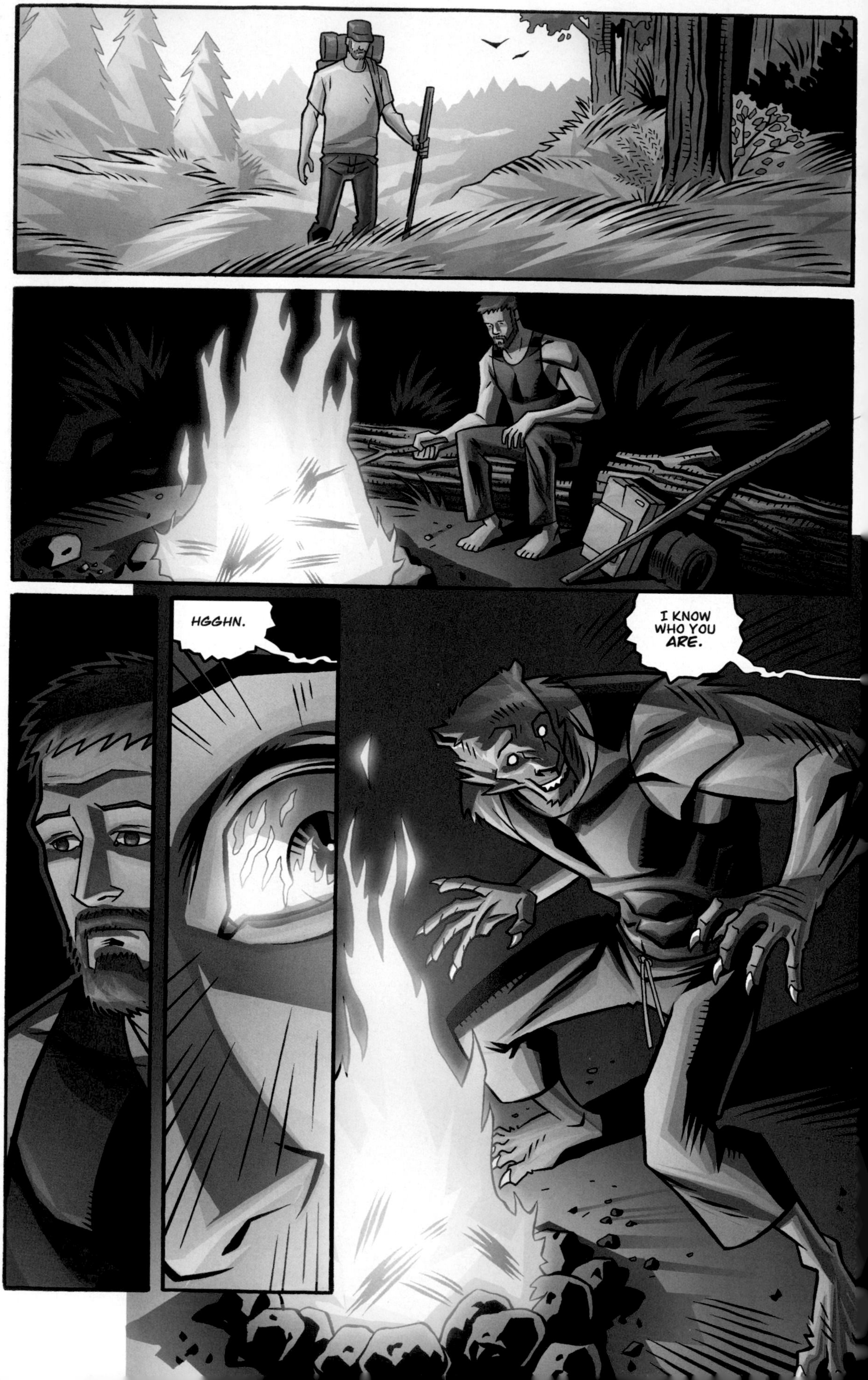
HGGHN.
I KNOW WHO YOU ARE.

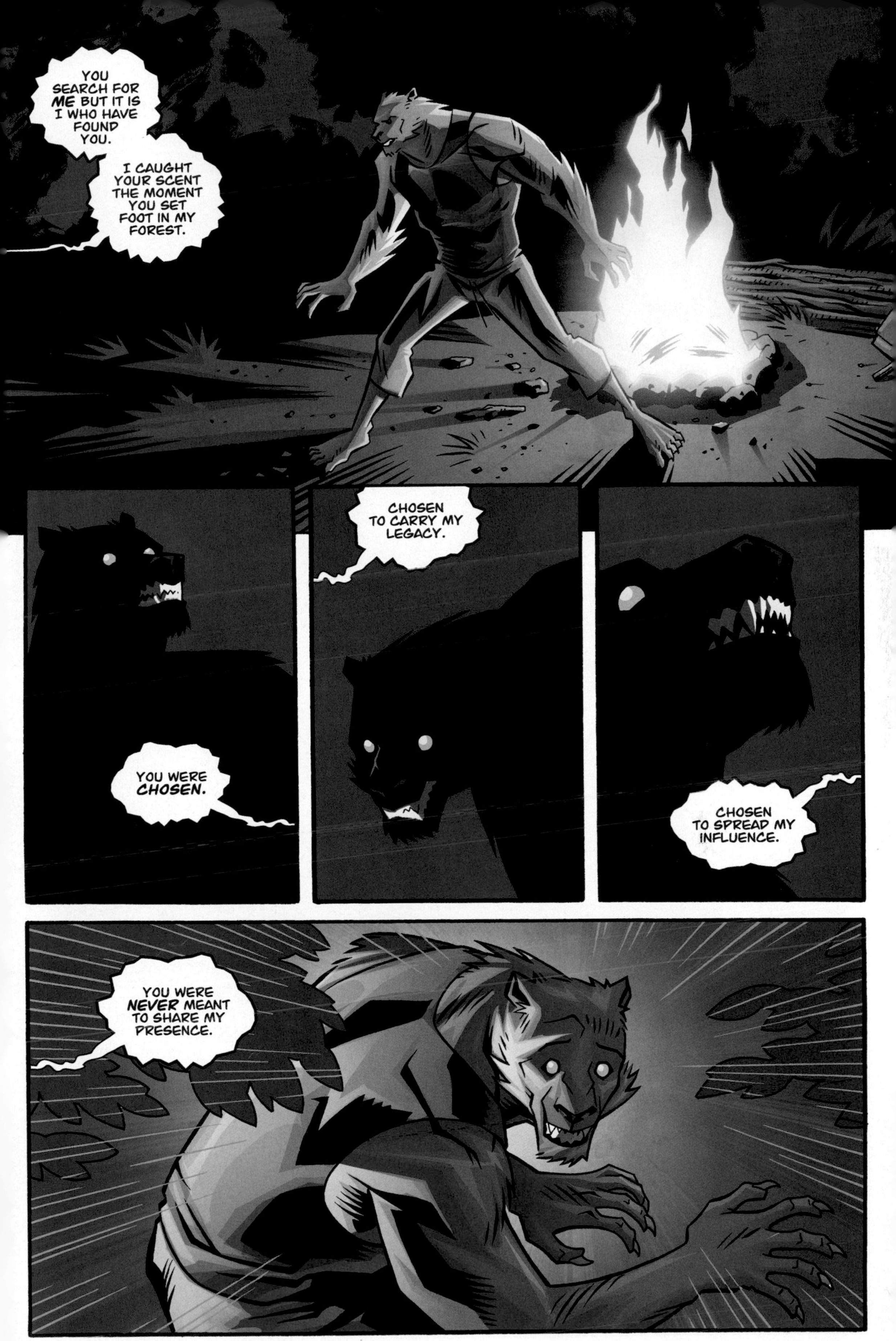
YOU SEARCH FOR ME BUT IT IS I WHO HAVE FOUND YOU.
I CAUGHT YOUR SCENT THE MOMENT YOU SET FOOT IN MY FOREST.
YOU WERE CHOSEN.
CHOSEN TO CARRY MY LEGACY.
CHOSEN TO SPREAD MY INFLUENCE.
YOU WERE NEVER MEANT TO SHARE MY PRESENCE.

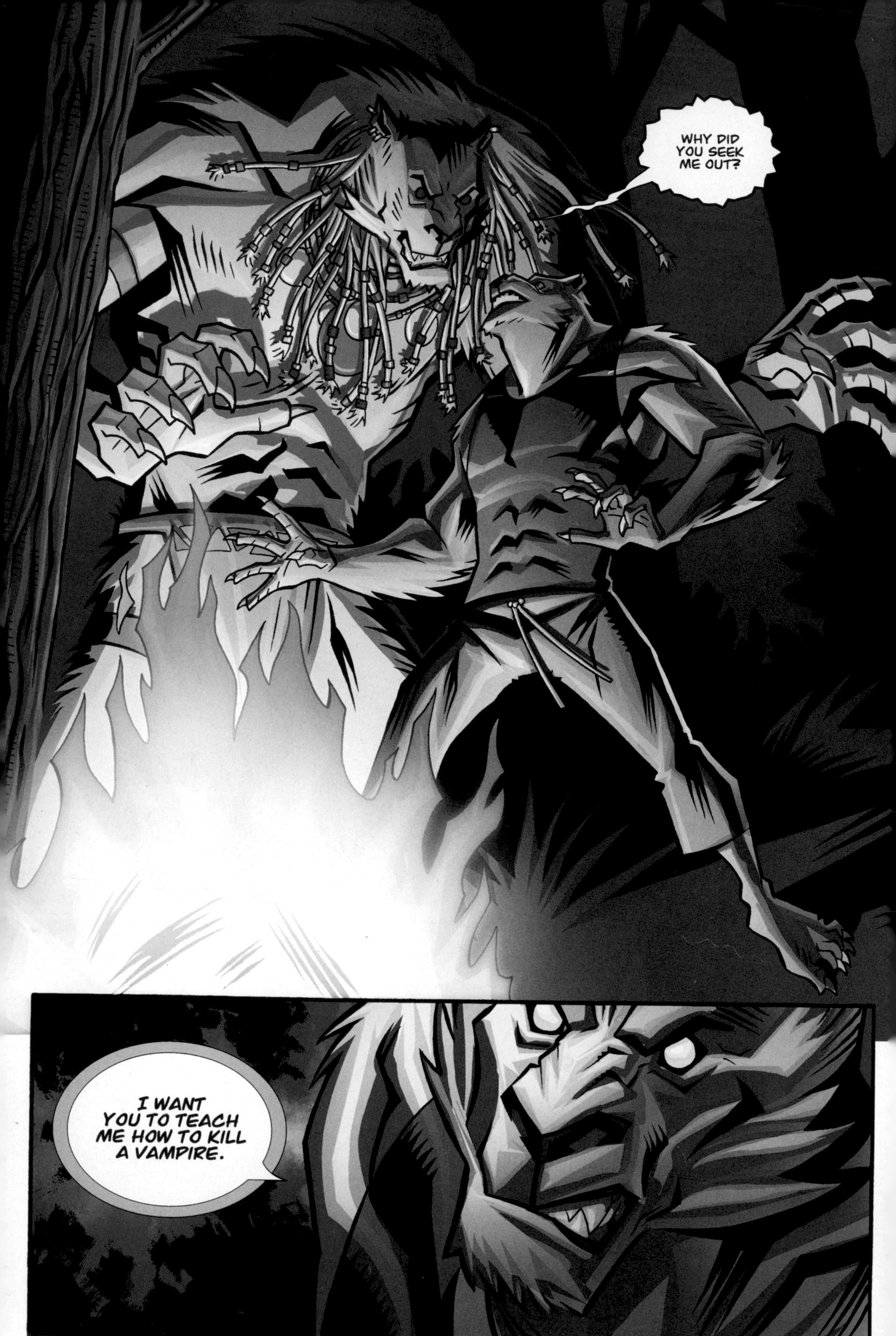
WHY DID YOU SEEK ME OUT?
I WANT YOU TO TEACH ME HOW TO KILL A VAMPIRE.

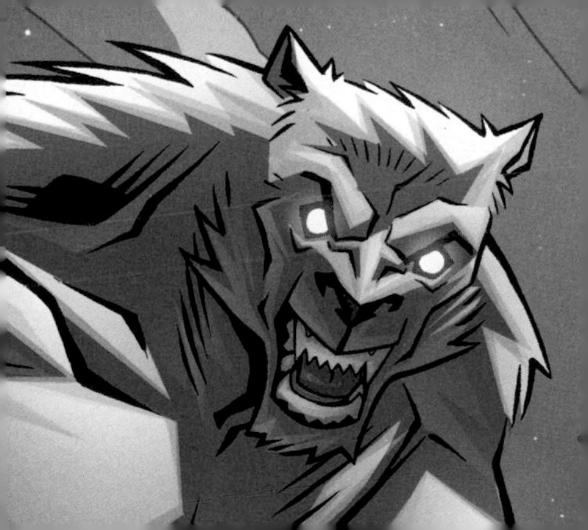

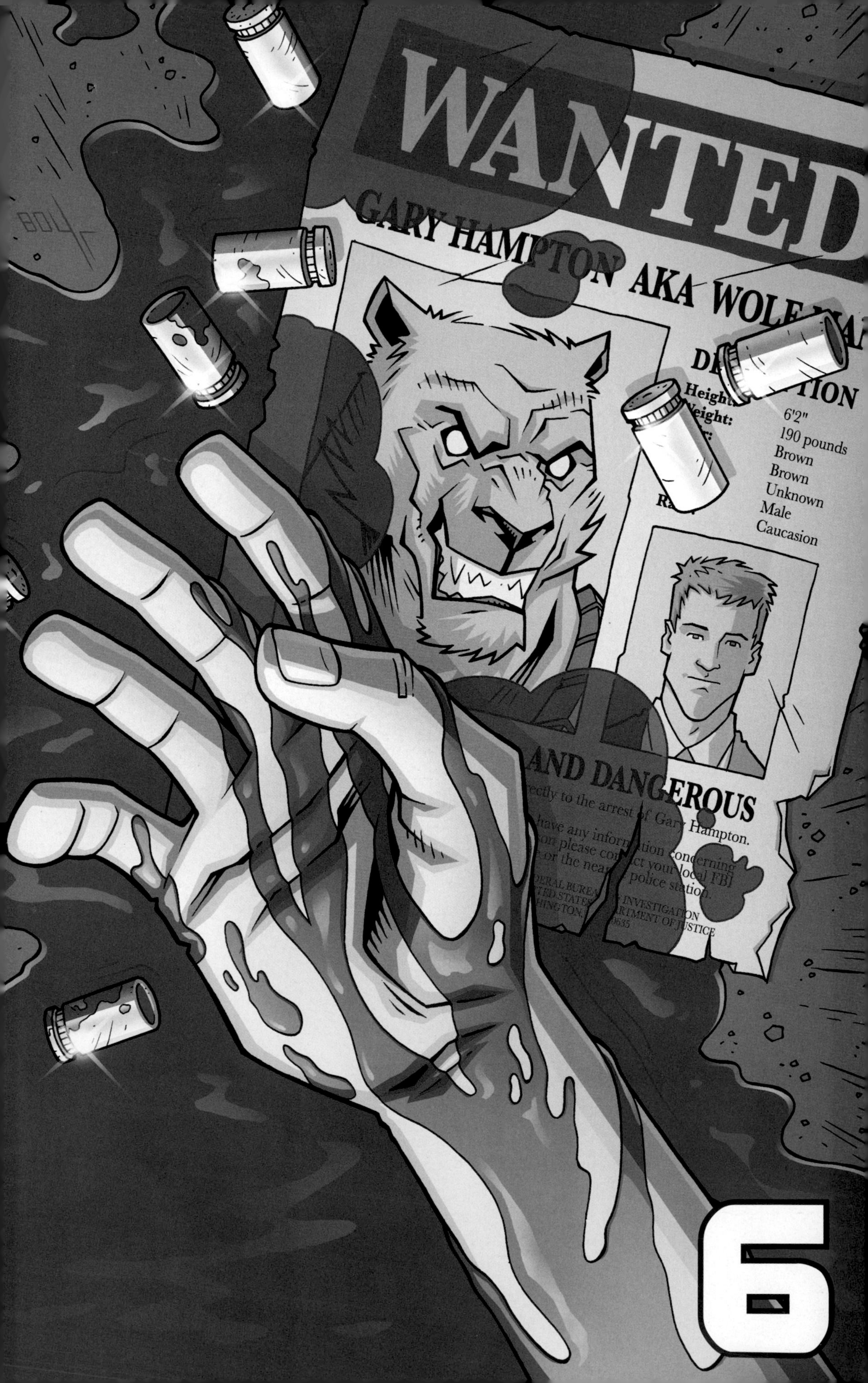
WANTED
GARY HAMPTON AKA WOLF MA
6'2"
190 pounds
Brown
Brown
Unknown
Male
Caucasion
AND DANGEROUS
have any information concerning
police station.
6

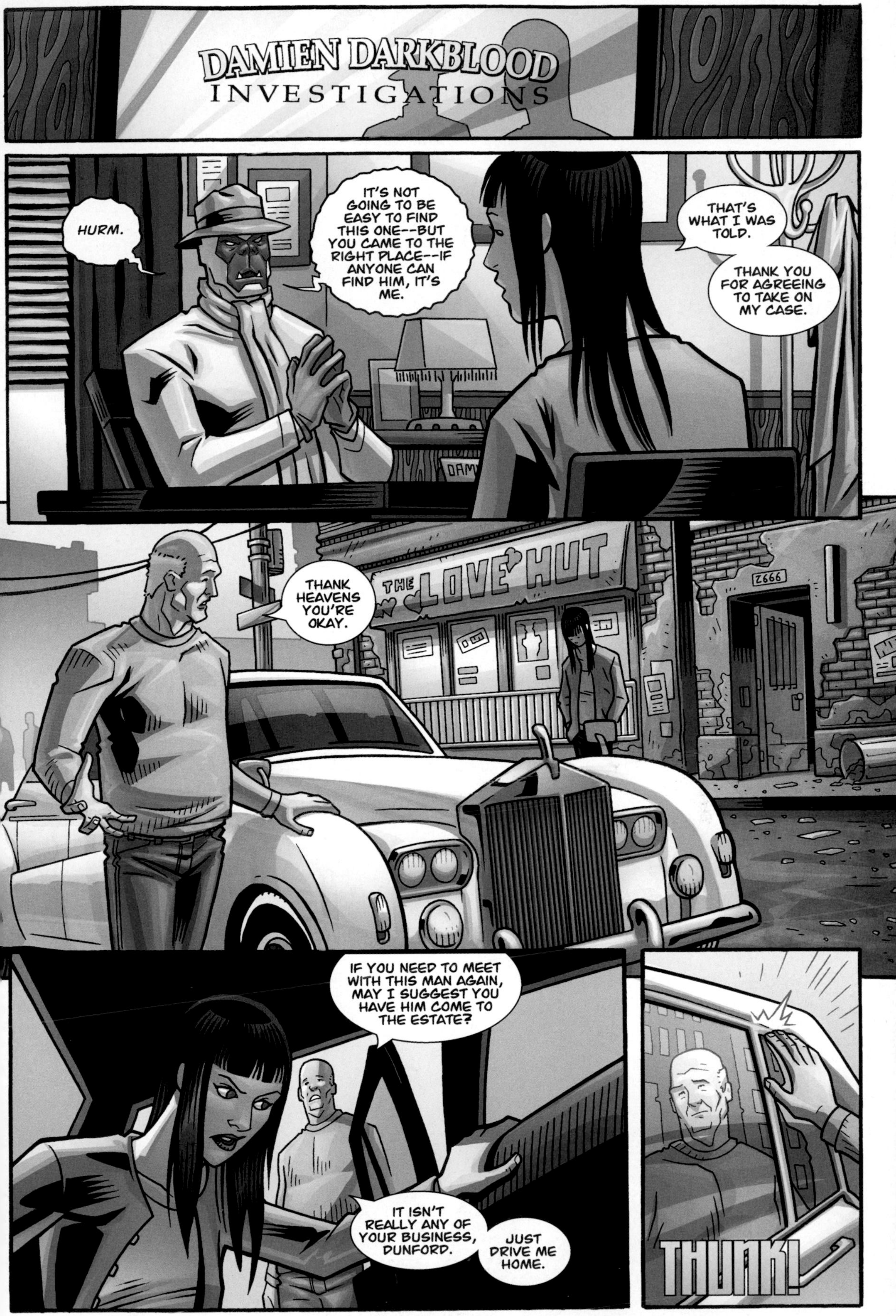
DAMIEN DARKBLOOD
INVESTIGATIONS
HURM.
IT'S NOT GOING TO BE EASY TO FIND THIS ONE--BUT YOU CAME TO THE RIGHT PLACE--IF ANYONE CAN FIND HIM, IT'S ME.
THAT'S WHAT I WAS TOLD.
THANK YOU FOR AGREEING TO TAKE ON MY CASE.
THE LOVE HUT
2666
THANK HEAVENS YOU'RE OKAY.
IF YOU NEED TO MEET WITH THIS MAN AGAIN, MAY I SUGGEST YOU HAVE HIM COME TO THE ESTATE?
IT ISN'T REALLY ANY OF YOUR BUSINESS, DUNFORD.
JUST DRIVE ME HOME.
THUNK!

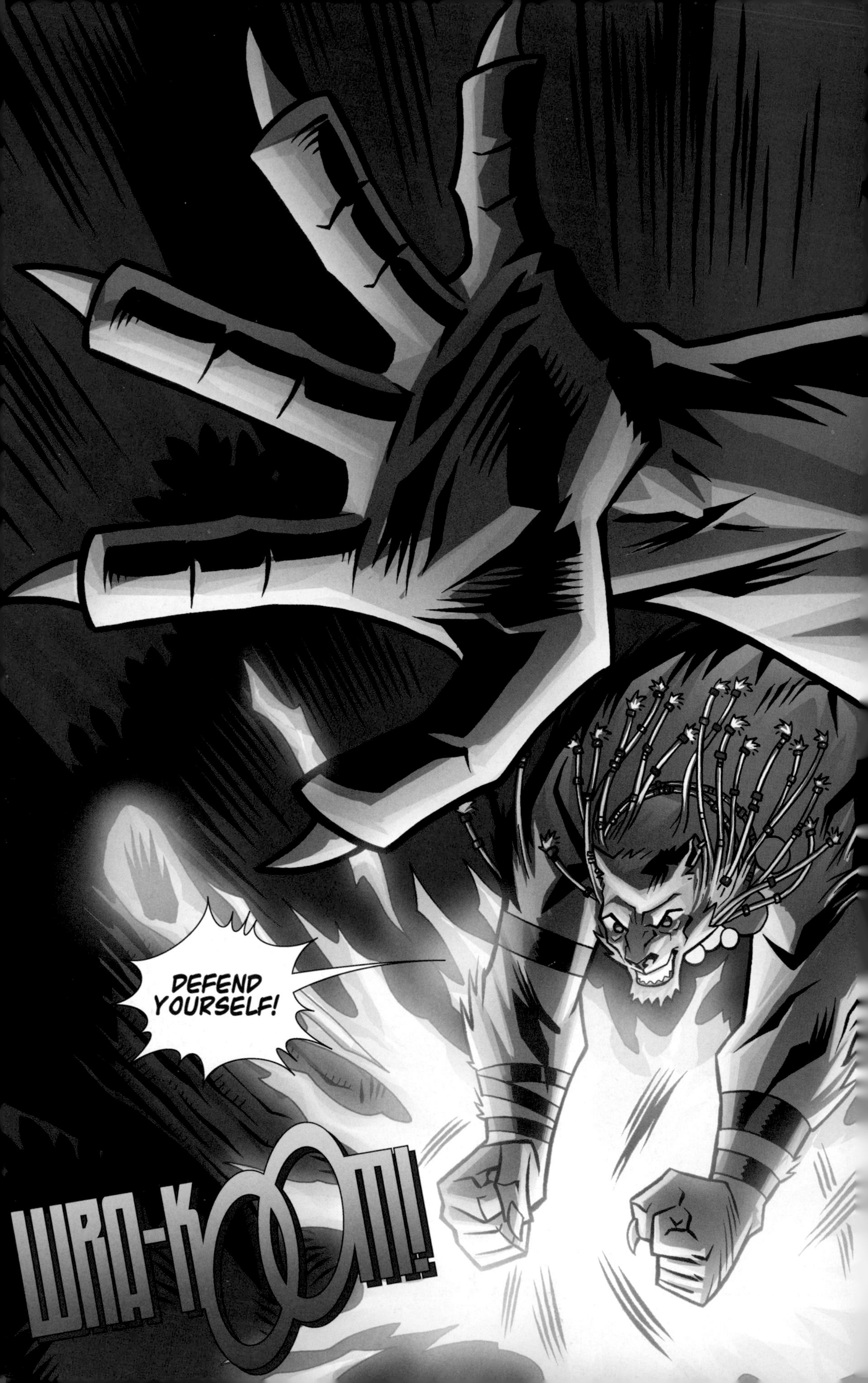
DEFEND YOURSELF!
WRA-KOOM!!

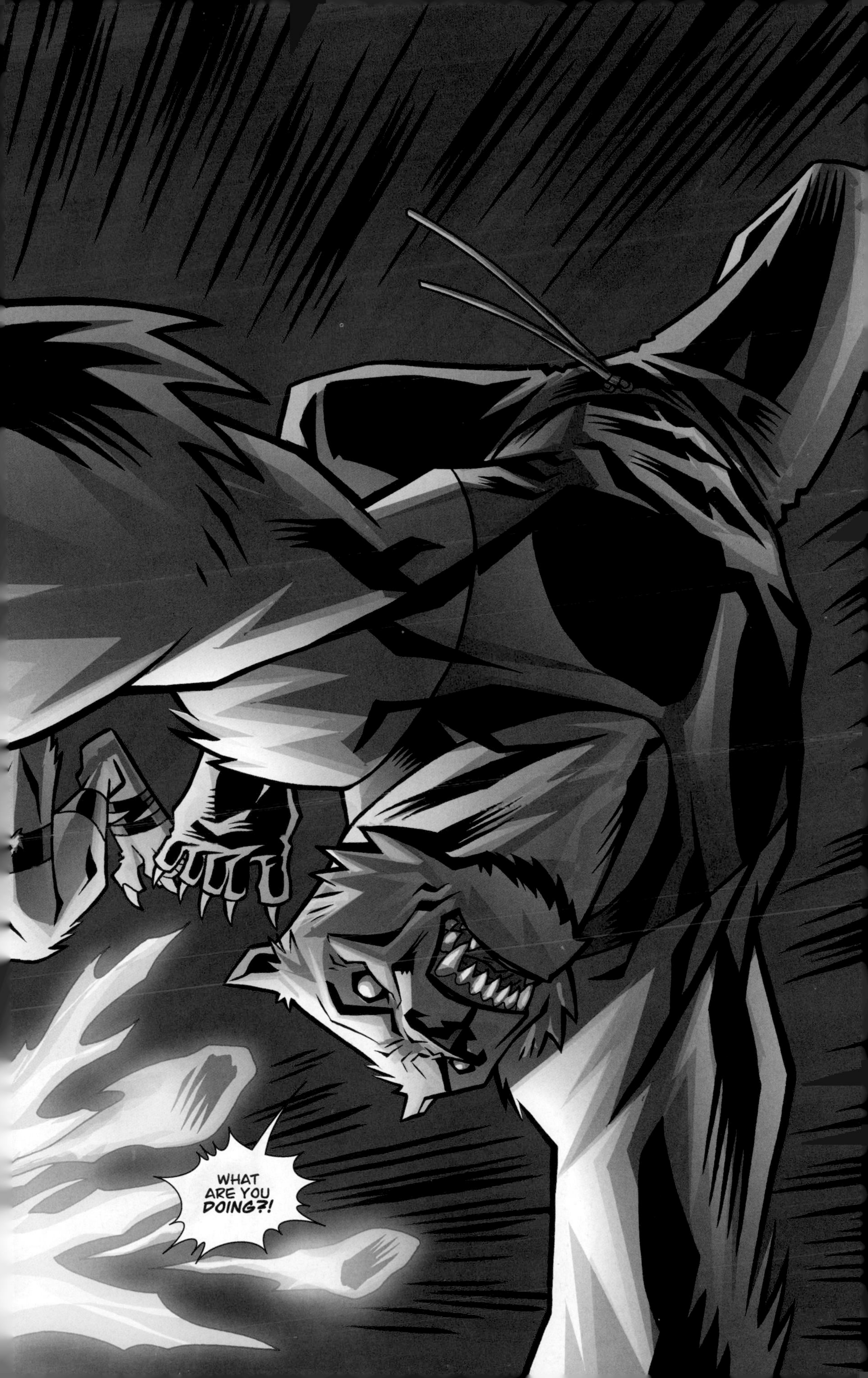
WHAT ARE YOU DOING?!

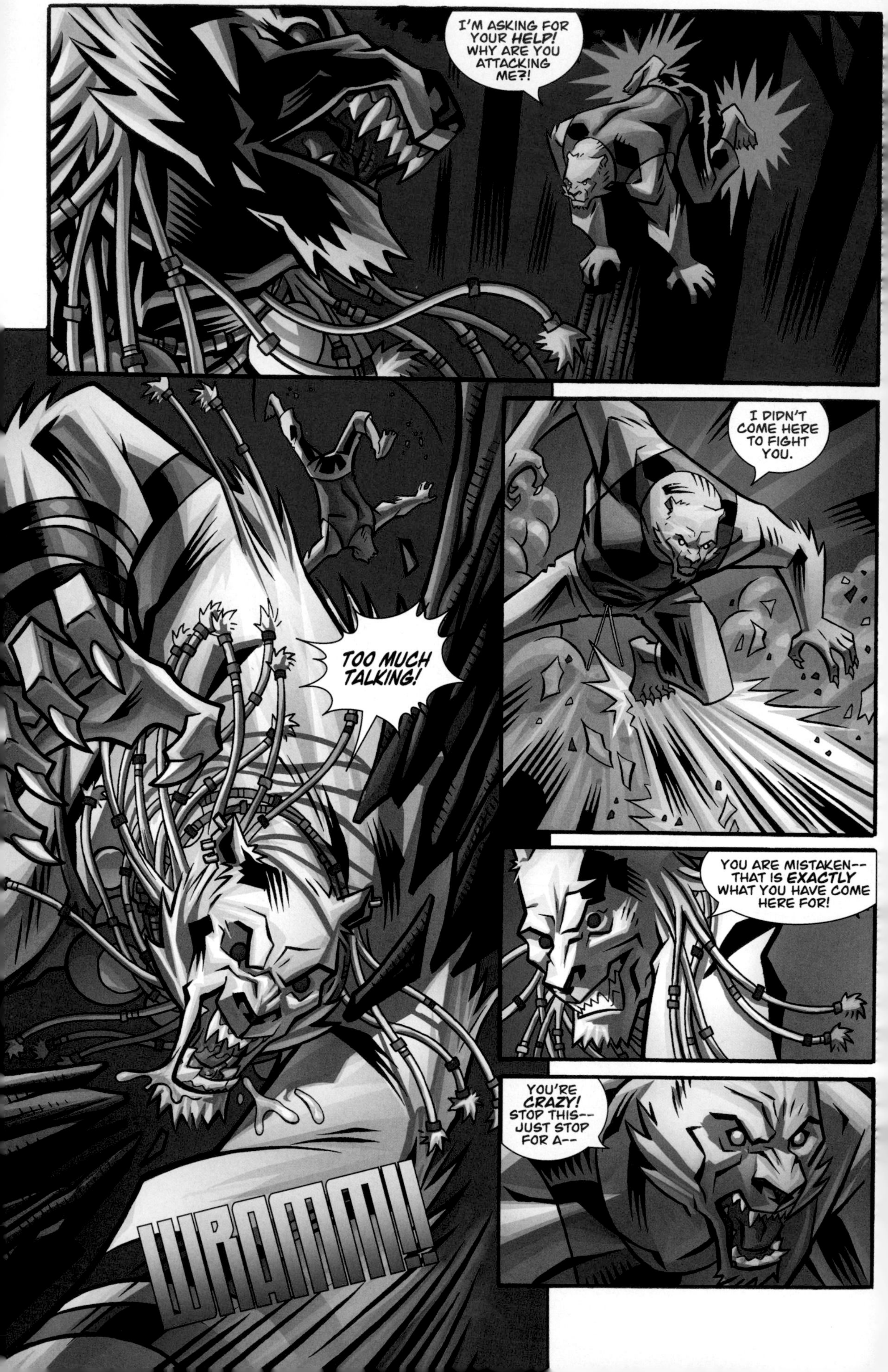
I'M ASKING FOR YOUR HELP! WHY ARE YOU ATTACKING ME?!
TOO MUCH TALKING!
I DIDN'T COME HERE TO FIGHT YOU.
YOU ARE MISTAKEN-- THAT IS EXACTLY WHAT YOU HAVE COME HERE FOR!
YOU'RE CRAZY! STOP THIS-- JUST STOP FOR A--
WHAMM!!

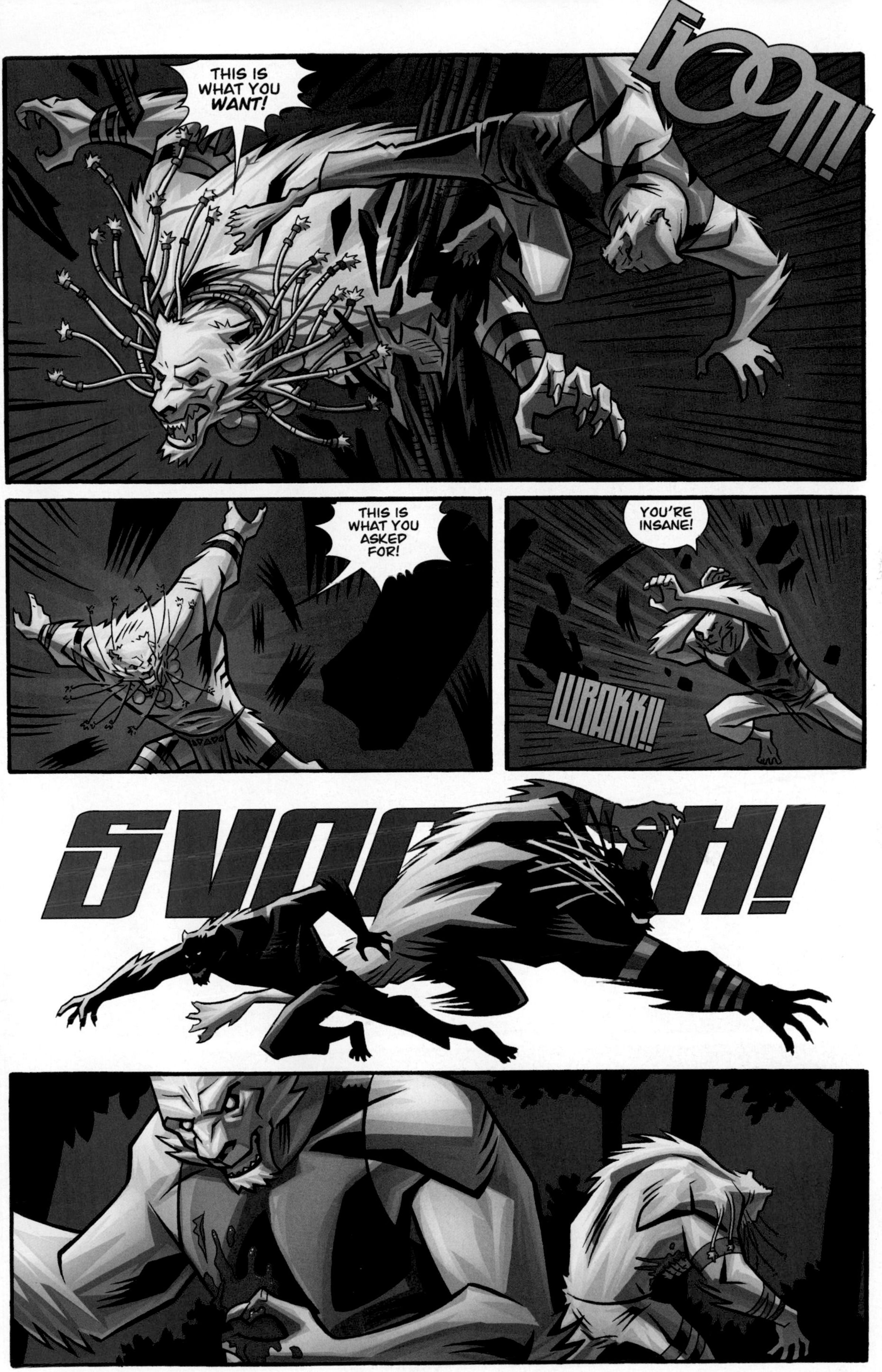
THIS IS WHAT YOU WANT!
BOOM!!
THIS IS WHAT YOU ASKED FOR!
YOU'RE INSANE!
WRAKK!!

IMPRESSIVE.

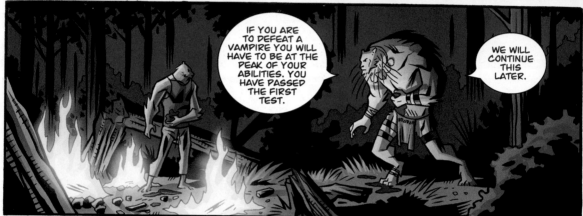

IF YOU ARE TO DEFEAT A VAMPIRE YOU WILL HAVE TO BE AT THE PEAK OF YOUR ABILITIES. YOU HAVE PASSED THE FIRST TEST.

WE WILL CONTINUE THIS LATER.

FSSSH!

I CAN'T DO THIS. I'M SCARED, MOMMY.

I NEED YOU TO DO THIS, HONEY. THEY DON'T KNOW ABOUT YOU. YOU CAN DISTRACT THEM.

DON'T WORRY, I CAN SHUT YOU DOWN BEFORE THEY TOUCH YOU.

OKAY, MOMMY.

I'M HUNGRY.

WHAT?! HOW'D YOU GET IN HERE, LITTLE GIRL?!

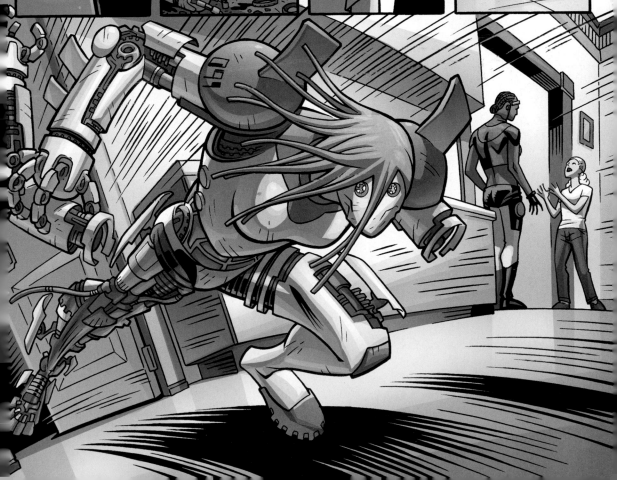

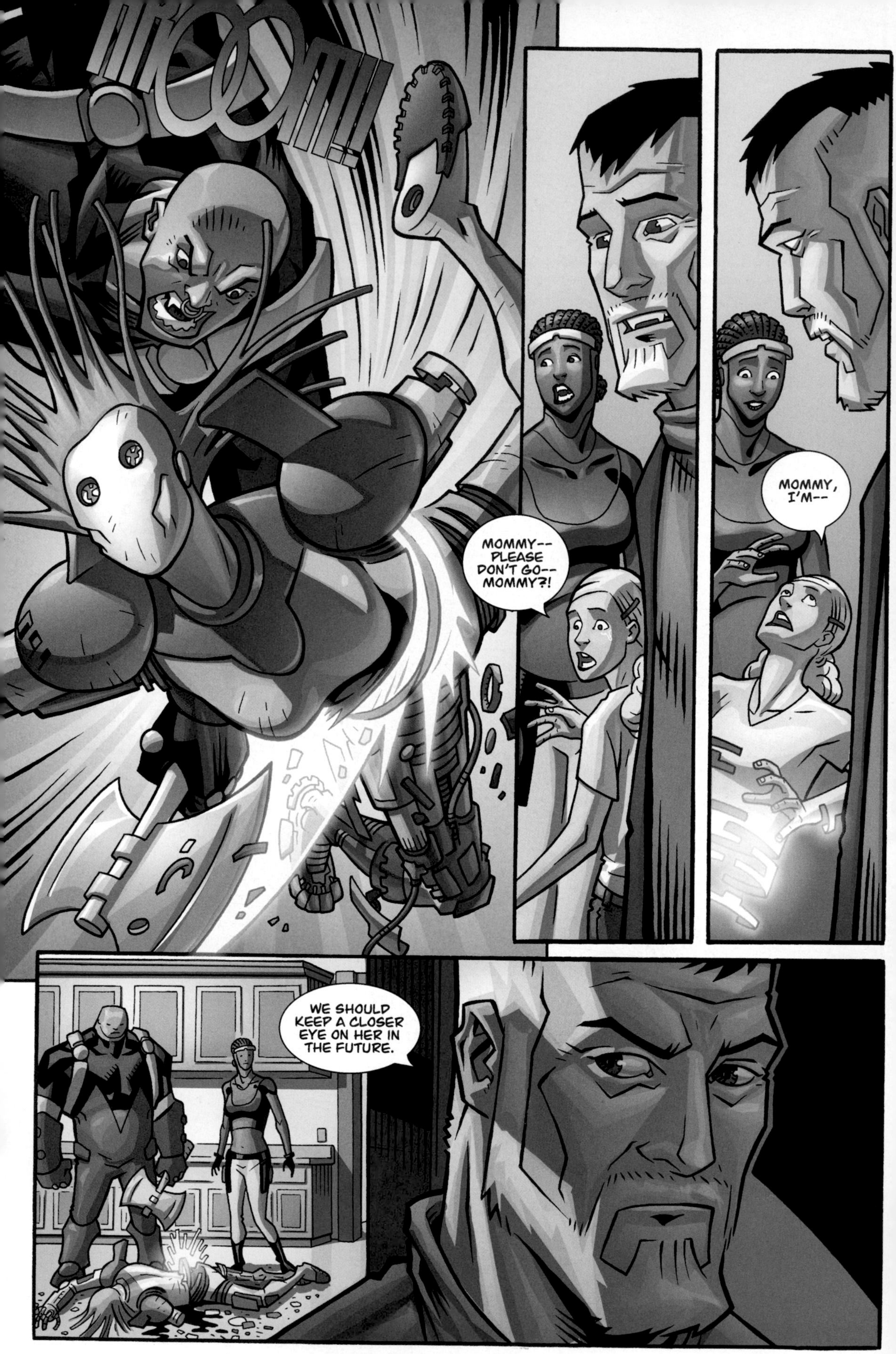
KRØØM!!
MOMMY-- PLEASE DON'T GO-- MOMMY?!
MOMMY, I'M--
WE SHOULD KEEP A CLOSER EYE ON HER IN THE FUTURE.

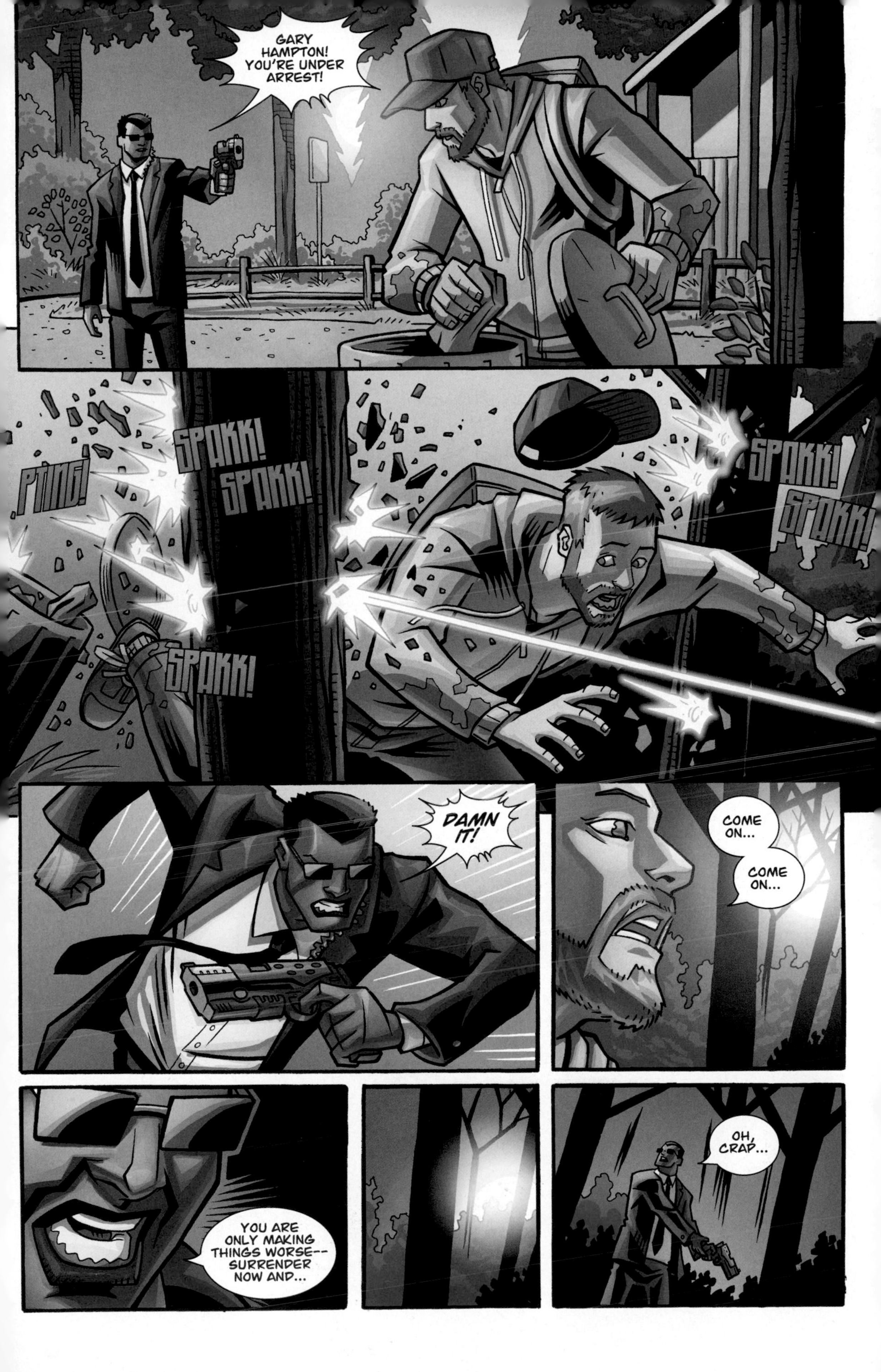
GARY HAMPTON! YOU'RE UNDER ARREST!
PTING!
SPAKK!
SPAKK!
SPAKK!
SPAKK!
SPAKK!
DAMN IT!
COME ON...
COME ON...
YOU ARE ONLY MAKING THINGS WORSE-- SURRENDER NOW AND...
OH, CRAP...

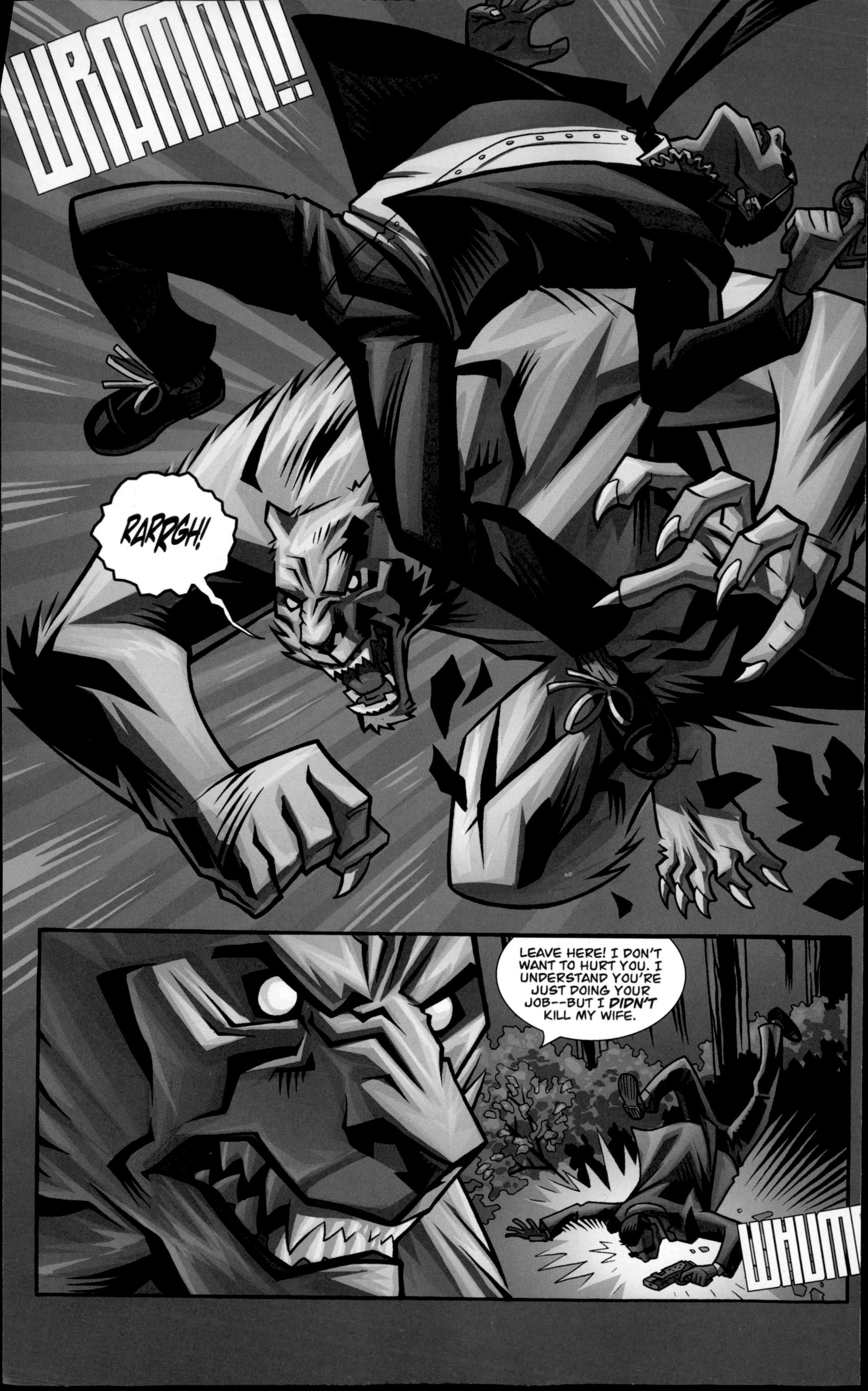
WHAMM!!
RARRGH!
LEAVE HERE! I DON'T WANT TO HURT YOU. I UNDERSTAND YOU'RE JUST DOING YOUR JOB--BUT I DIDN'T KILL MY WIFE.
WHUM

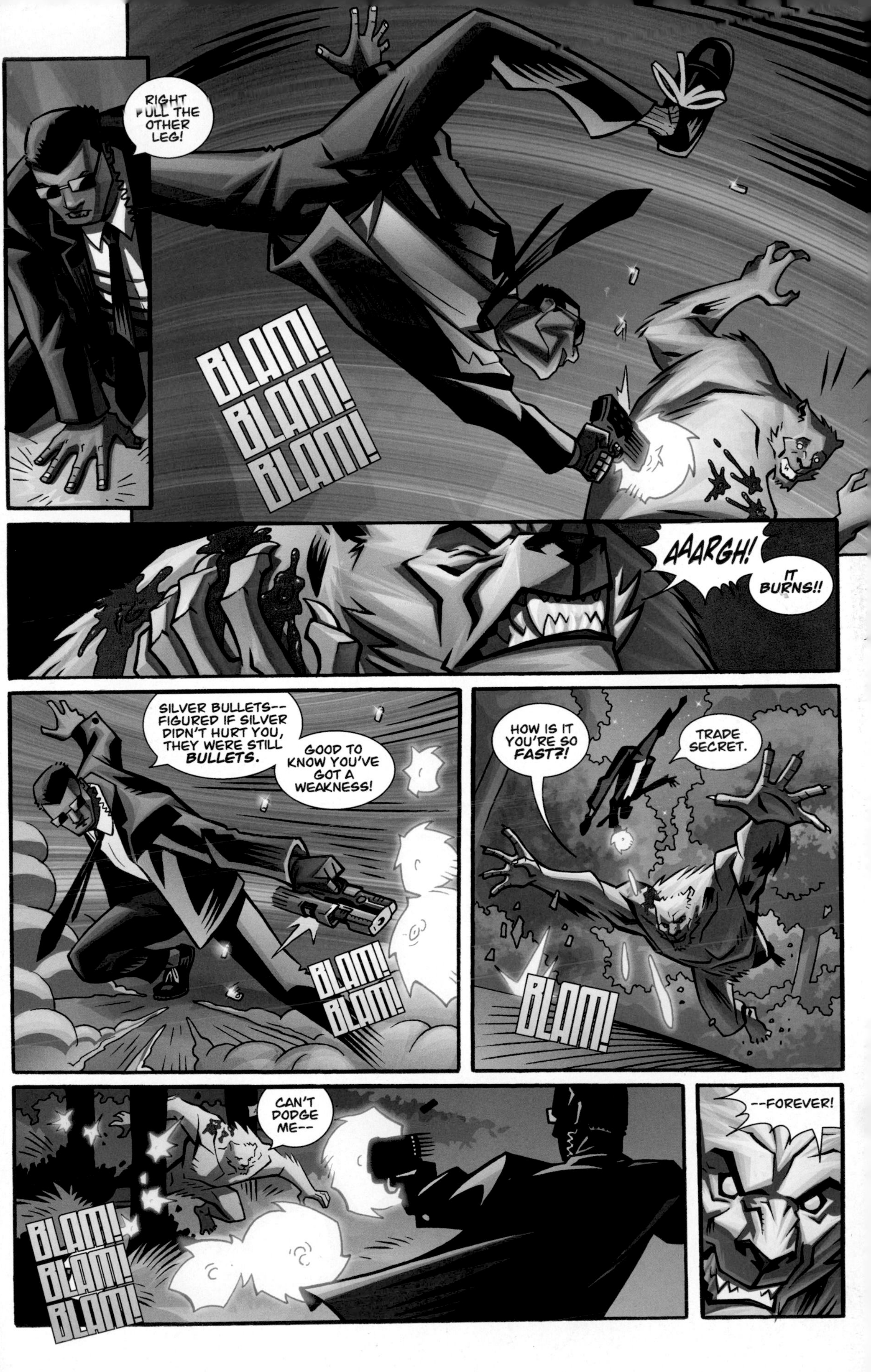
RIGHT PULL THE OTHER LEG!
BLAM! BLAM! BLAM!
AAARGH!
IT BURNS!!
SILVER BULLETS-- FIGURED IF SILVER DIDN'T HURT YOU, THEY WERE STILL BULLETS.
GOOD TO KNOW YOU'VE GOT A WEAKNESS!
BLAM! BLAM!
HOW IS IT YOU'RE SO FAST?!
TRADE SECRET.
BLAM!
CAN'T DODGE ME--
BLAM! BLAM! BLAM!
--FOREVER!

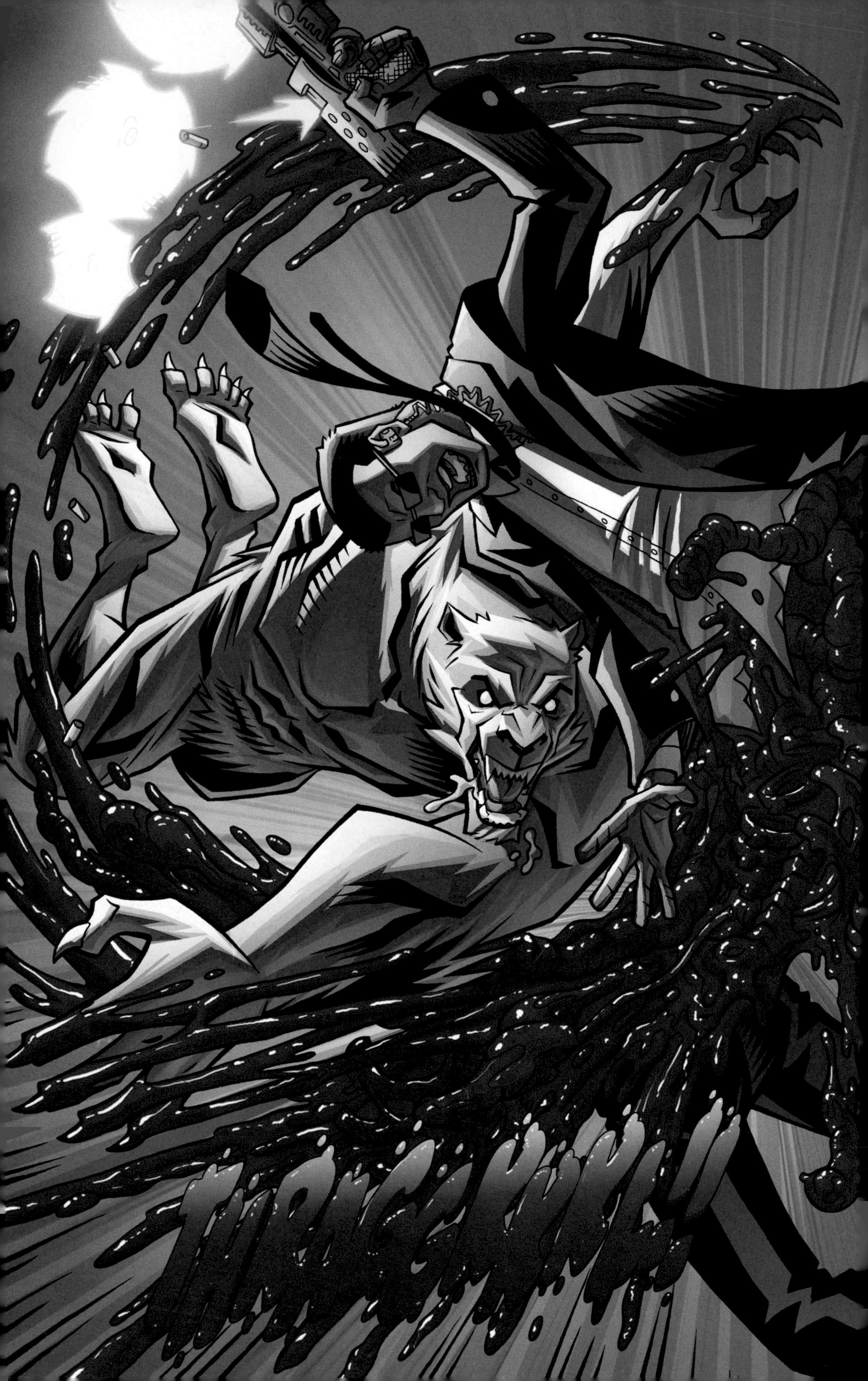

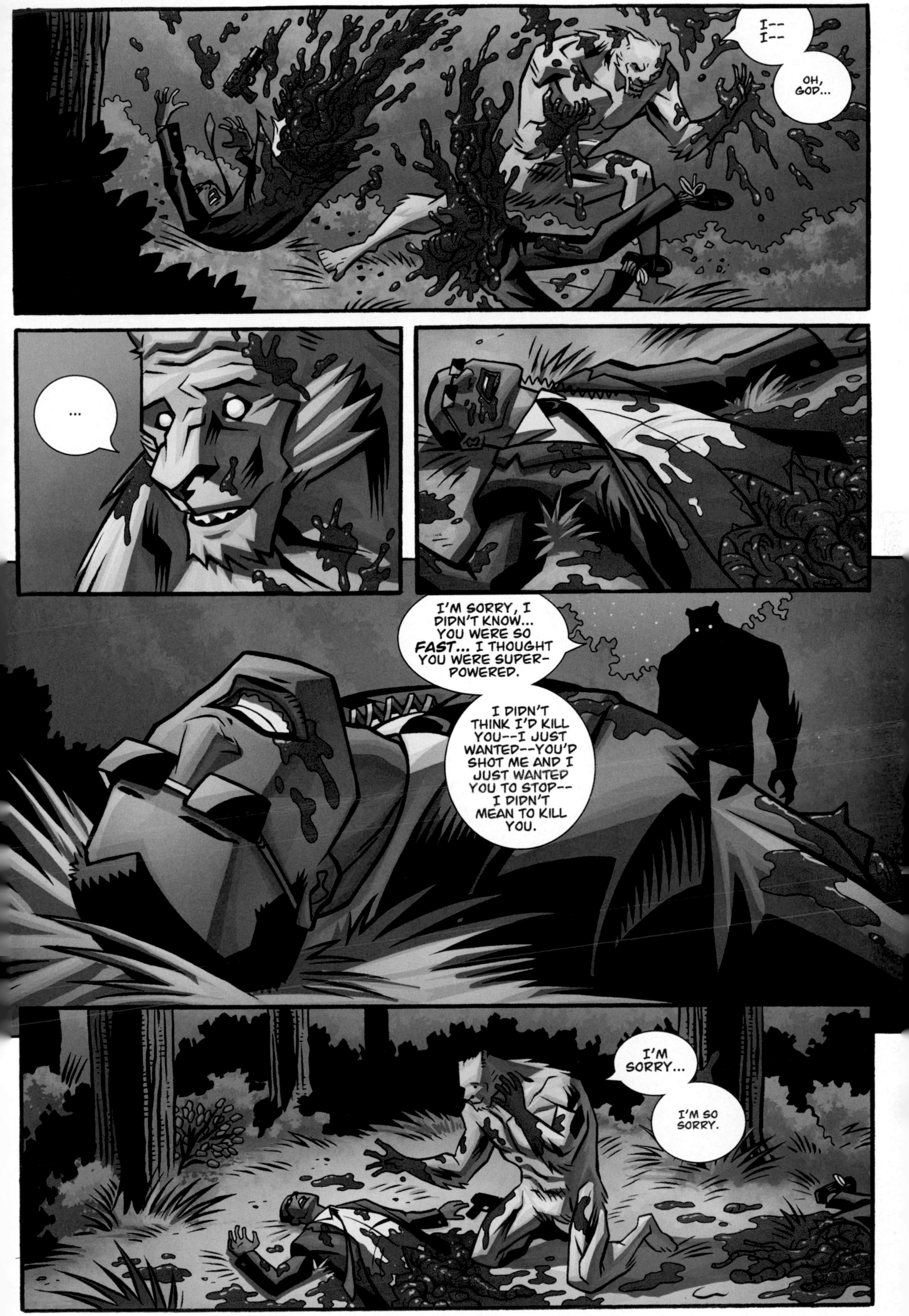
I--
I--
OH, GOD...
...
I'M SORRY, I DIDN'T KNOW... YOU WERE SO FAST... I THOUGHT YOU WERE SUPER-POWERED.
I DIDN'T THINK I'D KILL YOU--I JUST WANTED--YOU'D SHOT ME AND I JUST WANTED YOU TO STOP--I DIDN'T MEAN TO KILL YOU.
I'M SORRY...
I'M SO SORRY.

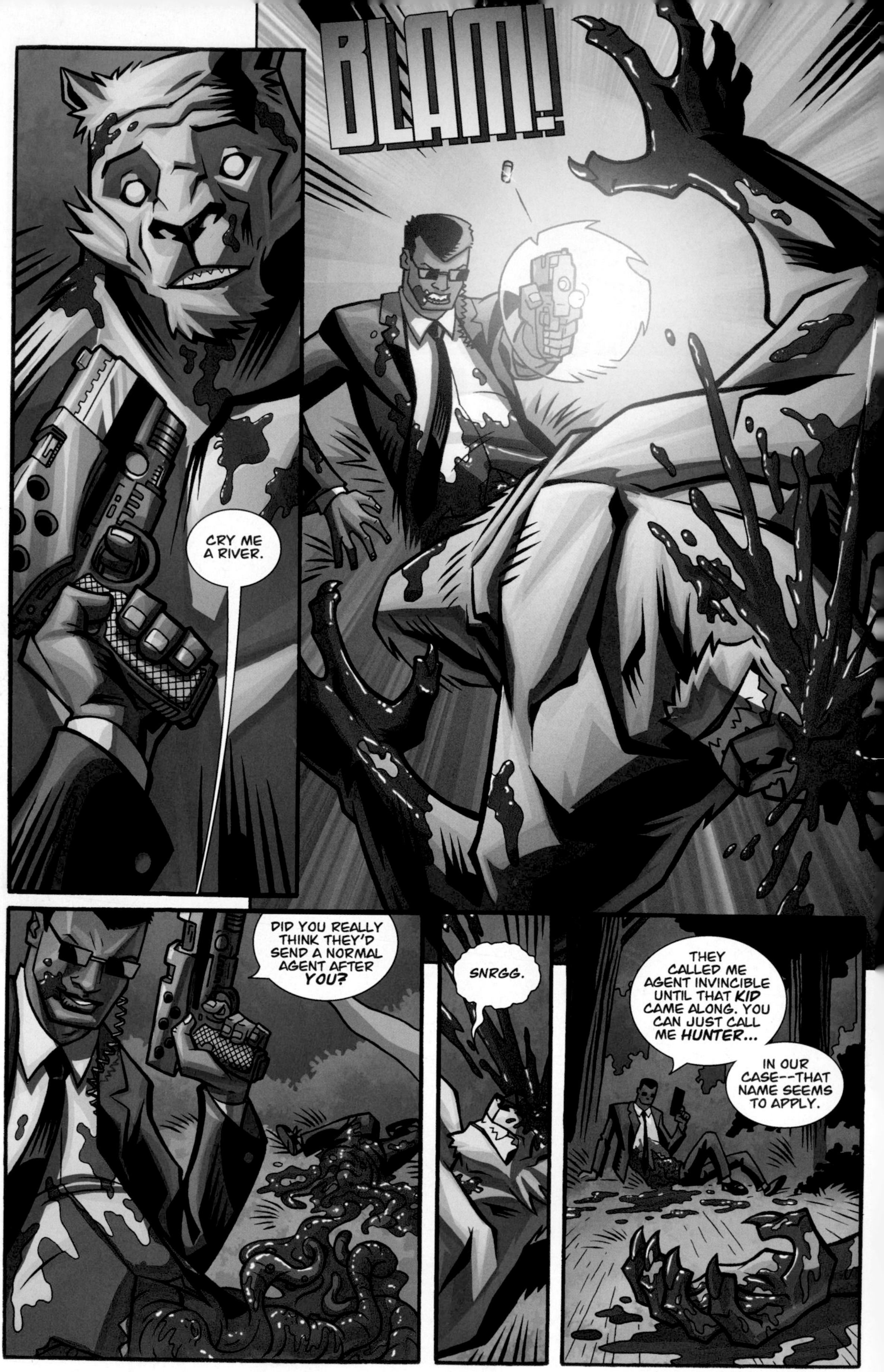
BLAM!!
CRY ME A RIVER.
DID YOU REALLY THINK THEY'D SEND A NORMAL AGENT AFTER *YOU?*
SNRGG.
THEY CALLED ME AGENT INVINCIBLE UNTIL THAT *KID* CAME ALONG. YOU CAN JUST CALL ME *HUNTER...*
IN OUR CASE--THAT NAME SEEMS TO APPLY.

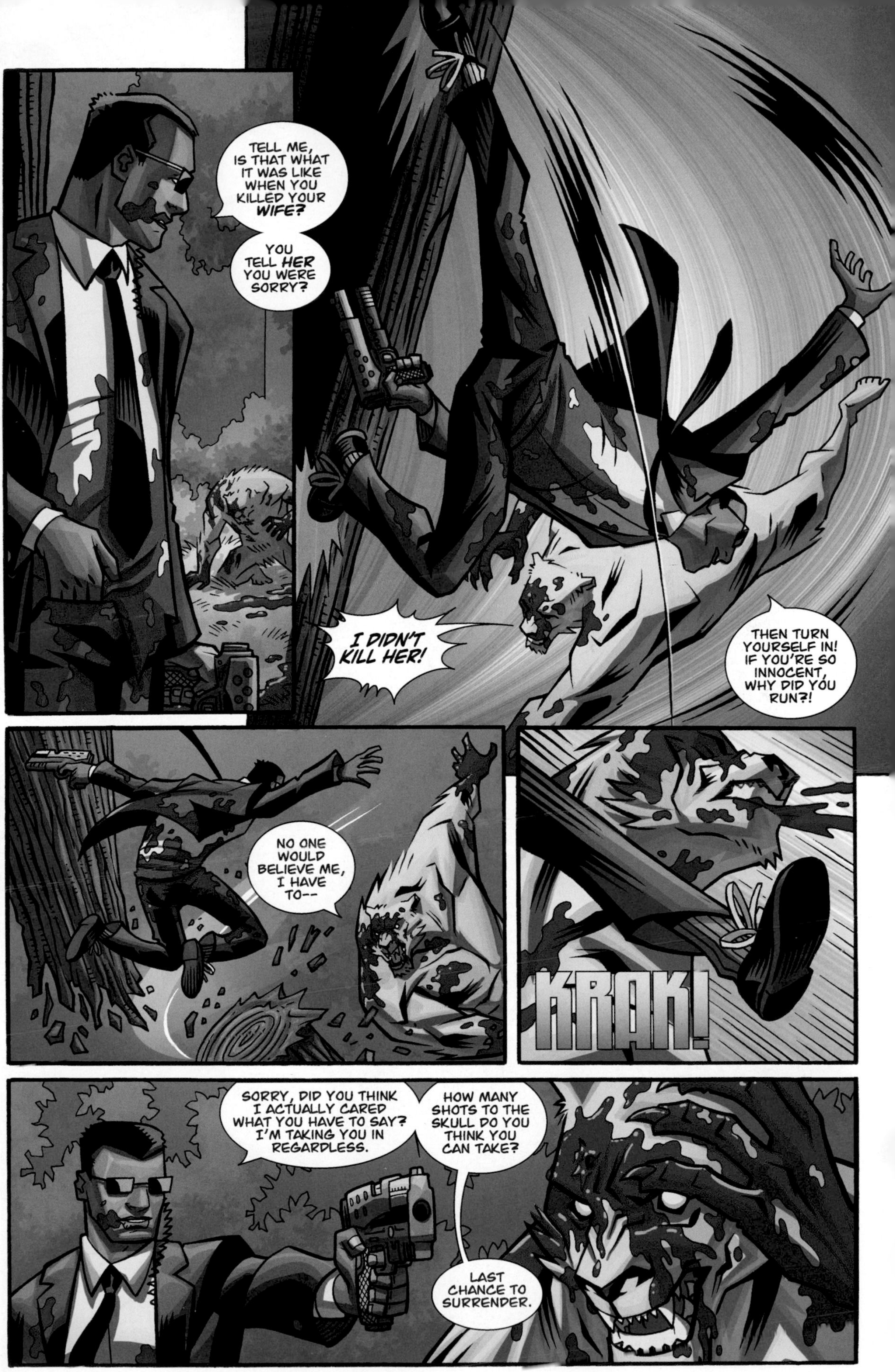
TELL ME, IS THAT WHAT IT WAS LIKE WHEN YOU KILLED YOUR WIFE?
YOU TELL HER YOU WERE SORRY?
I DIDN'T KILL HER!
THEN TURN YOURSELF IN! IF YOU'RE SO INNOCENT, WHY DID YOU RUN?!
NO ONE WOULD BELIEVE ME, I HAVE TO--
KRAK!
SORRY, DID YOU THINK I ACTUALLY CARED WHAT YOU HAVE TO SAY? I'M TAKING YOU IN REGARDLESS.
HOW MANY SHOTS TO THE SKULL DO YOU THINK YOU CAN TAKE?
LAST CHANCE TO SURRENDER.

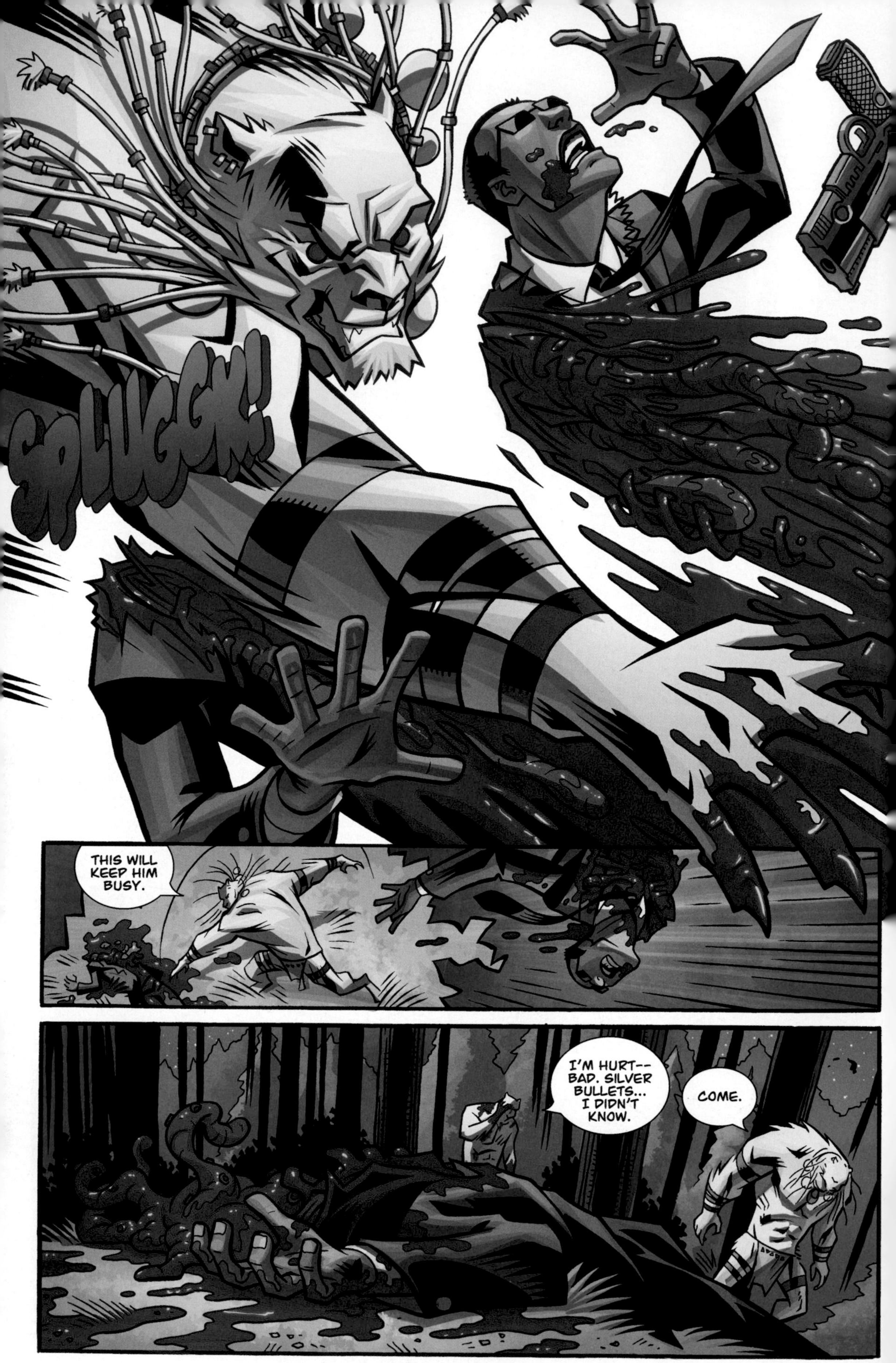
SPLUGGK!
THIS WILL KEEP HIM BUSY.
I'M HURT-- BAD. SILVER BULLETS... I DIDN'T KNOW.
COME.

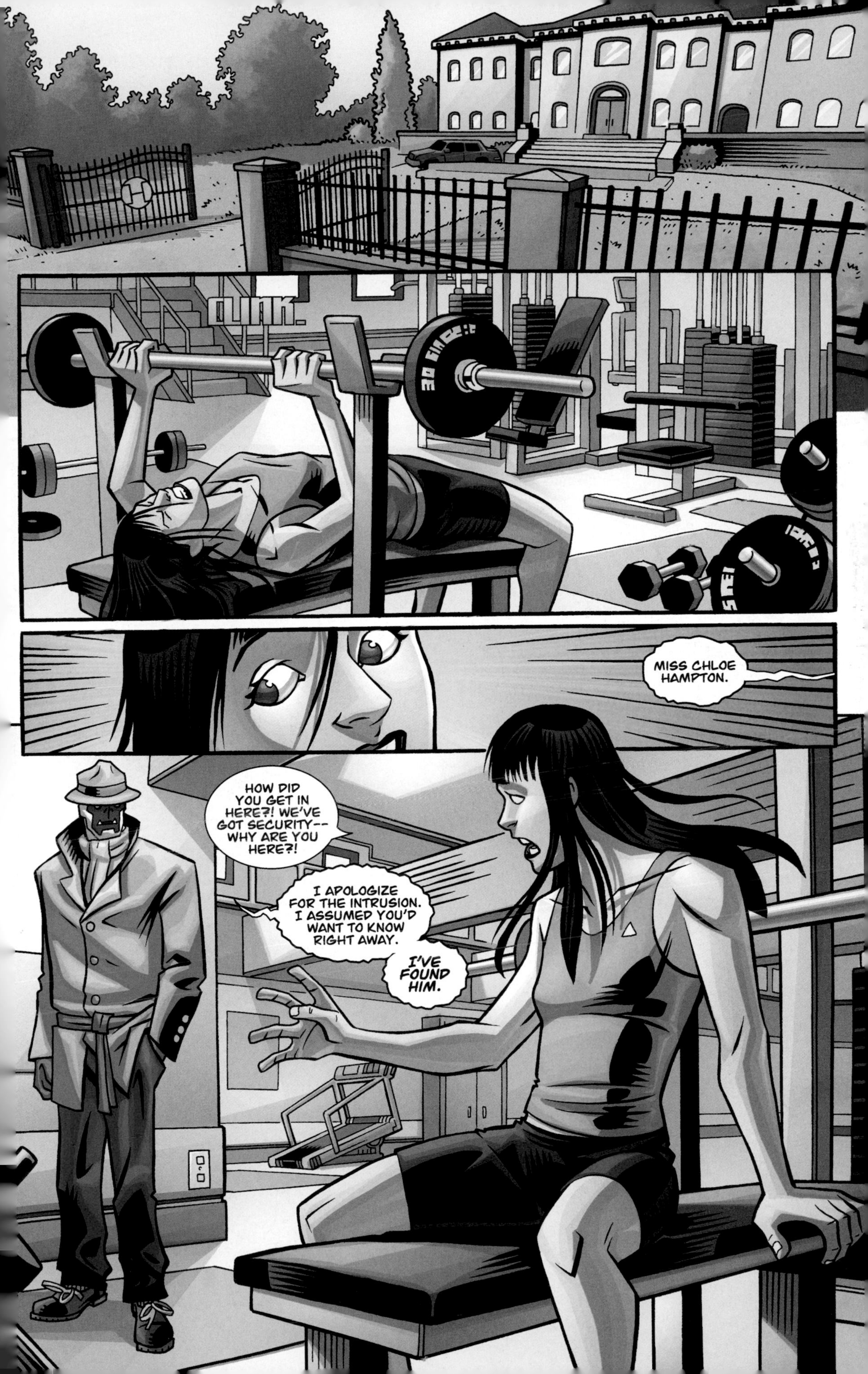
CLINK.
MISS CHLOE HAMPTON.
HOW DID YOU GET IN HERE?! WE'VE GOT SECURITY-- WHY ARE YOU HERE?!
I APOLOGIZE FOR THE INTRUSION. I ASSUMED YOU'D WANT TO KNOW RIGHT AWAY.
I'VE FOUND HIM.

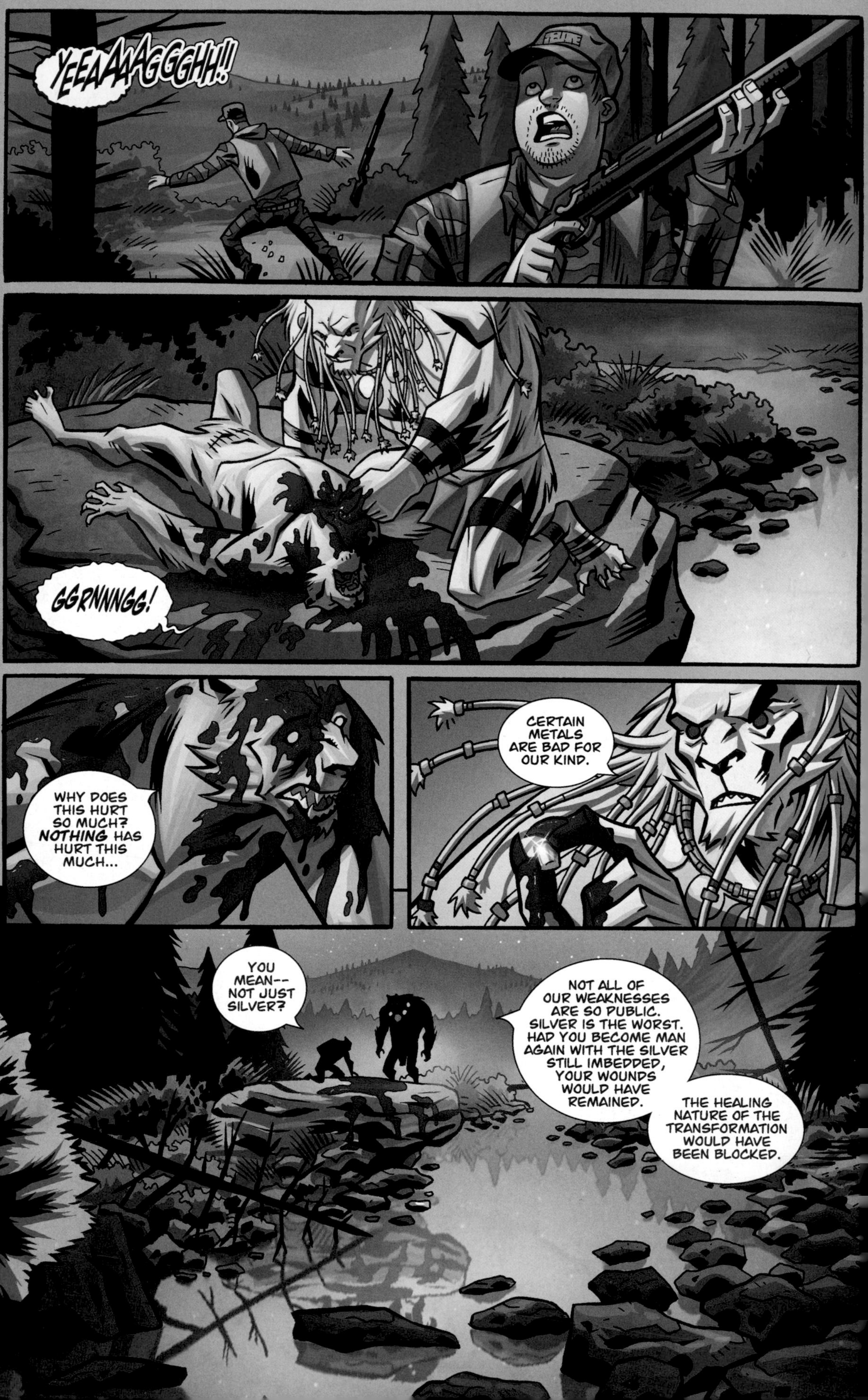
YEEAAAAGGGHH!!
GGRNNNGG!
WHY DOES THIS HURT SO MUCH? NOTHING HAS HURT THIS MUCH...
CERTAIN METALS ARE BAD FOR OUR KIND.
YOU MEAN-- NOT JUST SILVER?
NOT ALL OF OUR WEAKNESSES ARE SO PUBLIC. SILVER IS THE WORST. HAD YOU BECOME MAN AGAIN WITH THE SILVER STILL IMBEDDED, YOUR WOUNDS WOULD HAVE REMAINED.
THE HEALING NATURE OF THE TRANSFORMATION WOULD HAVE BEEN BLOCKED.

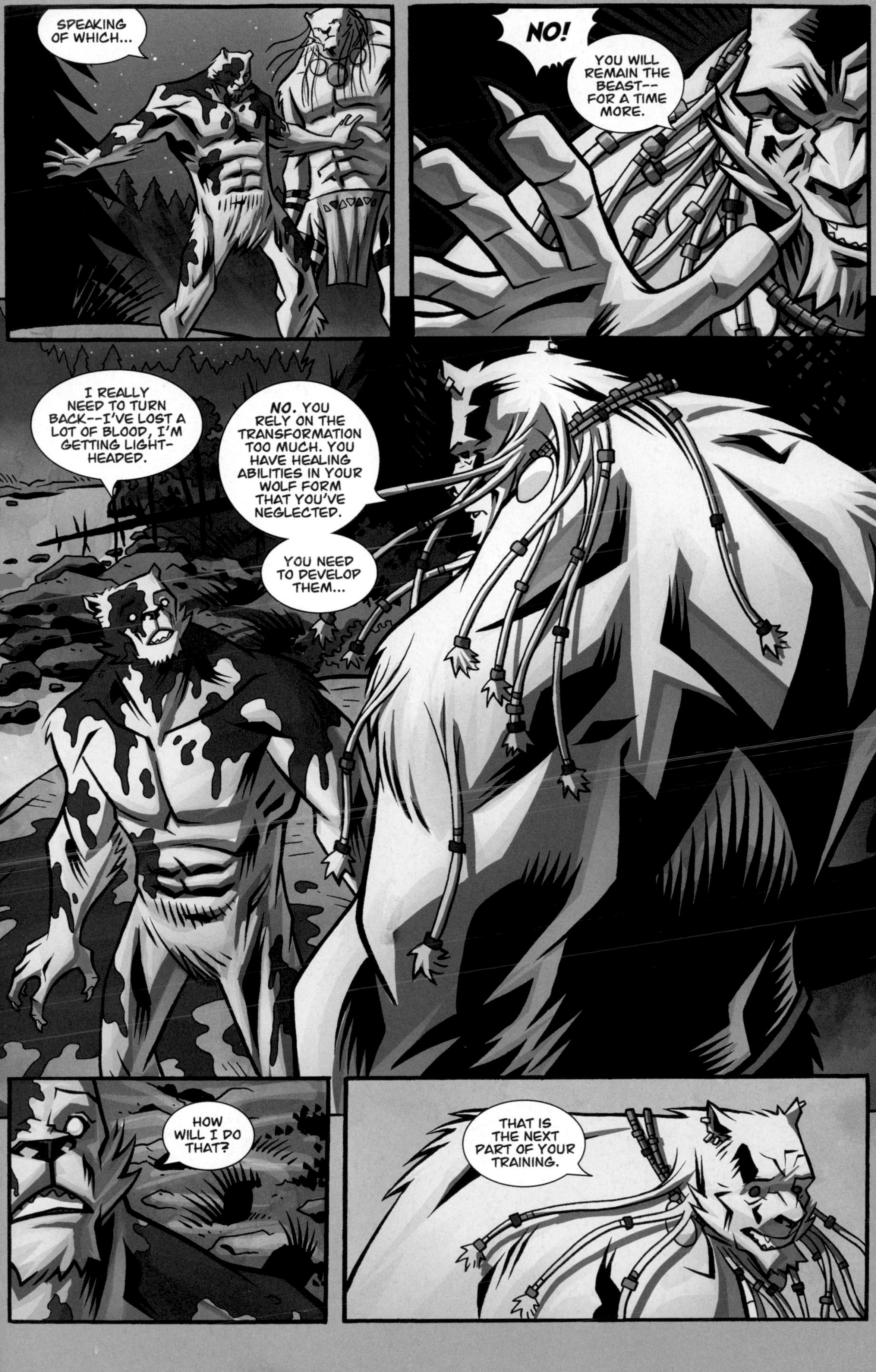
SPEAKING OF WHICH...
NO!
YOU WILL REMAIN THE BEAST-- FOR A TIME MORE.
I REALLY NEED TO TURN BACK--I'VE LOST A LOT OF BLOOD, I'M GETTING LIGHT-HEADED.
NO. YOU RELY ON THE TRANSFORMATION TOO MUCH. YOU HAVE HEALING ABILITIES IN YOUR WOLF FORM THAT YOU'VE NEGLECTED.
YOU NEED TO DEVELOP THEM...
HOW WILL I DO THAT?
THAT IS THE NEXT PART OF YOUR TRAINING.

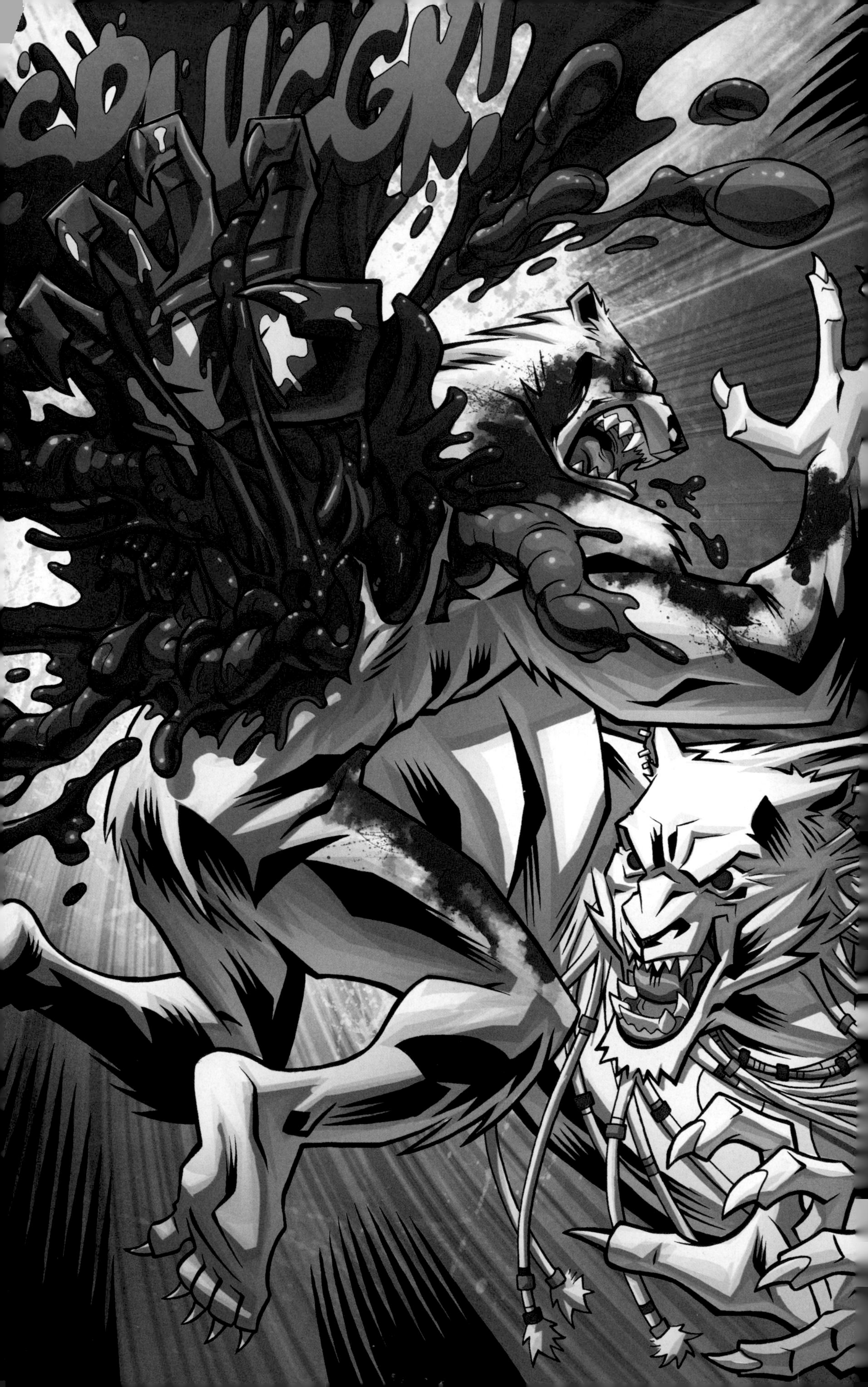

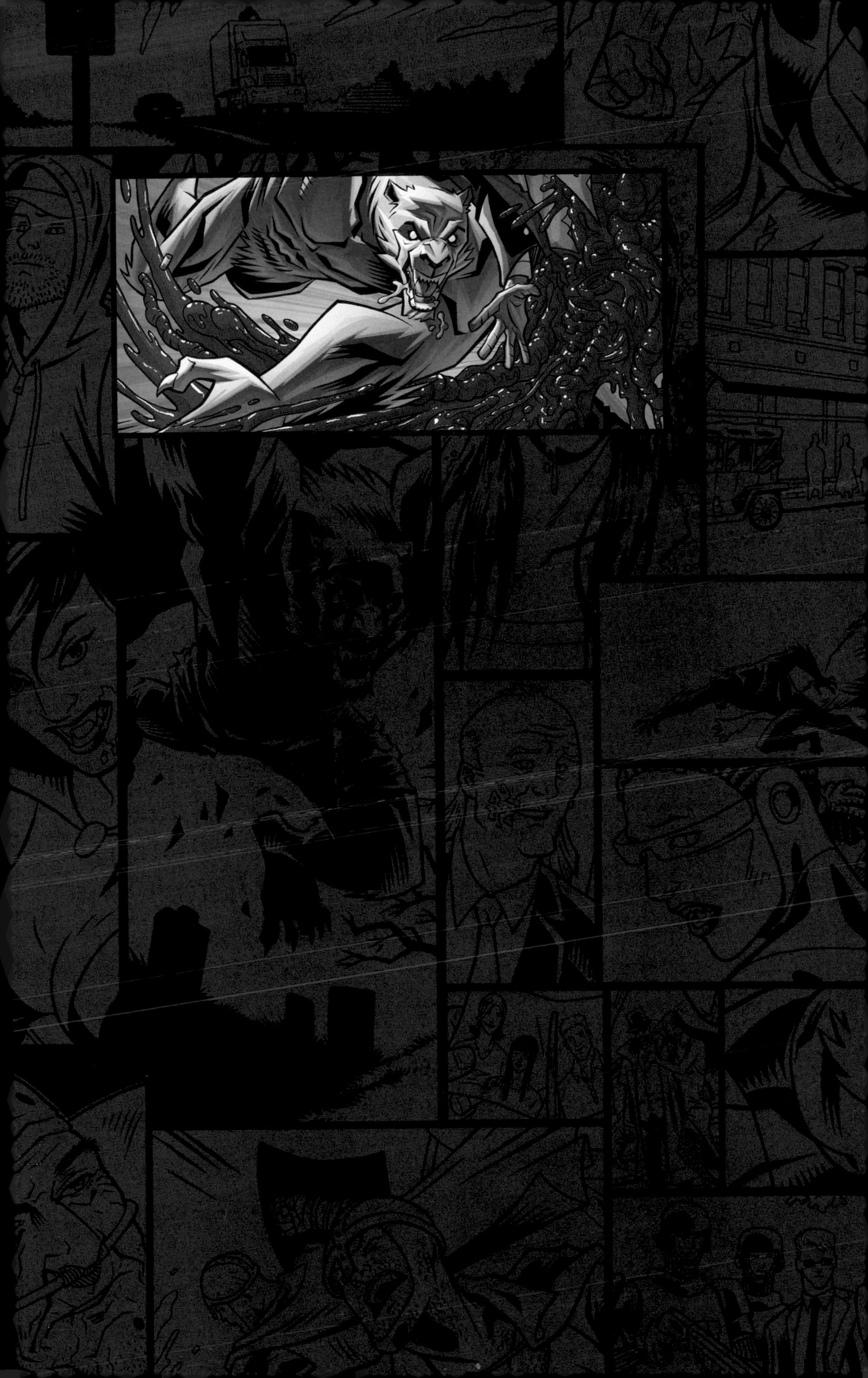

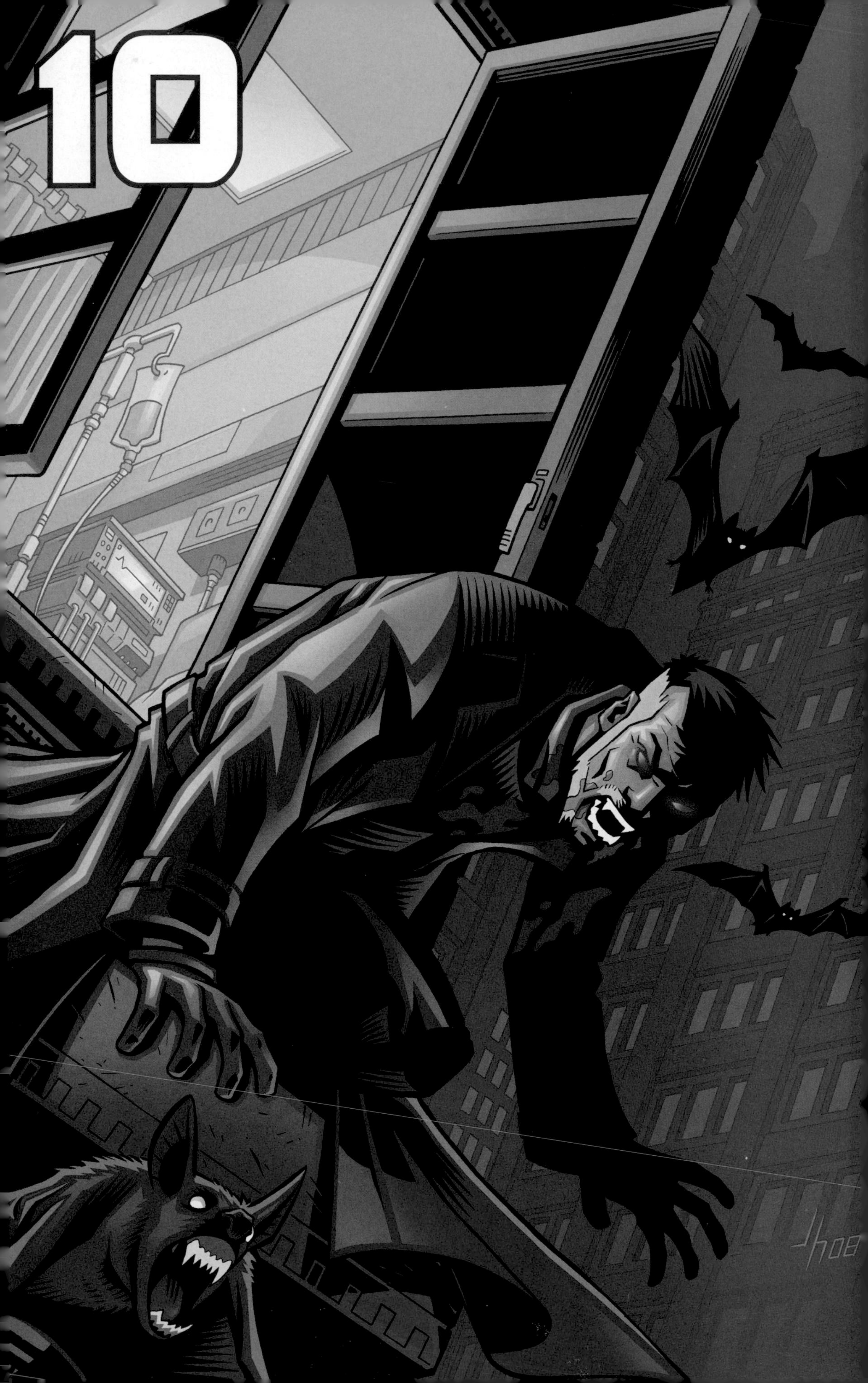
10

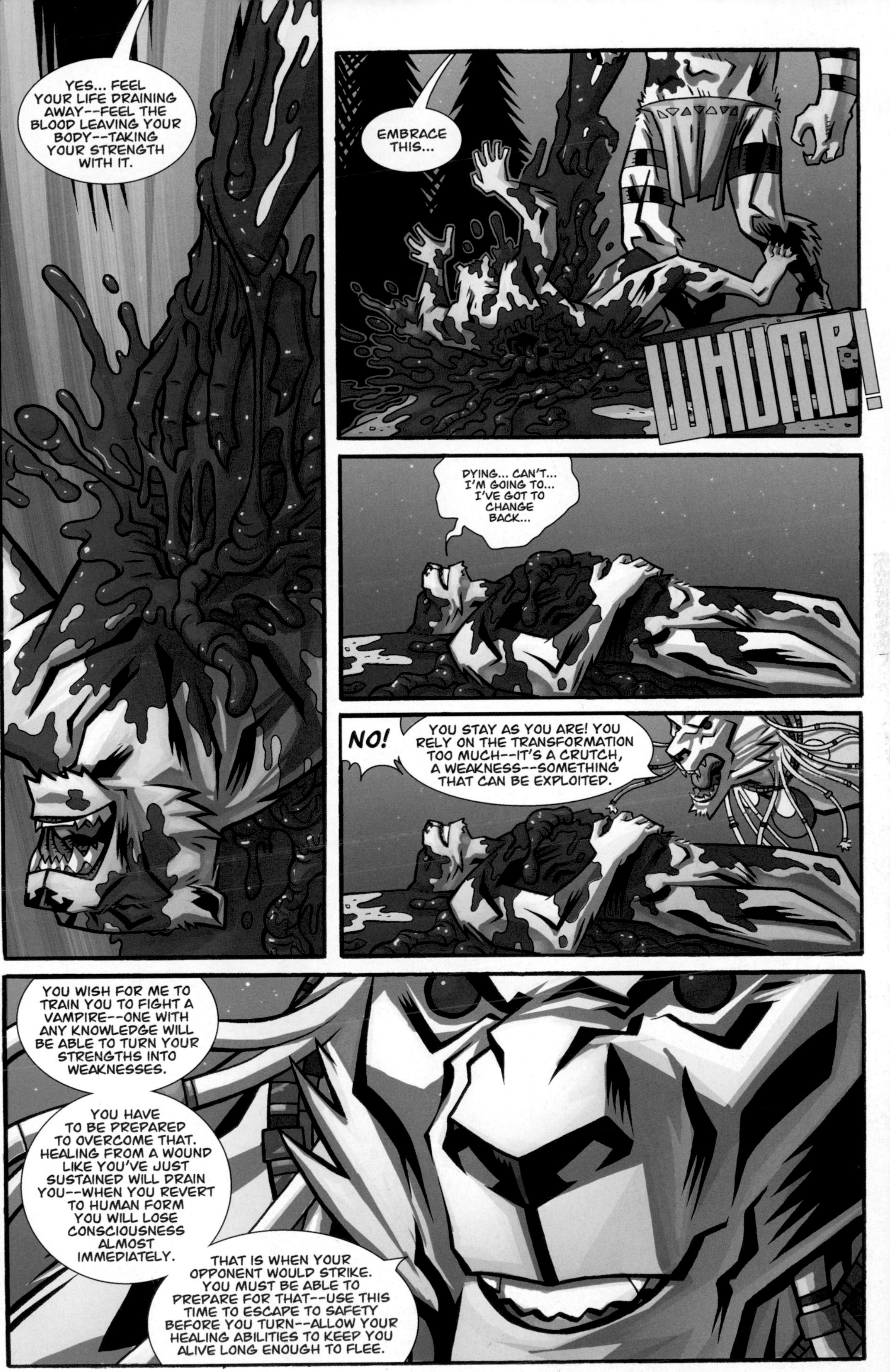
YES... FEEL YOUR LIFE DRAINING AWAY--FEEL THE BLOOD LEAVING YOUR BODY--TAKING YOUR STRENGTH WITH IT.
EMBRACE THIS...
WHUMP!
DYING... CAN'T... I'M GOING TO... I'VE GOT TO CHANGE BACK...
NO!
YOU STAY AS YOU ARE! YOU RELY ON THE TRANSFORMATION TOO MUCH--IT'S A CRUTCH, A WEAKNESS--SOMETHING THAT CAN BE EXPLOITED.
YOU WISH FOR ME TO TRAIN YOU TO FIGHT A VAMPIRE--ONE WITH ANY KNOWLEDGE WILL BE ABLE TO TURN YOUR STRENGTHS INTO WEAKNESSES.
YOU HAVE TO BE PREPARED TO OVERCOME THAT. HEALING FROM A WOUND LIKE YOU'VE JUST SUSTAINED WILL DRAIN YOU--WHEN YOU REVERT TO HUMAN FORM YOU WILL LOSE CONSCIOUSNESS ALMOST IMMEDIATELY.
THAT IS WHEN YOUR OPPONENT WOULD STRIKE. YOU MUST BE ABLE TO PREPARE FOR THAT--USE THIS TIME TO ESCAPE TO SAFETY BEFORE YOU TURN--ALLOW YOUR HEALING ABILITIES TO KEEP YOU ALIVE LONG ENOUGH TO FLEE.

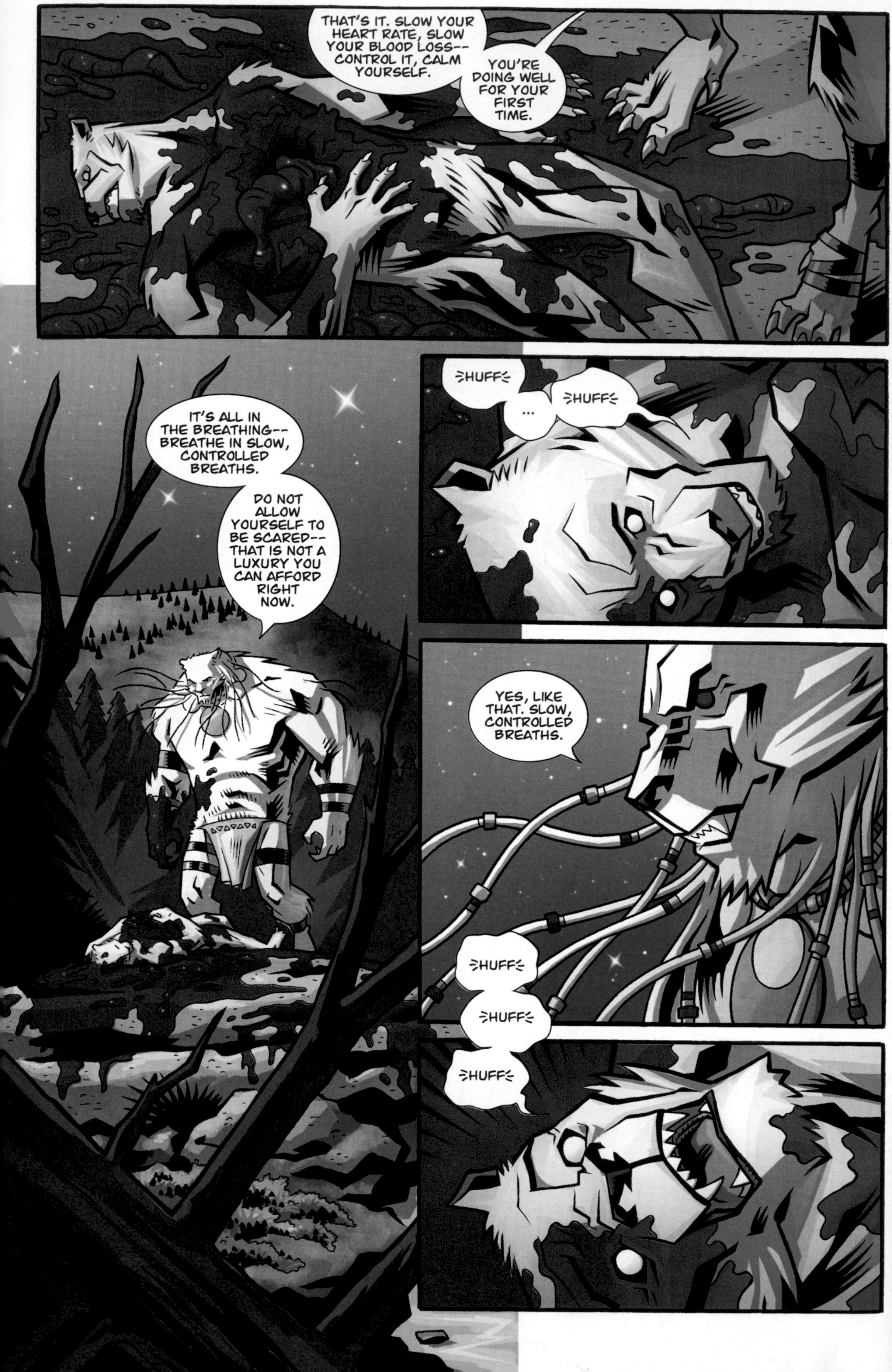
THAT'S IT. SLOW YOUR HEART RATE, SLOW YOUR BLOOD LOSS-- CONTROL IT, CALM YOURSELF.
YOU'RE DOING WELL FOR YOUR FIRST TIME.
IT'S ALL IN THE BREATHING-- BREATHE IN SLOW, CONTROLLED BREATHS.
DO NOT ALLOW YOURSELF TO BE SCARED-- THAT IS NOT A LUXURY YOU CAN AFFORD RIGHT NOW.
HUFF
...
HUFF
YES, LIKE THAT. SLOW, CONTROLLED BREATHS.
HUFF
HUFF
HUFF

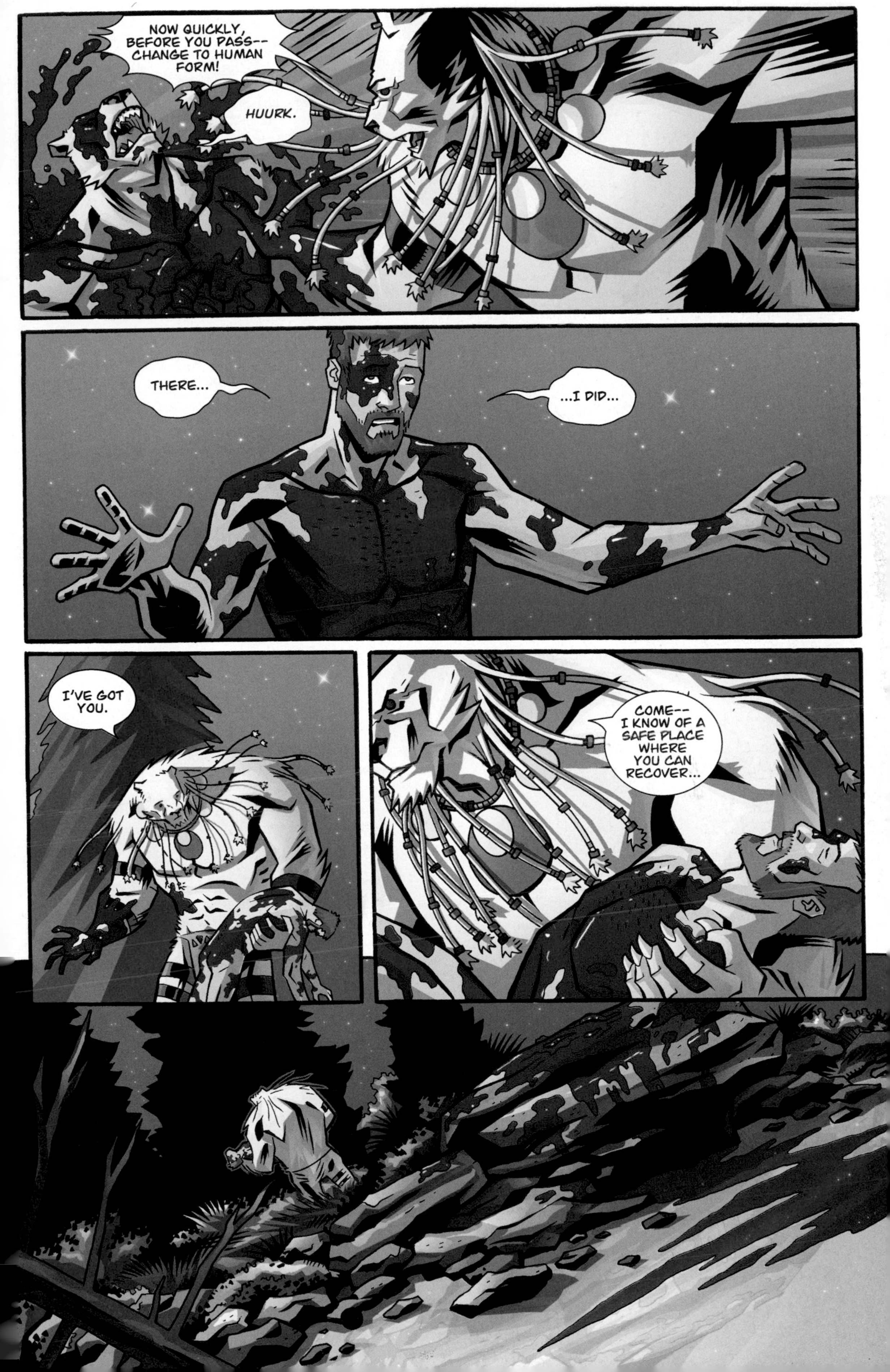
NOW QUICKLY, BEFORE YOU PASS-- CHANGE TO HUMAN FORM!
HUURK.
THERE...
...I DID...
I'VE GOT YOU.
COME-- I KNOW OF A SAFE PLACE WHERE YOU CAN RECOVER...

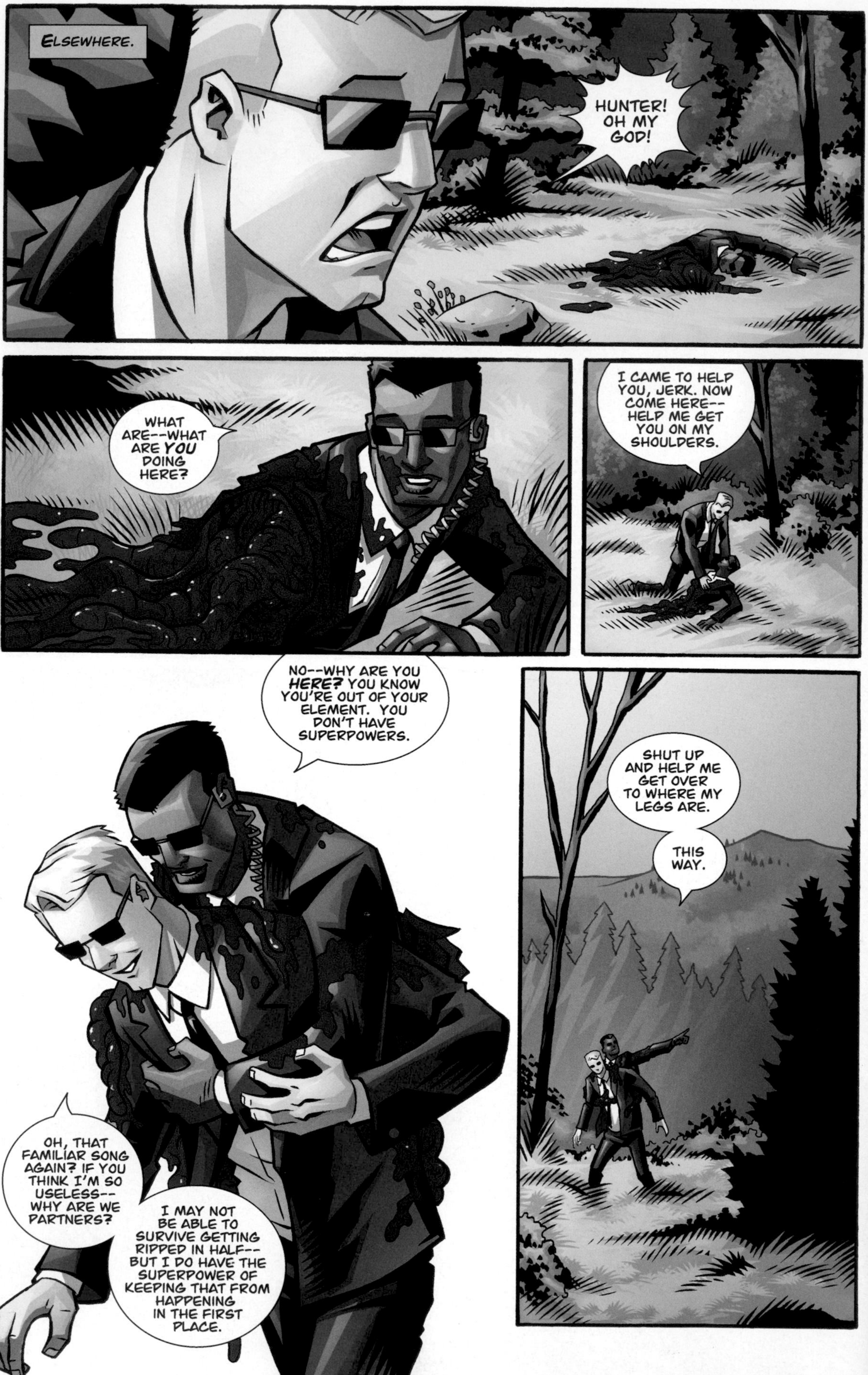
ELSEWHERE.
HUNTER! OH MY GOD!
WHAT ARE--WHAT ARE YOU DOING HERE?
I CAME TO HELP YOU, JERK. NOW COME HERE-- HELP ME GET YOU ON MY SHOULDERS.
NO--WHY ARE YOU HERE? YOU KNOW YOU'RE OUT OF YOUR ELEMENT. YOU DON'T HAVE SUPERPOWERS.
OH, THAT FAMILIAR SONG AGAIN? IF YOU THINK I'M SO USELESS-- WHY ARE WE PARTNERS?
I MAY NOT BE ABLE TO SURVIVE GETTING RIPPED IN HALF-- BUT I DO HAVE THE SUPERPOWER OF KEEPING THAT FROM HAPPENING IN THE FIRST PLACE.
SHUT UP AND HELP ME GET OVER TO WHERE MY LEGS ARE.
THIS WAY.

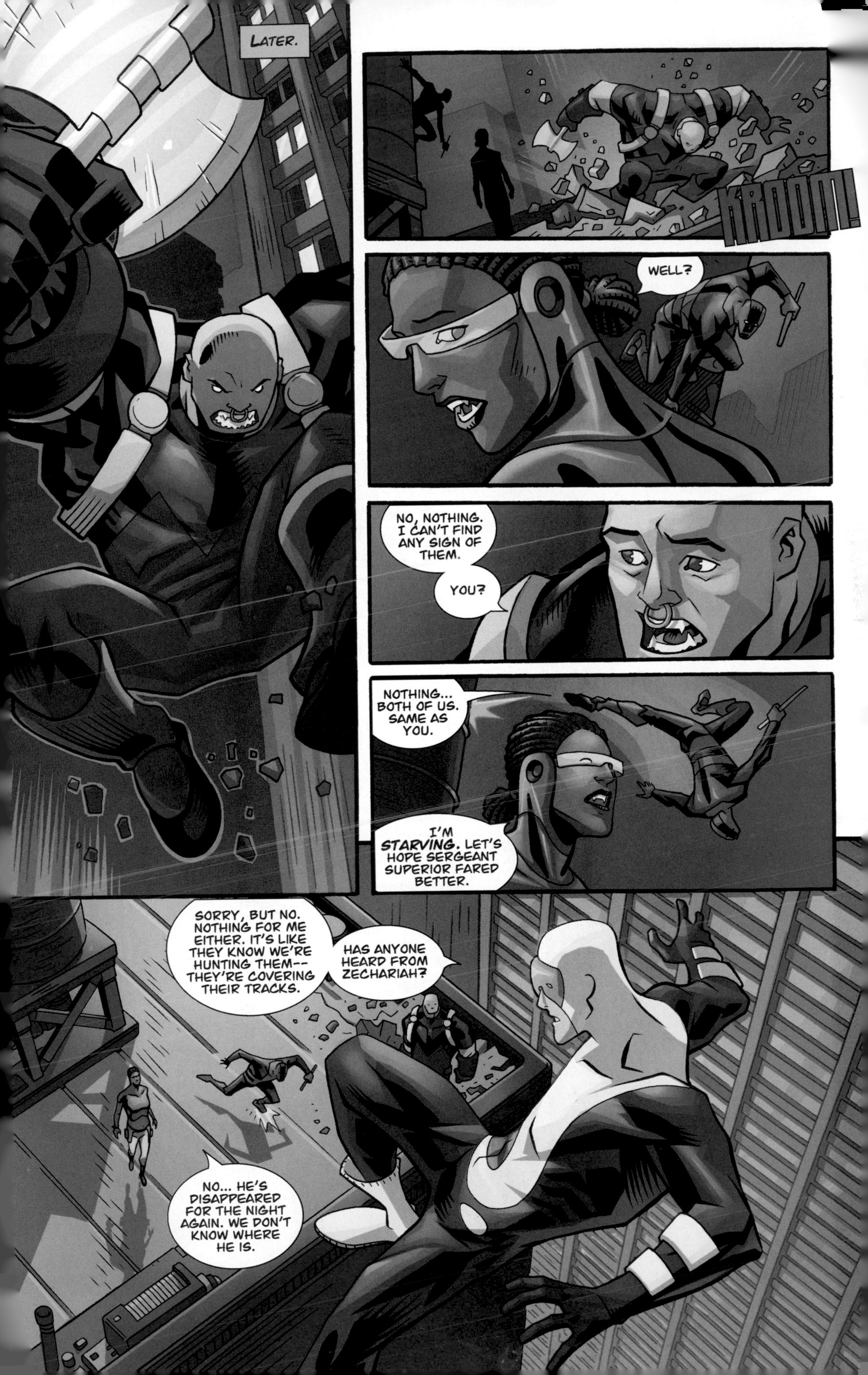
LATER.
KROOM!
WELL?
NO, NOTHING. I CAN'T FIND ANY SIGN OF THEM.
YOU?
NOTHING... BOTH OF US. SAME AS YOU.
I'M STARVING. LET'S HOPE SERGEANT SUPERIOR FARED BETTER.
SORRY, BUT NO. NOTHING FOR ME EITHER. IT'S LIKE THEY KNOW WE'RE HUNTING THEM-- THEY'RE COVERING THEIR TRACKS.
HAS ANYONE HEARD FROM ZECHARIAH?
NO... HE'S DISAPPEARED FOR THE NIGHT AGAIN. WE DON'T KNOW WHERE HE IS.

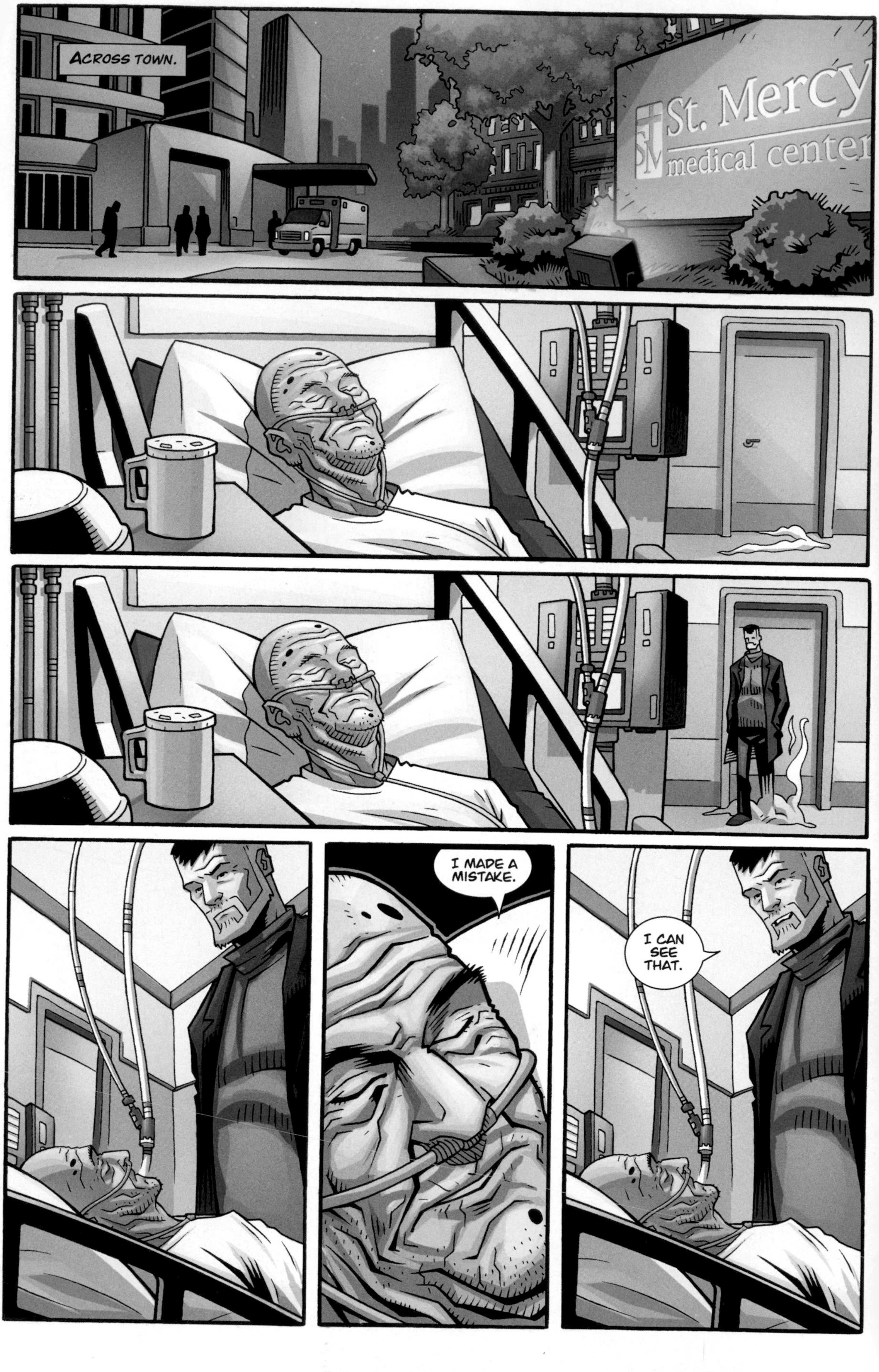
ACROSS TOWN.
St. Mercy medical center
I MADE A MISTAKE.
I CAN SEE THAT.

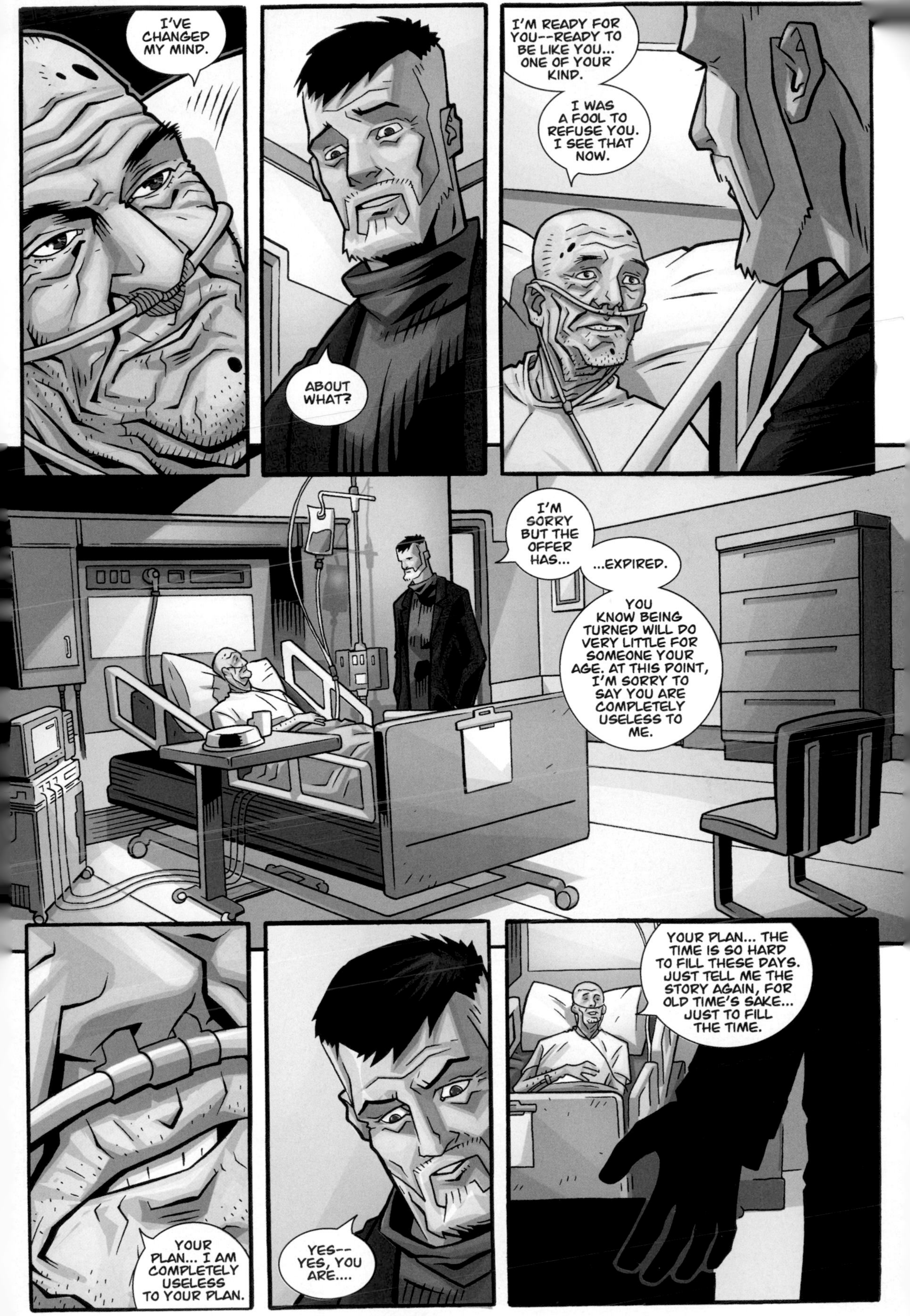
I'VE CHANGED MY MIND.
ABOUT WHAT?
I'M READY FOR YOU--READY TO BE LIKE YOU... ONE OF YOUR KIND.
I WAS A FOOL TO REFUSE YOU. I SEE THAT NOW.
I'M SORRY BUT THE OFFER HAS...
...EXPIRED.
YOU KNOW BEING TURNED WILL DO VERY LITTLE FOR SOMEONE YOUR AGE. AT THIS POINT, I'M SORRY TO SAY YOU ARE COMPLETELY USELESS TO ME.
YOUR PLAN... I AM COMPLETELY USELESS TO YOUR PLAN.
YES-- YES, YOU ARE....
YOUR PLAN... THE TIME IS SO HARD TO FILL THESE DAYS. JUST TELL ME THE STORY AGAIN, FOR OLD TIME'S SAKE... JUST TO FILL THE TIME.

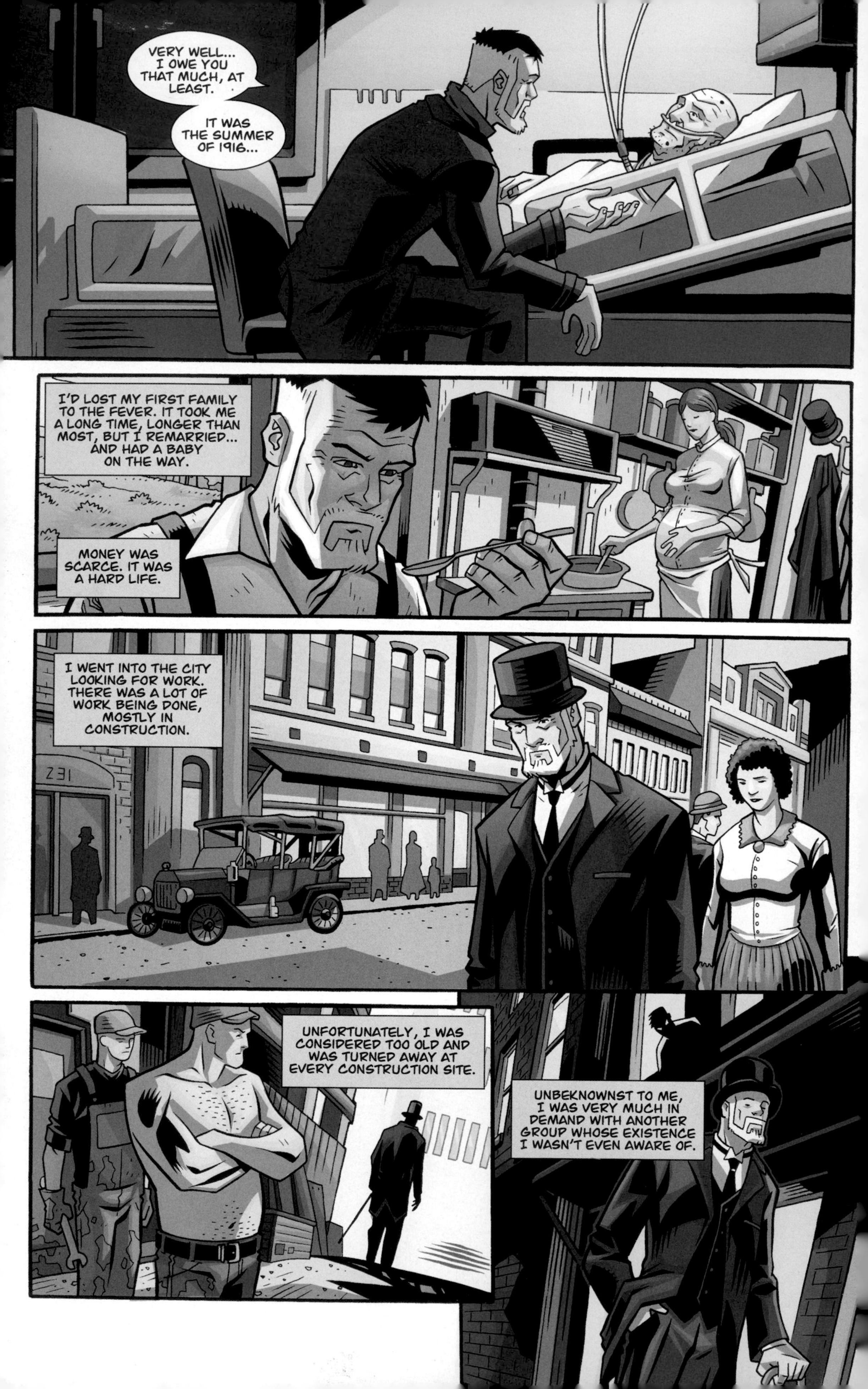
VERY WELL... I OWE YOU THAT MUCH, AT LEAST.
IT WAS THE SUMMER OF 1916...
I'D LOST MY FIRST FAMILY TO THE FEVER. IT TOOK ME A LONG TIME, LONGER THAN MOST, BUT I REMARRIED... AND HAD A BABY ON THE WAY.
MONEY WAS SCARCE. IT WAS A HARD LIFE.
I WENT INTO THE CITY LOOKING FOR WORK. THERE WAS A LOT OF WORK BEING DONE, MOSTLY IN CONSTRUCTION.
231
UNFORTUNATELY, I WAS CONSIDERED TOO OLD AND WAS TURNED AWAY AT EVERY CONSTRUCTION SITE.
UNBEKNOWNST TO ME, I WAS VERY MUCH IN DEMAND WITH ANOTHER GROUP WHOSE EXISTENCE I WASN'T EVEN AWARE OF.

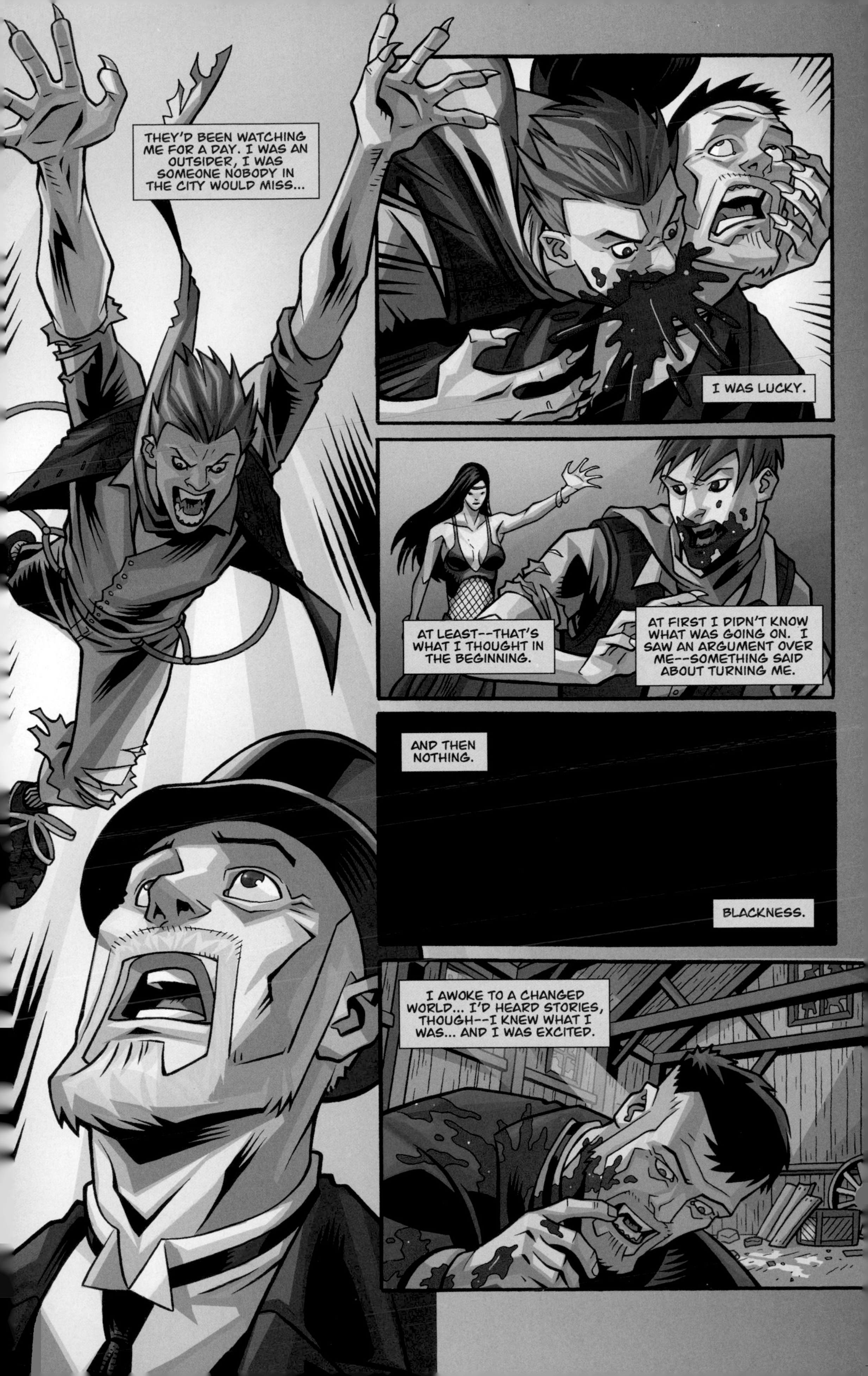
THEY'D BEEN WATCHING ME FOR A DAY. I WAS AN OUTSIDER, I WAS SOMEONE NOBODY IN THE CITY WOULD MISS...
I WAS LUCKY.
AT LEAST--THAT'S WHAT I THOUGHT IN THE BEGINNING.
AT FIRST I DIDN'T KNOW WHAT WAS GOING ON. I SAW AN ARGUMENT OVER ME--SOMETHING SAID ABOUT TURNING ME.
AND THEN NOTHING.
BLACKNESS.
I AWOKE TO A CHANGED WORLD... I'D HEARD STORIES, THOUGH--I KNEW WHAT I WAS... AND I WAS EXCITED.

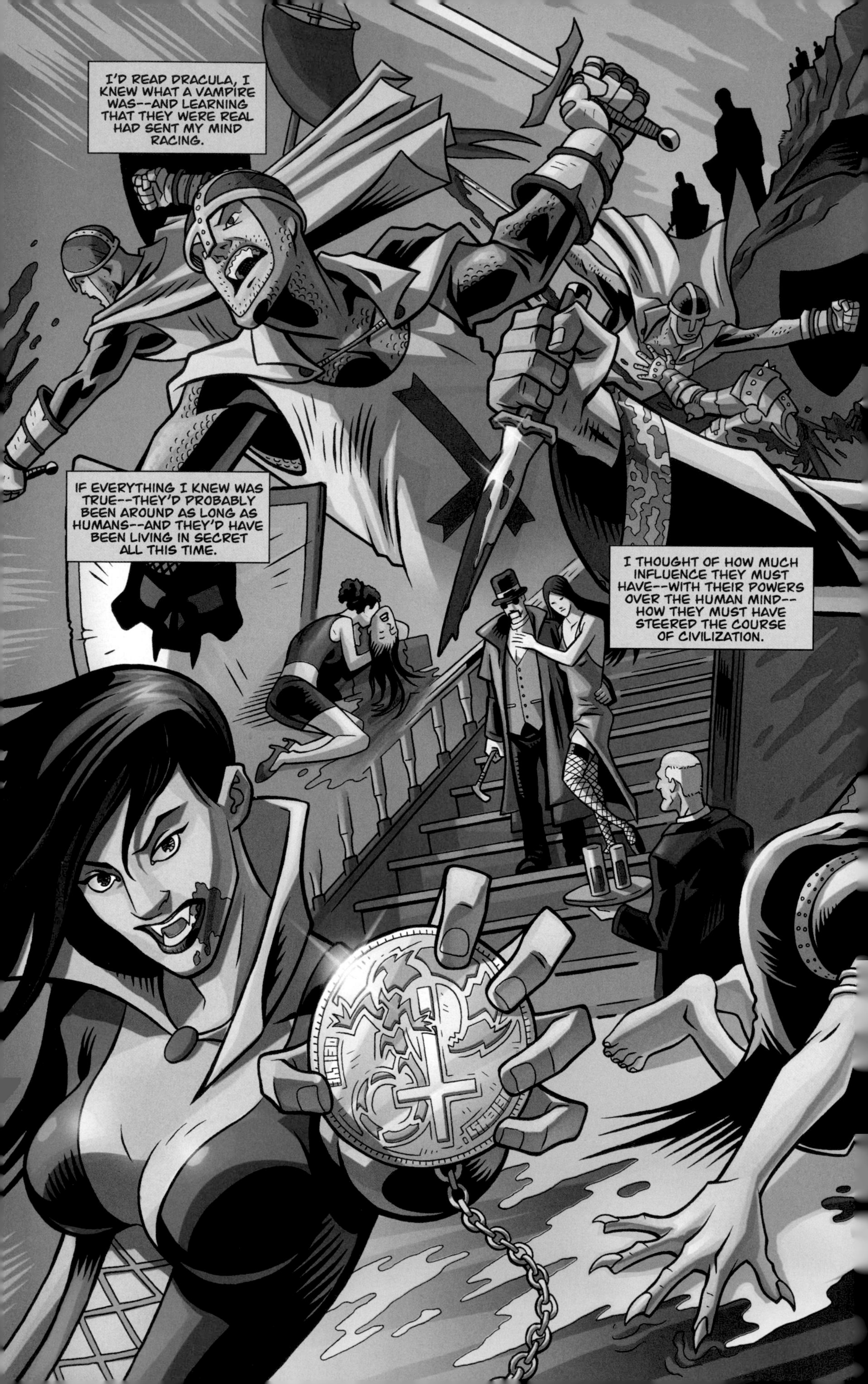
I'D READ DRACULA, I KNEW WHAT A VAMPIRE WAS--AND LEARNING THAT THEY WERE REAL HAD SENT MY MIND RACING.
IF EVERYTHING I KNEW WAS TRUE--THEY'D PROBABLY BEEN AROUND AS LONG AS HUMANS--AND THEY'D HAVE BEEN LIVING IN SECRET ALL THIS TIME.
I THOUGHT OF HOW MUCH INFLUENCE THEY MUST HAVE--WITH THEIR POWERS OVER THE HUMAN MIND--HOW THEY MUST HAVE STEERED THE COURSE OF CIVILIZATION.

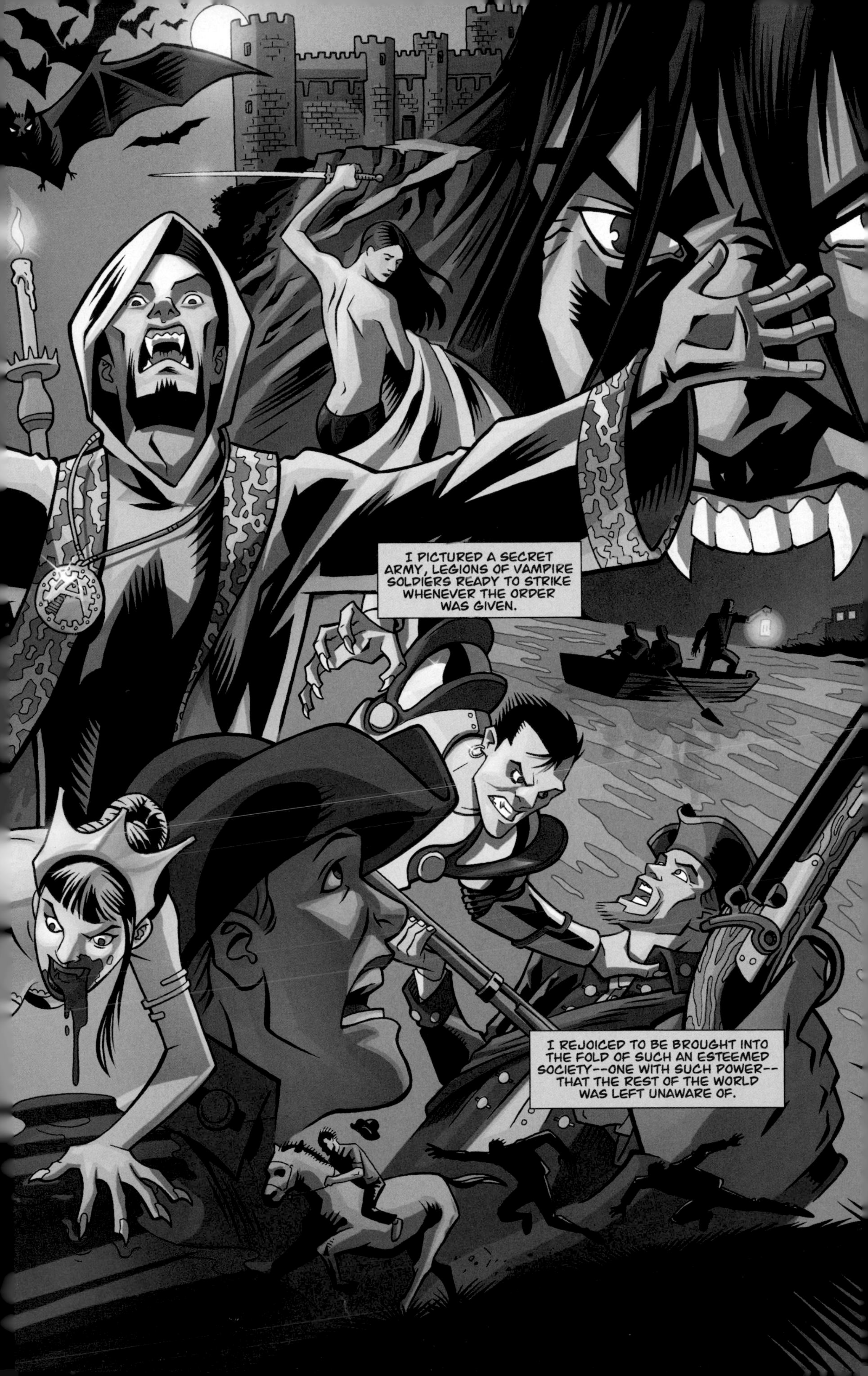
I PICTURED A SECRET ARMY, LEGIONS OF VAMPIRE SOLDIERS READY TO STRIKE WHENEVER THE ORDER WAS GIVEN.
I REJOICED TO BE BROUGHT INTO THE FOLD OF SUCH AN ESTEEMED SOCIETY--ONE WITH SUCH POWER--THAT THE REST OF THE WORLD WAS LEFT UNAWARE OF.

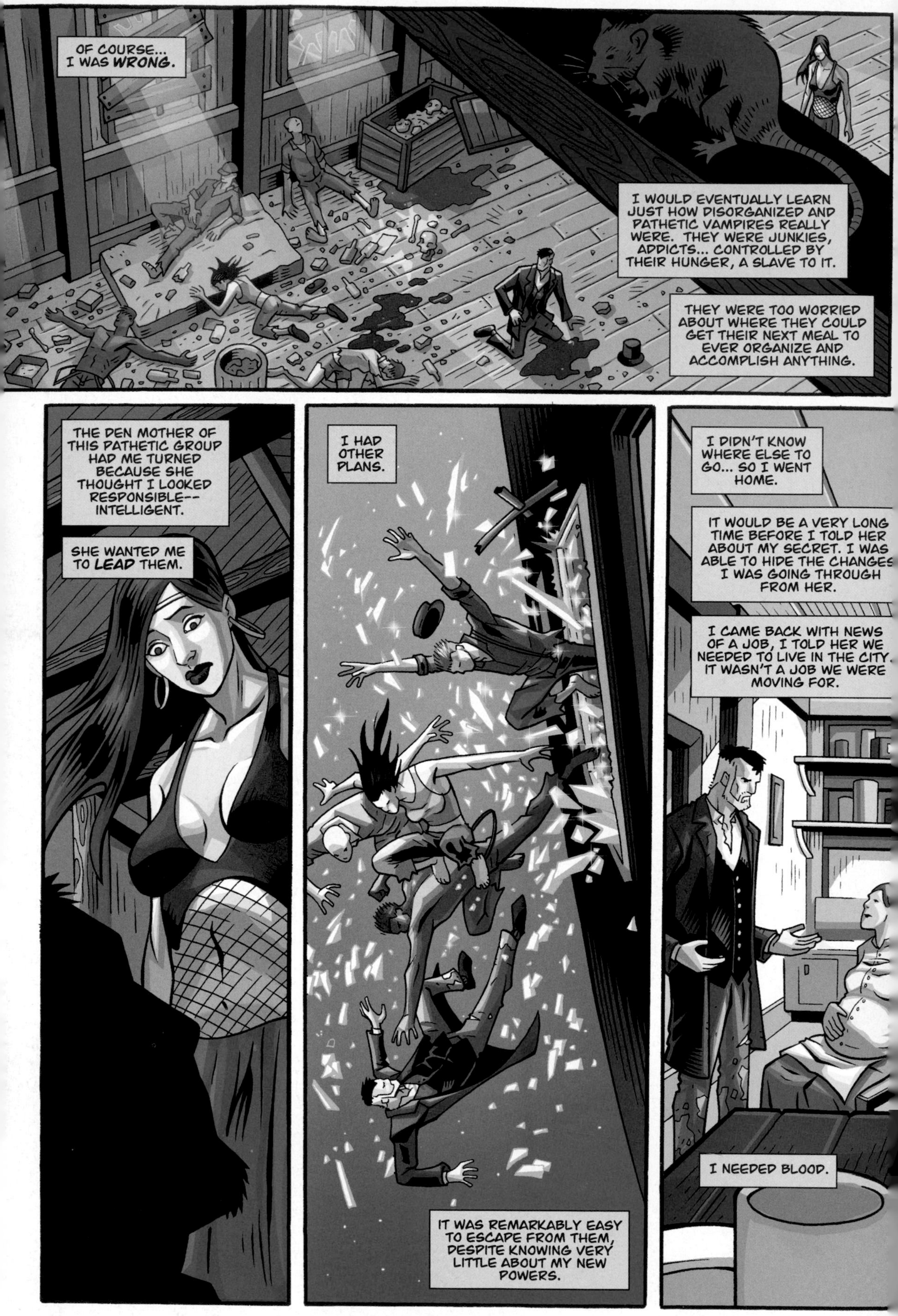
OF COURSE... I WAS WRONG.
I WOULD EVENTUALLY LEARN JUST HOW DISORGANIZED AND PATHETIC VAMPIRES REALLY WERE. THEY WERE JUNKIES, ADDICTS... CONTROLLED BY THEIR HUNGER, A SLAVE TO IT.
THEY WERE TOO WORRIED ABOUT WHERE THEY COULD GET THEIR NEXT MEAL TO EVER ORGANIZE AND ACCOMPLISH ANYTHING.
THE DEN MOTHER OF THIS PATHETIC GROUP HAD ME TURNED BECAUSE SHE THOUGHT I LOOKED RESPONSIBLE-- INTELLIGENT.
SHE WANTED ME TO LEAD THEM.
I HAD OTHER PLANS.
IT WAS REMARKABLY EASY TO ESCAPE FROM THEM, DESPITE KNOWING VERY LITTLE ABOUT MY NEW POWERS.
I DIDN'T KNOW WHERE ELSE TO GO... SO I WENT HOME.
IT WOULD BE A VERY LONG TIME BEFORE I TOLD HER ABOUT MY SECRET. I WAS ABLE TO HIDE THE CHANGES I WAS GOING THROUGH FROM HER.
I CAME BACK WITH NEWS OF A JOB, I TOLD HER WE NEEDED TO LIVE IN THE CITY. IT WASN'T A JOB WE WERE MOVING FOR.
I NEEDED BLOOD.

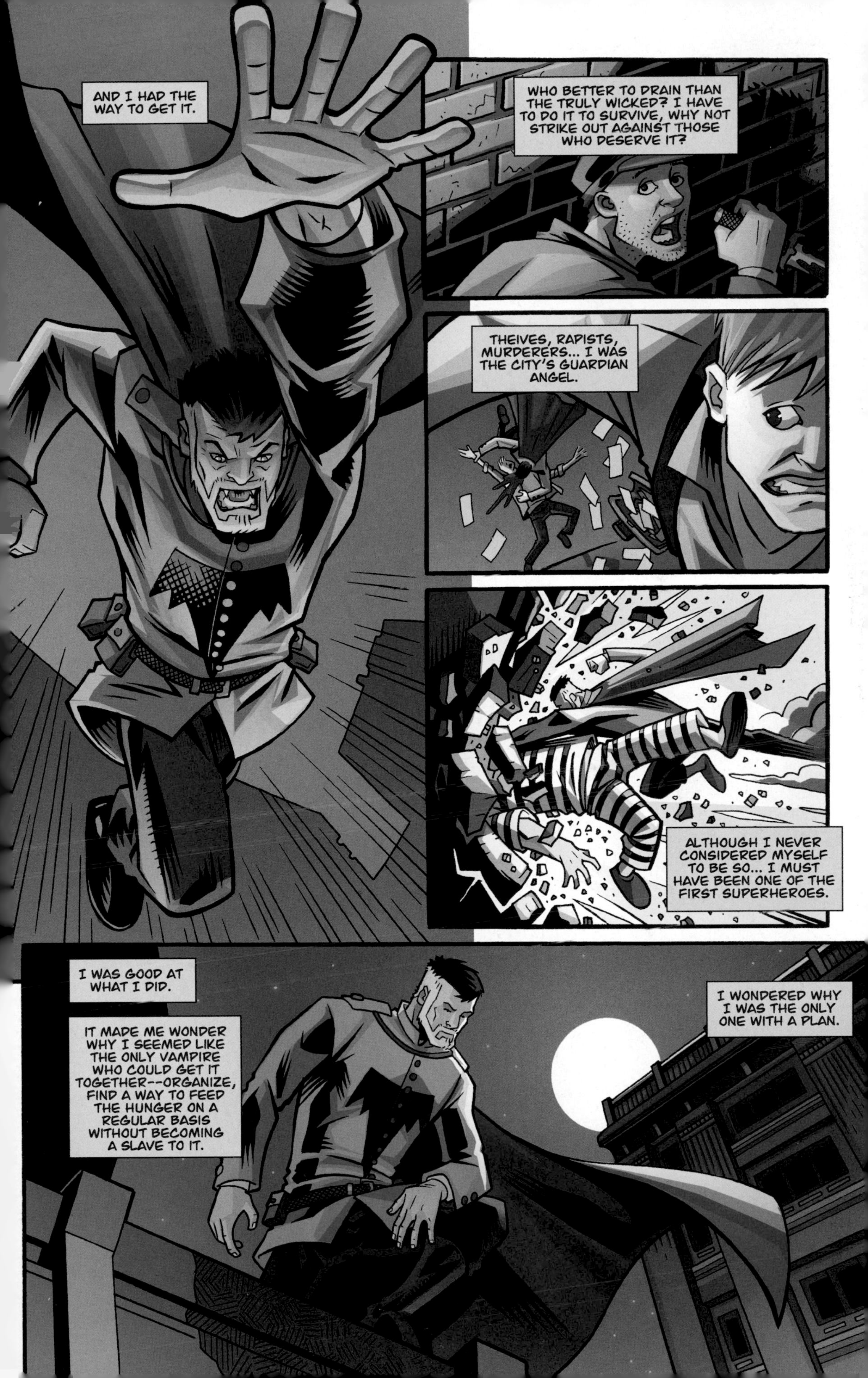
AND I HAD THE WAY TO GET IT.
WHO BETTER TO DRAIN THAN THE TRULY WICKED? I HAVE TO DO IT TO SURVIVE, WHY NOT STRIKE OUT AGAINST THOSE WHO DESERVE IT?
THEIVES, RAPISTS, MURDERERS... I WAS THE CITY'S GUARDIAN ANGEL.
ALTHOUGH I NEVER CONSIDERED MYSELF TO BE SO... I MUST HAVE BEEN ONE OF THE FIRST SUPERHEROES.
I WAS GOOD AT WHAT I DID.
IT MADE ME WONDER WHY I SEEMED LIKE THE ONLY VAMPIRE WHO COULD GET IT TOGETHER--ORGANIZE, FIND A WAY TO FEED THE HUNGER ON A REGULAR BASIS WITHOUT BECOMING A SLAVE TO IT.
I WONDERED WHY I WAS THE ONLY ONE WITH A PLAN.

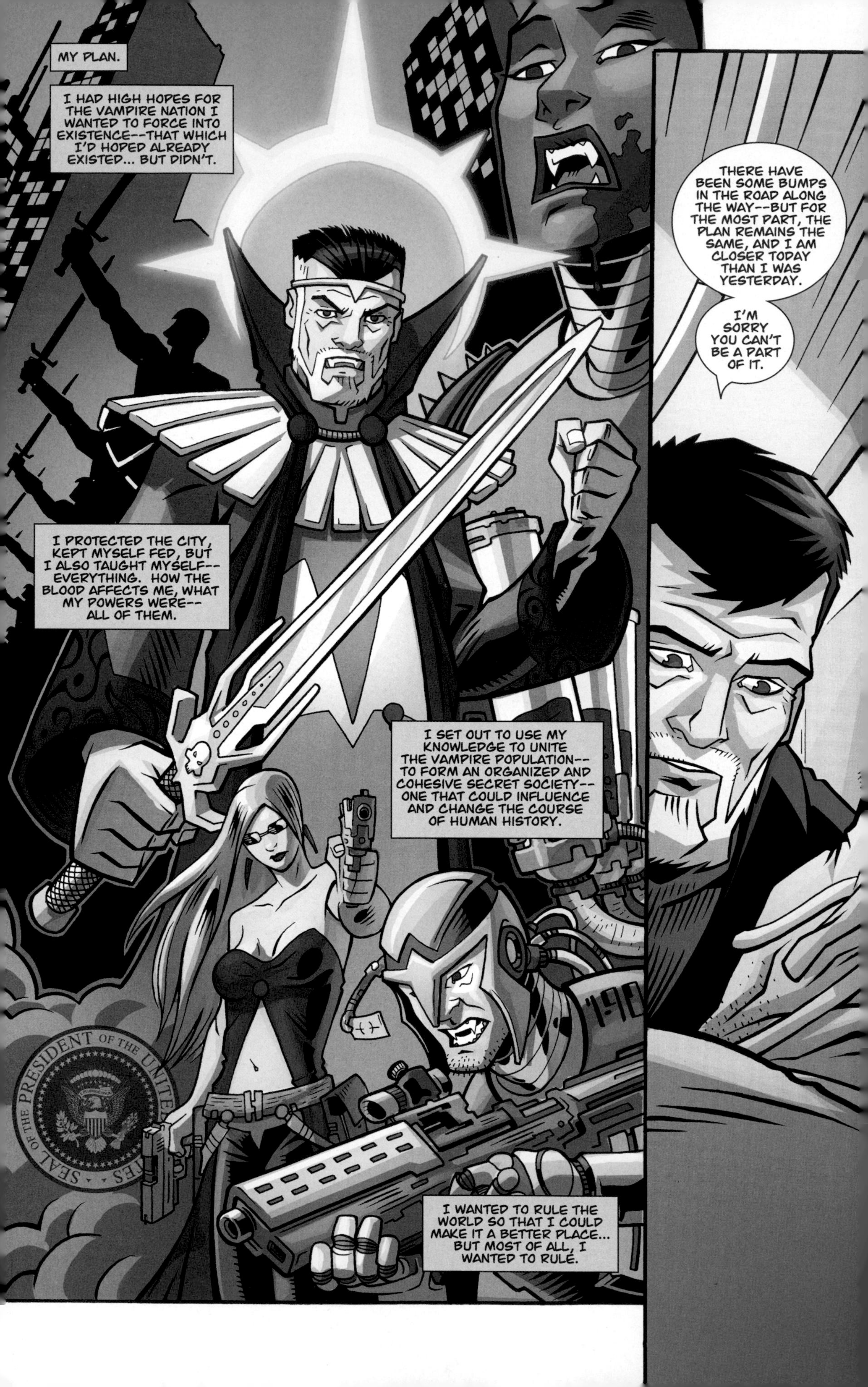

MY PLAN.
I HAD HIGH HOPES FOR THE VAMPIRE NATION I WANTED TO FORCE INTO EXISTENCE--THAT WHICH I'D HOPED ALREADY EXISTED... BUT DIDN'T.
I PROTECTED THE CITY, KEPT MYSELF FED, BUT I ALSO TAUGHT MYSELF--EVERYTHING. HOW THE BLOOD AFFECTS ME, WHAT MY POWERS WERE--ALL OF THEM.
I SET OUT TO USE MY KNOWLEDGE TO UNITE THE VAMPIRE POPULATION--TO FORM AN ORGANIZED AND COHESIVE SECRET SOCIETY--ONE THAT COULD INFLUENCE AND CHANGE THE COURSE OF HUMAN HISTORY.
I WANTED TO RULE THE WORLD SO THAT I COULD MAKE IT A BETTER PLACE... BUT MOST OF ALL, I WANTED TO RULE.
SEAL OF THE PRESIDENT OF THE UNITED STATES
THERE HAVE BEEN SOME BUMPS IN THE ROAD ALONG THE WAY--BUT FOR THE MOST PART, THE PLAN REMAINS THE SAME, AND I AM CLOSER TODAY THAN I WAS YESTERDAY.
I'M SORRY YOU CAN'T BE A PART OF IT.

NOT AS--

≥COUGH!≤

NOT AS SORRY AS I AM.

DON'T BE SO SURE...

IF YOU CAN'T TURN ME-- COULD YOU AT LEAST--?

THAT'S WHY I'M HERE.

BEEP. BEEP. BEEP.

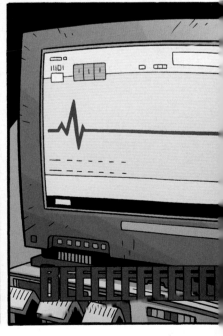

BEEEEEEEEEEE

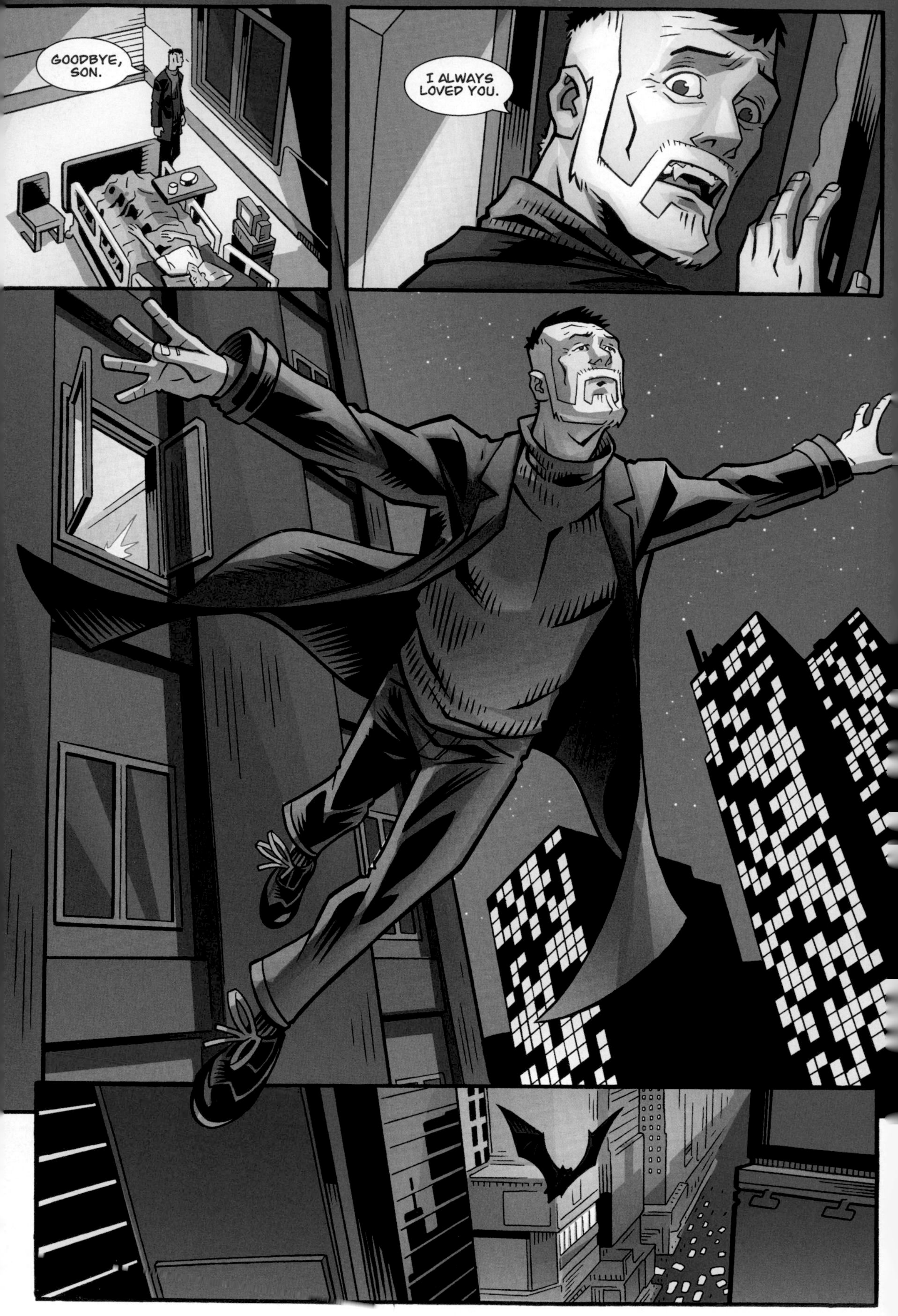
GOODBYE, SON.
I ALWAYS LOVED YOU.

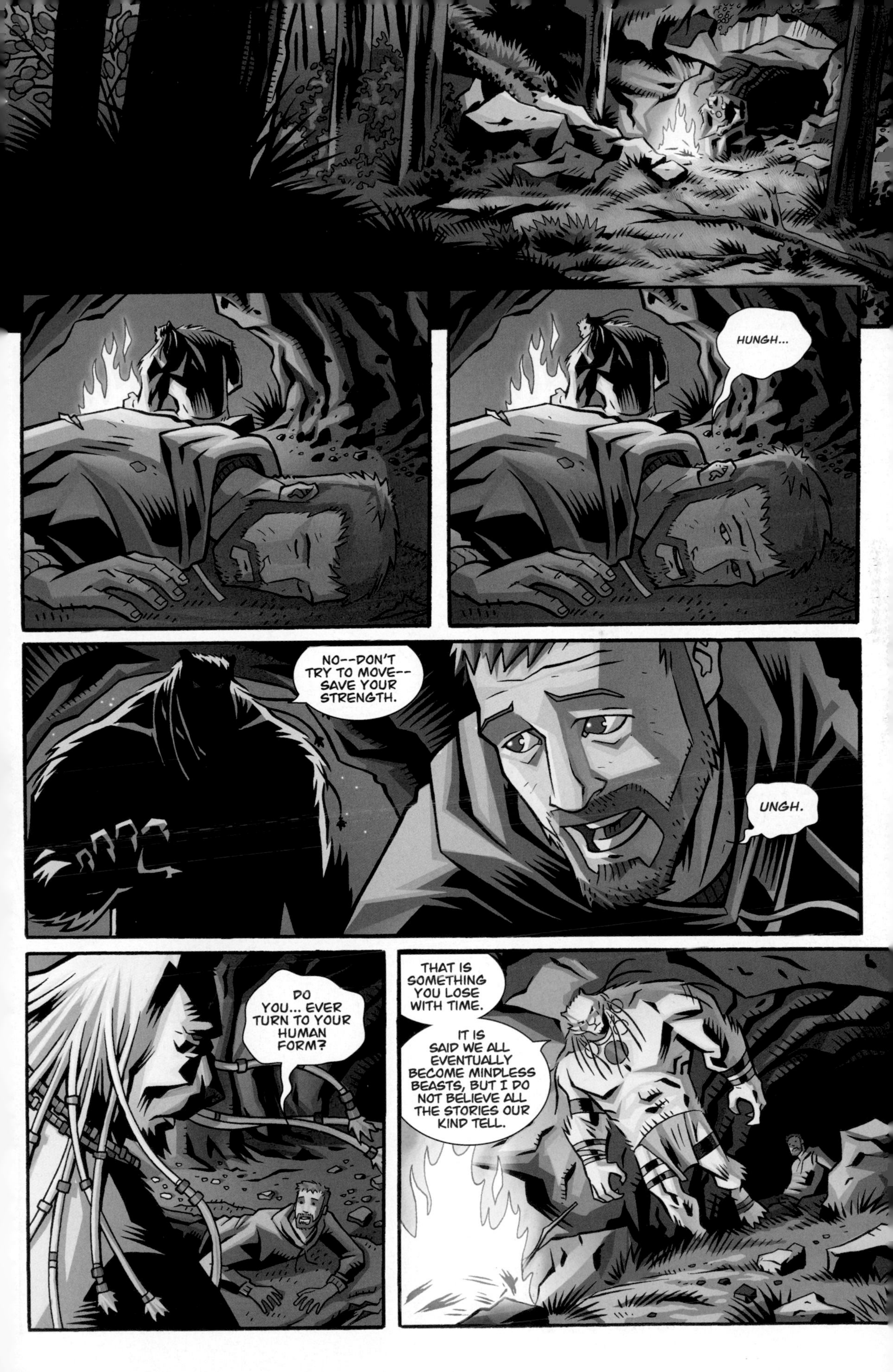
HUNGH...
NO--DON'T TRY TO MOVE-- SAVE YOUR STRENGTH.
UNGH.
DO YOU... EVER TURN TO YOUR HUMAN FORM?
THAT IS SOMETHING YOU LOSE WITH TIME.
IT IS SAID WE ALL EVENTUALLY BECOME MINDLESS BEASTS, BUT I DO NOT BELIEVE ALL THE STORIES OUR KIND TELL.

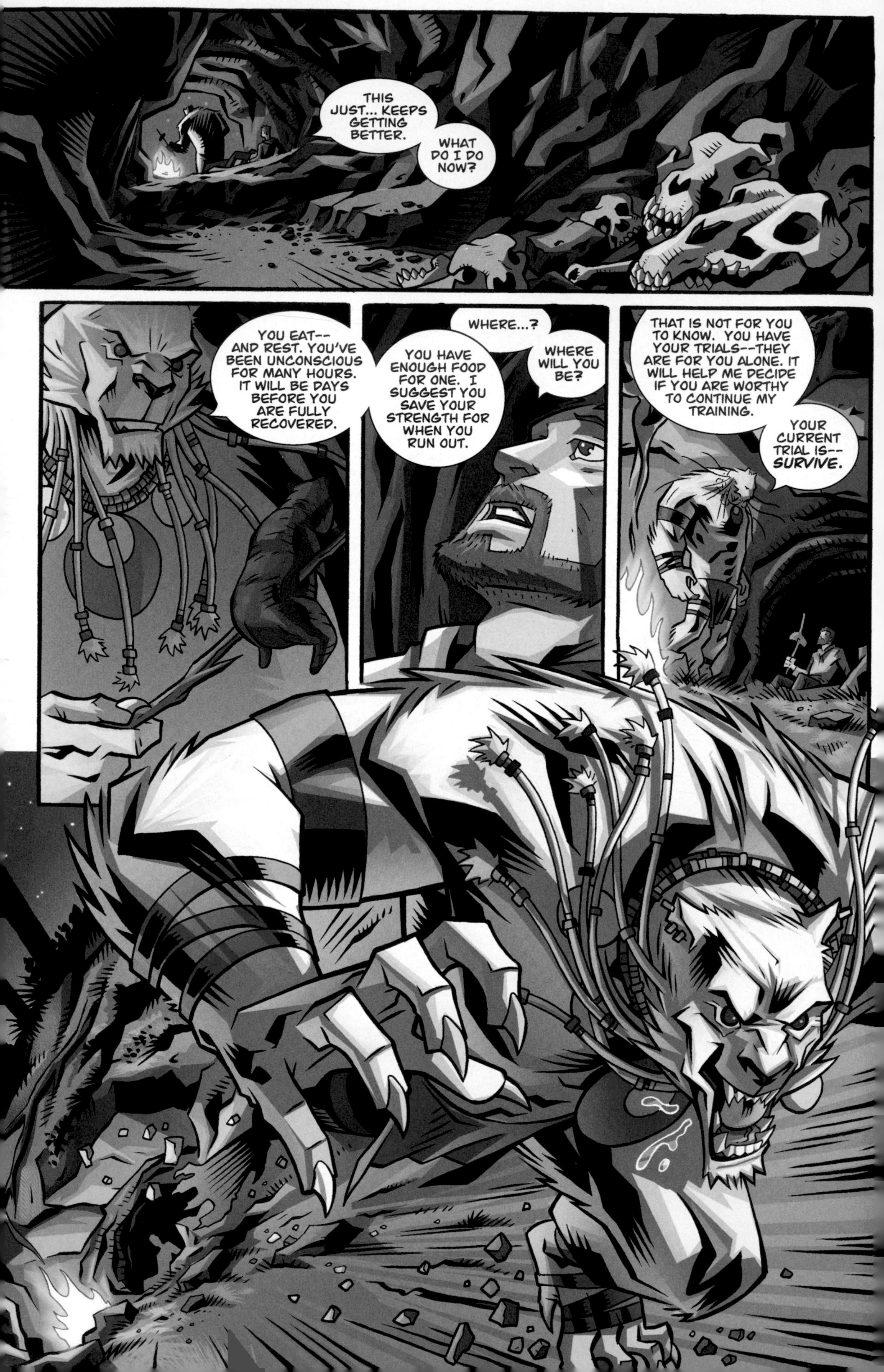
THIS JUST... KEEPS GETTING BETTER.
WHAT DO I DO NOW?
YOU EAT--AND REST. YOU'VE BEEN UNCONSCIOUS FOR MANY HOURS. IT WILL BE DAYS BEFORE YOU ARE FULLY RECOVERED.
WHERE...?
YOU HAVE ENOUGH FOOD FOR ONE. I SUGGEST YOU SAVE YOUR STRENGTH FOR WHEN YOU RUN OUT.
WHERE WILL YOU BE?
THAT IS NOT FOR YOU TO KNOW. YOU HAVE YOUR TRIALS--THEY ARE FOR YOU ALONE. IT WILL HELP ME DECIDE IF YOU ARE WORTHY TO CONTINUE MY TRAINING.
YOUR CURRENT TRIAL IS--**SURVIVE.**

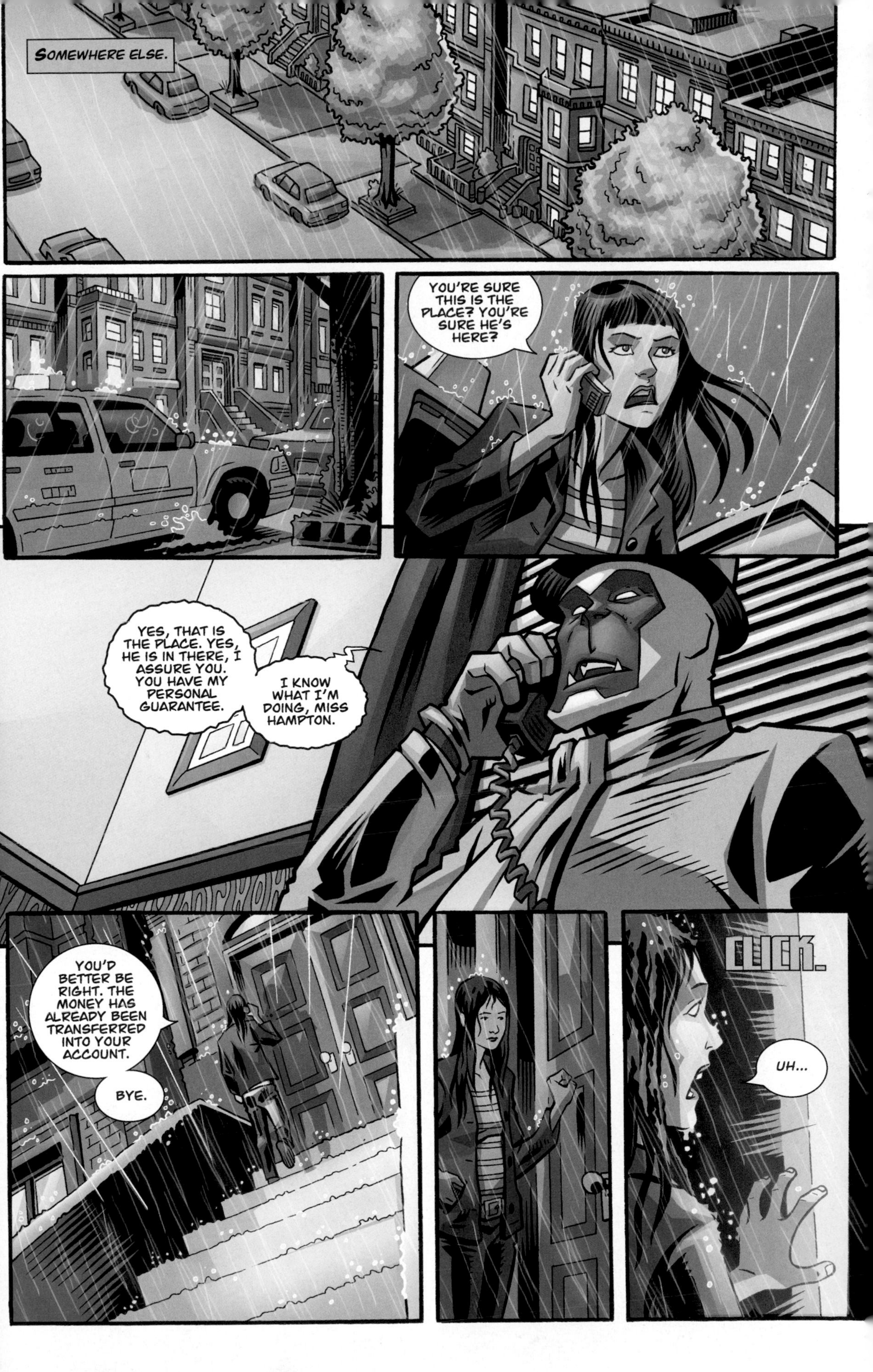
SOMEWHERE ELSE.
YOU'RE SURE THIS IS THE PLACE? YOU'RE SURE HE'S HERE?
YES, THAT IS THE PLACE. YES, HE IS IN THERE, I ASSURE YOU. YOU HAVE MY PERSONAL GUARANTEE.
I KNOW WHAT I'M DOING, MISS HAMPTON.
YOU'D BETTER BE RIGHT. THE MONEY HAS ALREADY BEEN TRANSFERRED INTO YOUR ACCOUNT.
BYE.
CLICK.
UH...

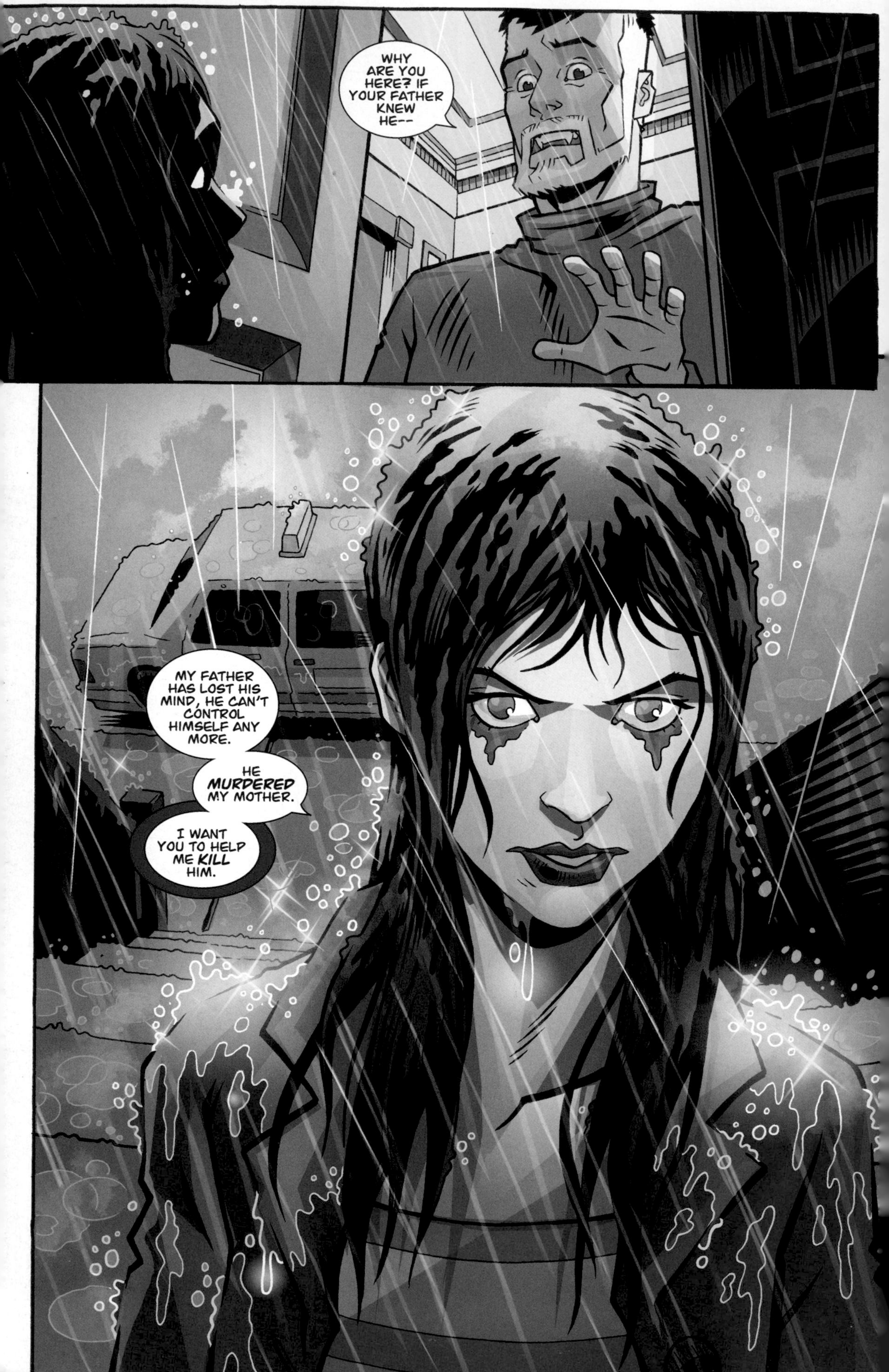
WHY ARE YOU HERE? IF YOUR FATHER KNEW HE--
MY FATHER HAS LOST HIS MIND, HE CAN'T CONTROL HIMSELF ANY MORE.
HE MURDERED MY MOTHER.
I WANT YOU TO HELP ME KILL HIM.

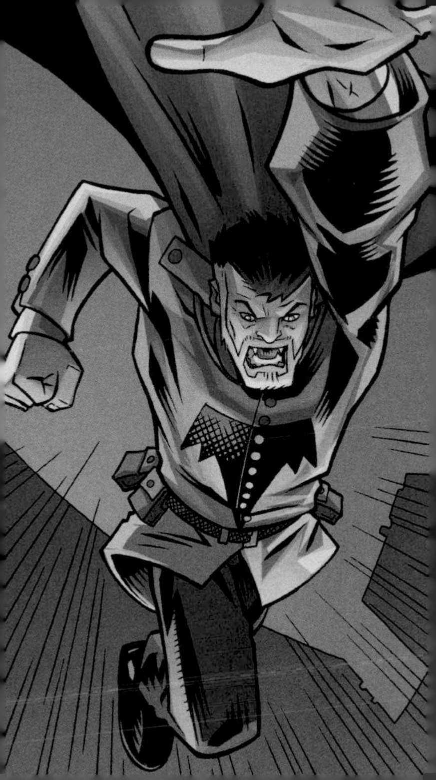

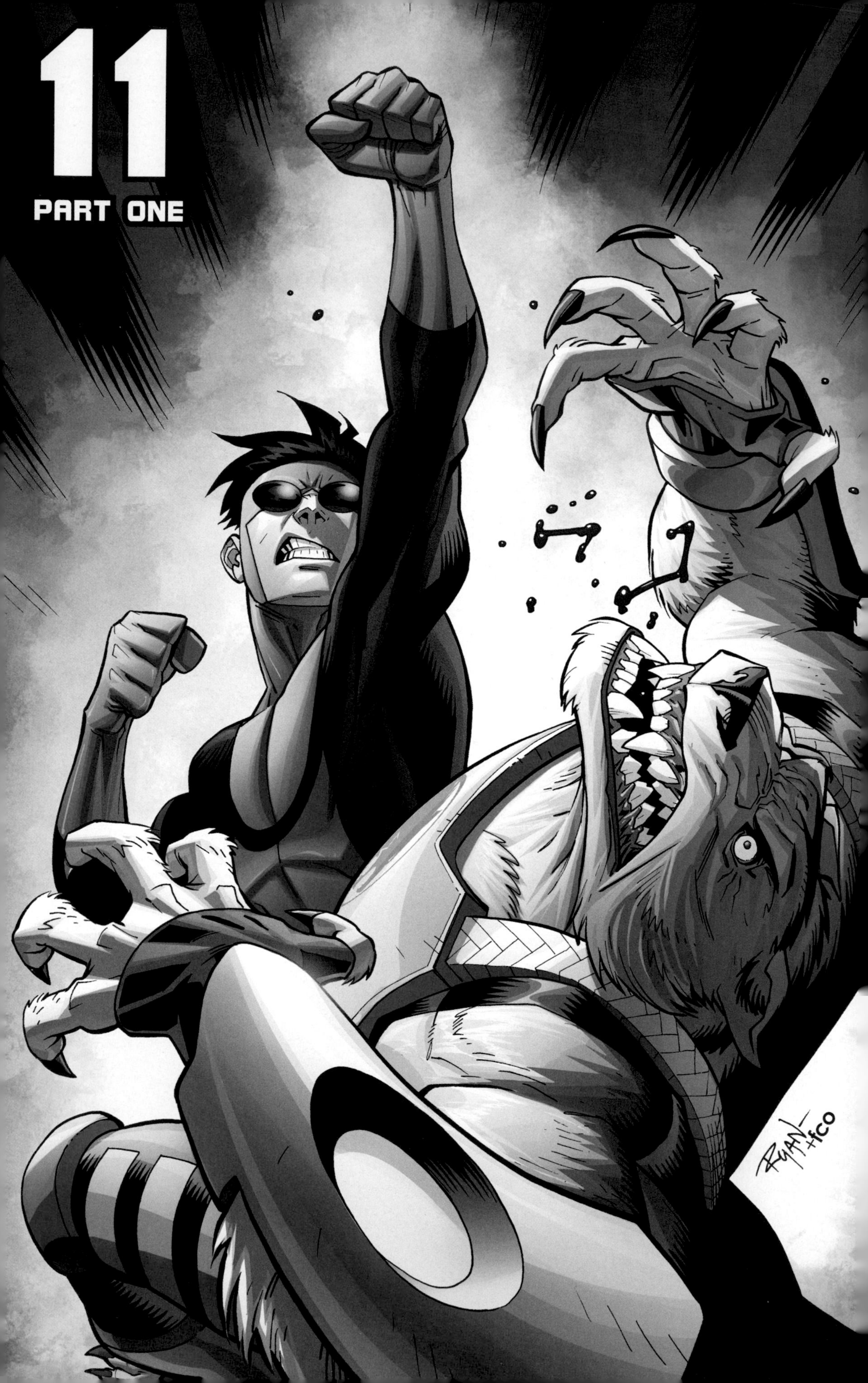
11
PART ONE
RYAN +FCO

THE SECRET BASE OF THE TEAM FORMERLY KNOWN AS THE TEEN TEAM.

WE'VE BEEN HERE ALMOST ALL DAY. HOW MUCH LONGER IS THIS GOING TO TAKE?

YEAH, ROBOT, REALLY... WOULD IT SPEED THINGS UP IF YOU--I DON'T KNOW... HELPED... YOURSELF?

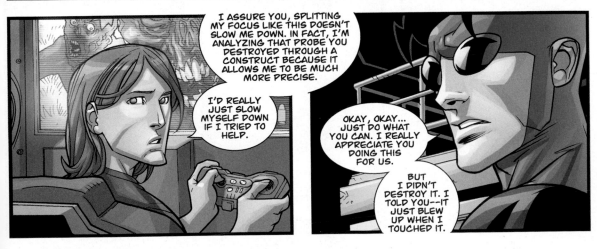

I ASSURE YOU, SPLITTING MY FOCUS LIKE THIS DOESN'T SLOW ME DOWN. IN FACT, I'M ANALYZING THAT PROBE YOU DESTROYED THROUGH A CONSTRUCT BECAUSE IT ALLOWS ME TO BE MUCH MORE PRECISE.

I'D REALLY JUST SLOW MYSELF DOWN IF I TRIED TO HELP.

OKAY, OKAY... JUST DO WHAT YOU CAN. I REALLY APPRECIATE YOU DOING THIS FOR US.

BUT I DIDN'T DESTROY IT. I TOLD YOU--IT JUST BLEW UP WHEN I TOUCHED IT.

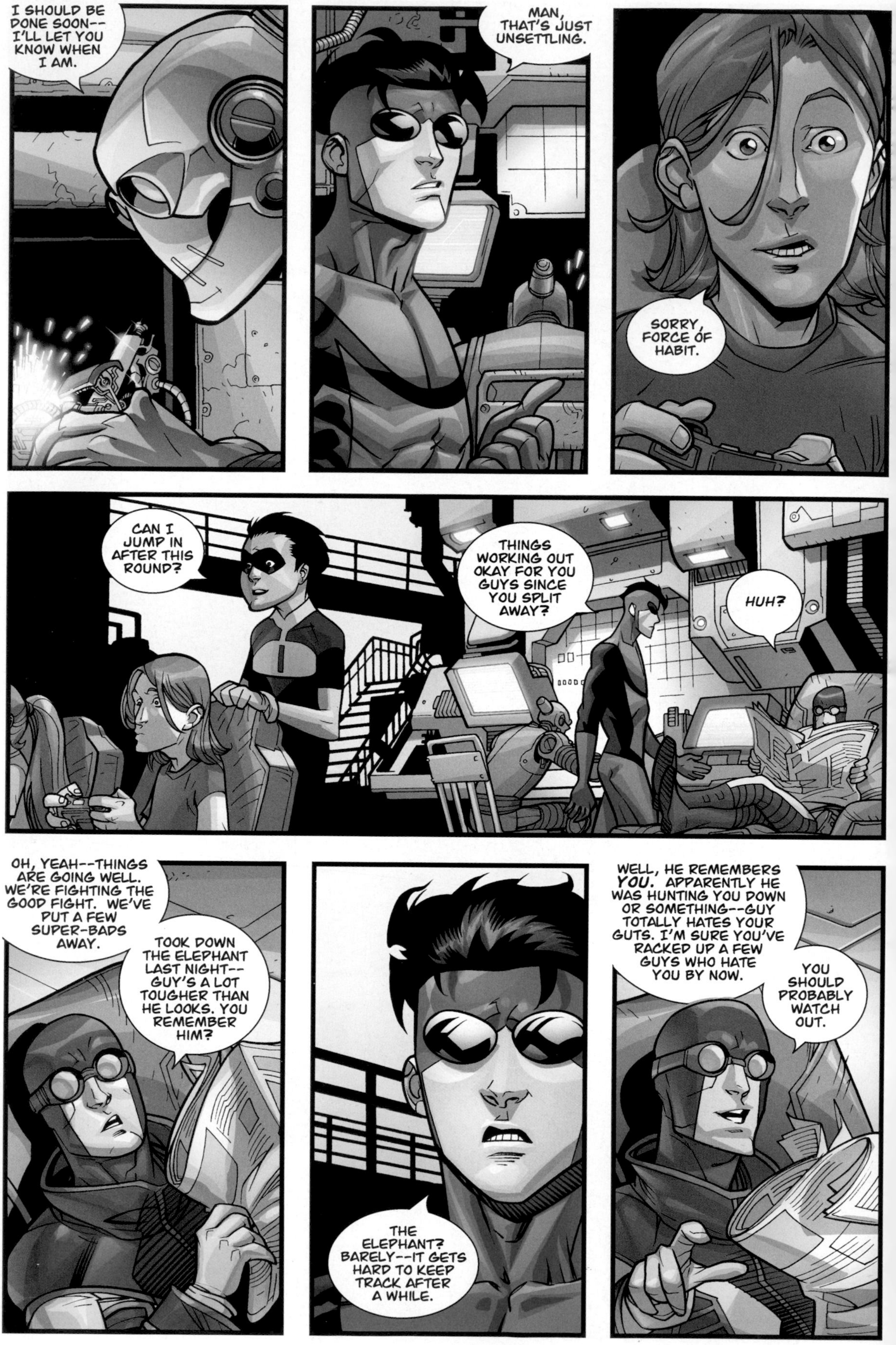
I SHOULD BE DONE SOON-- I'LL LET YOU KNOW WHEN I AM.
MAN, THAT'S JUST UNSETTLING.
SORRY, FORCE OF HABIT.
CAN I JUMP IN AFTER THIS ROUND?
THINGS WORKING OUT OKAY FOR YOU GUYS SINCE YOU SPLIT AWAY?
HUH?
OH, YEAH--THINGS ARE GOING WELL. WE'RE FIGHTING THE GOOD FIGHT. WE'VE PUT A FEW SUPER-BADS AWAY.
TOOK DOWN THE ELEPHANT LAST NIGHT--GUY'S A LOT TOUGHER THAN HE LOOKS. YOU REMEMBER HIM?
THE ELEPHANT? BARELY--IT GETS HARD TO KEEP TRACK AFTER A WHILE.
WELL, HE REMEMBERS YOU. APPARENTLY HE WAS HUNTING YOU DOWN OR SOMETHING--GUY TOTALLY HATES YOUR GUTS. I'M SURE YOU'VE RACKED UP A FEW GUYS WHO HATE YOU BY NOW.
YOU SHOULD PROBABLY WATCH OUT.

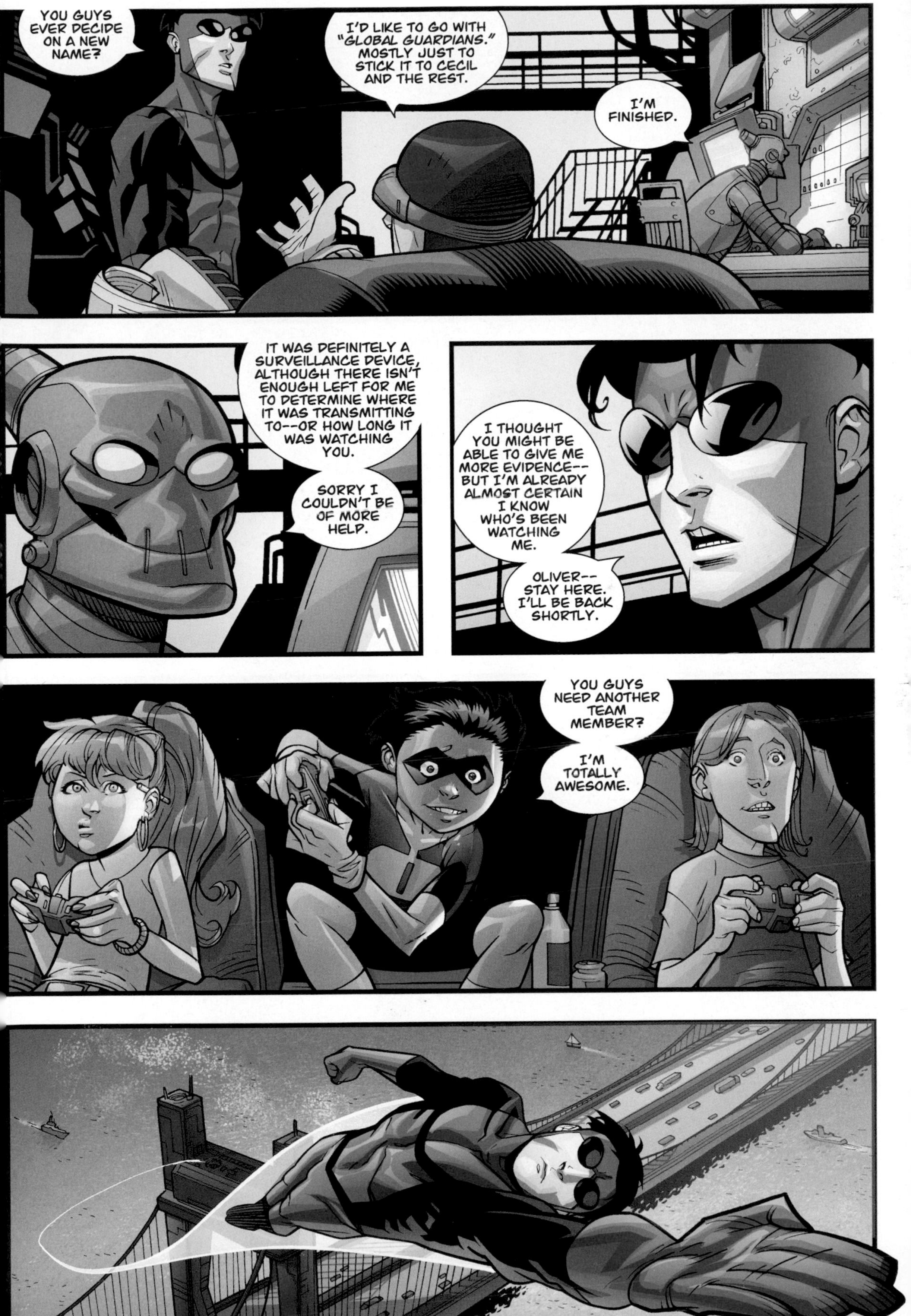
YOU GUYS EVER DECIDE ON A NEW NAME?
I'D LIKE TO GO WITH "GLOBAL GUARDIANS." MOSTLY JUST TO STICK IT TO CECIL AND THE REST.
I'M FINISHED.
IT WAS DEFINITELY A SURVEILLANCE DEVICE, ALTHOUGH THERE ISN'T ENOUGH LEFT FOR ME TO DETERMINE WHERE IT WAS TRANSMITTING TO--OR HOW LONG IT WAS WATCHING YOU.
SORRY I COULDN'T BE OF MORE HELP.
I THOUGHT YOU MIGHT BE ABLE TO GIVE ME MORE EVIDENCE--BUT I'M ALREADY ALMOST CERTAIN I KNOW WHO'S BEEN WATCHING ME.
OLIVER--STAY HERE. I'LL BE BACK SHORTLY.
YOU GUYS NEED ANOTHER TEAM MEMBER?
I'M TOTALLY AWESOME.

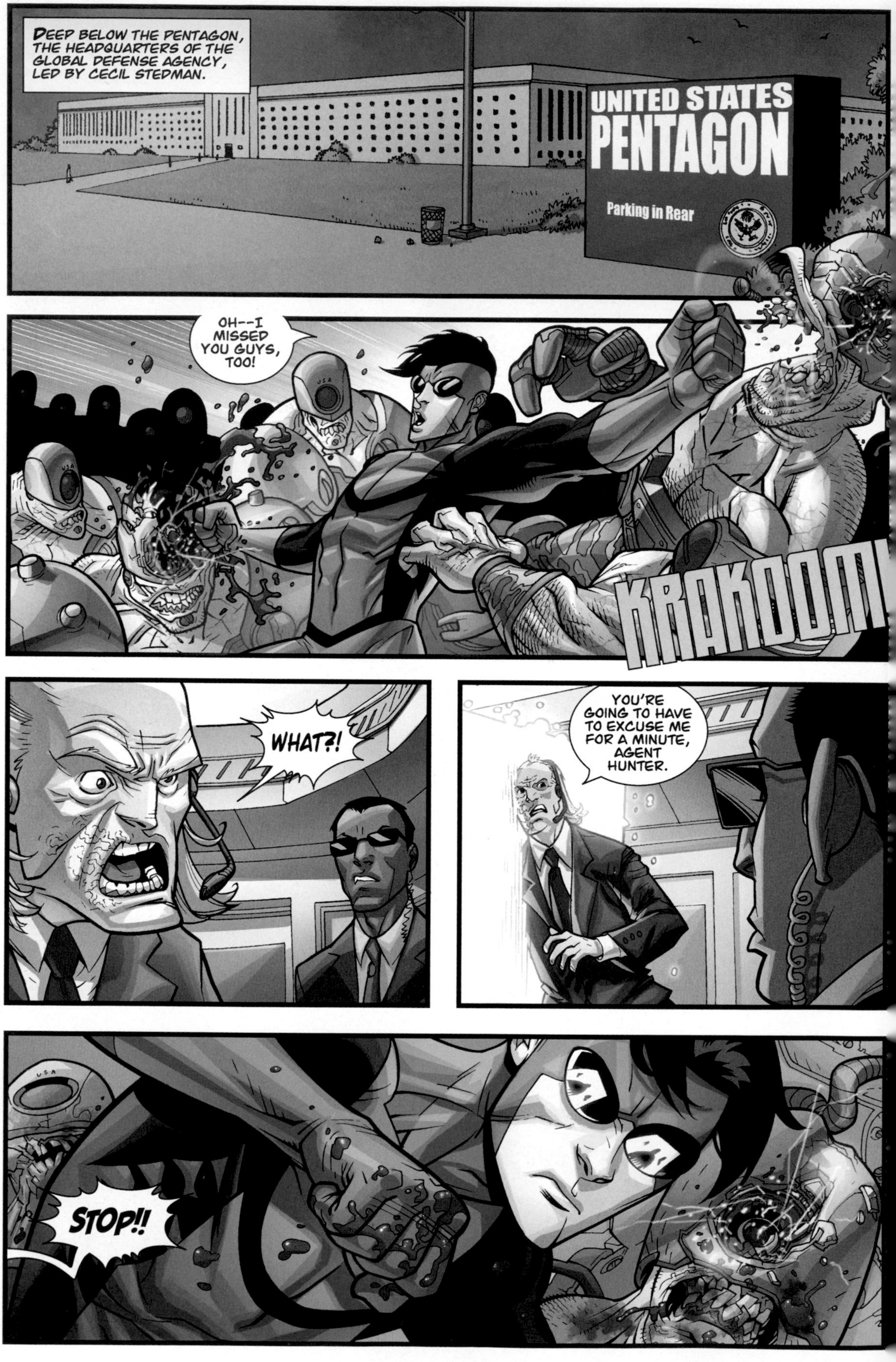
DEEP BELOW THE PENTAGON, THE HEADQUARTERS OF THE GLOBAL DEFENSE AGENCY, LED BY CECIL STEDMAN.
UNITED STATES PENTAGON
Parking in Rear
OH--I MISSED YOU GUYS, TOO!
KRAKOOM
WHAT?!
YOU'RE GOING TO HAVE TO EXCUSE ME FOR A MINUTE, AGENT HUNTER.
STOP!!

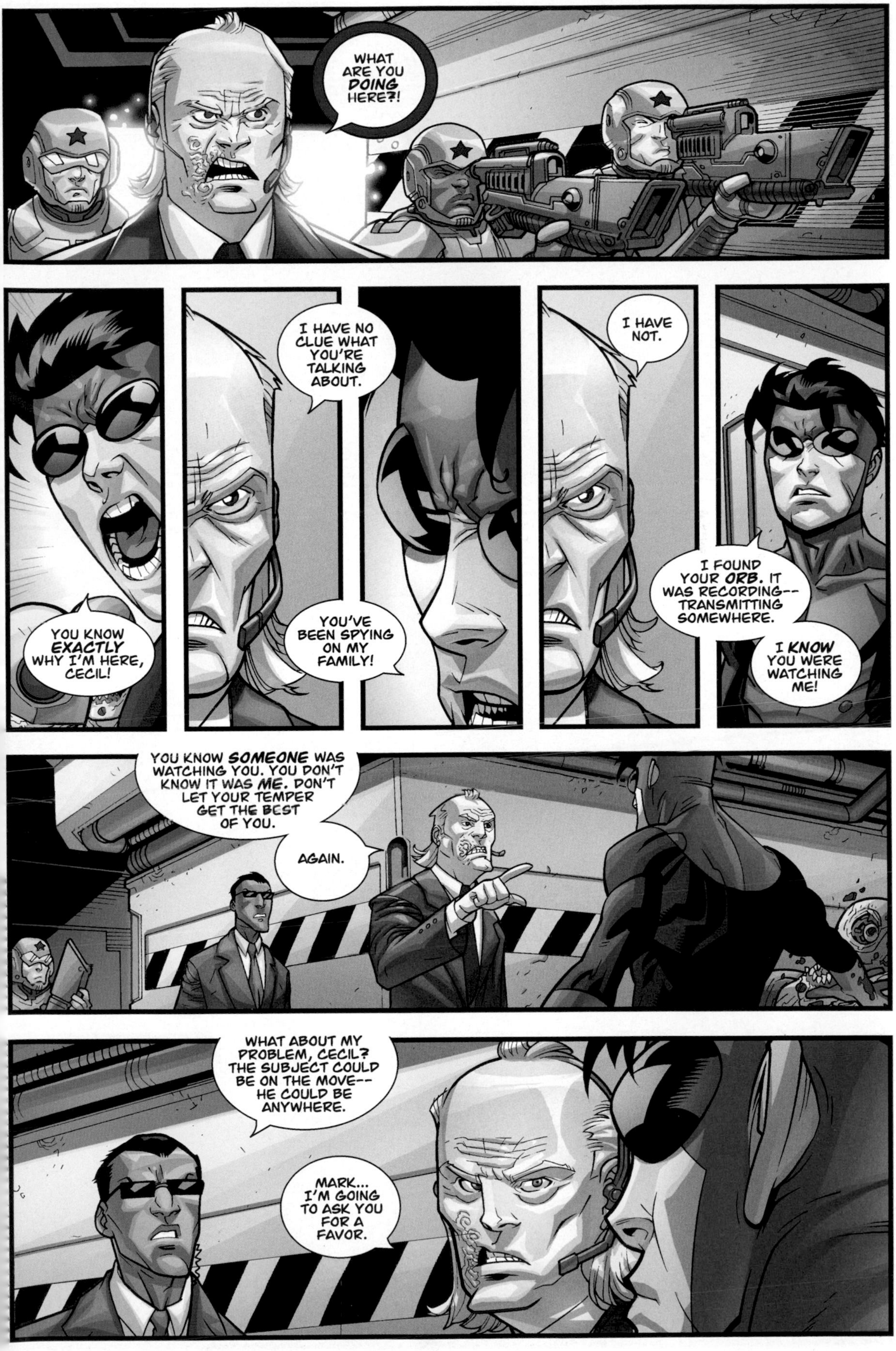

WHAT ARE YOU DOING HERE?!
YOU KNOW EXACTLY WHY I'M HERE, CECIL!
I HAVE NO CLUE WHAT YOU'RE TALKING ABOUT.
YOU'VE BEEN SPYING ON MY FAMILY!
I HAVE NOT.
I FOUND YOUR ORB. IT WAS RECORDING-- TRANSMITTING SOMEWHERE.
I KNOW YOU WERE WATCHING ME!
YOU KNOW SOMEONE WAS WATCHING YOU. YOU DON'T KNOW IT WAS ME. DON'T LET YOUR TEMPER GET THE BEST OF YOU.
AGAIN.
WHAT ABOUT MY PROBLEM, CECIL? THE SUBJECT COULD BE ON THE MOVE-- HE COULD BE ANYWHERE.
MARK... I'M GOING TO ASK YOU FOR A FAVOR.

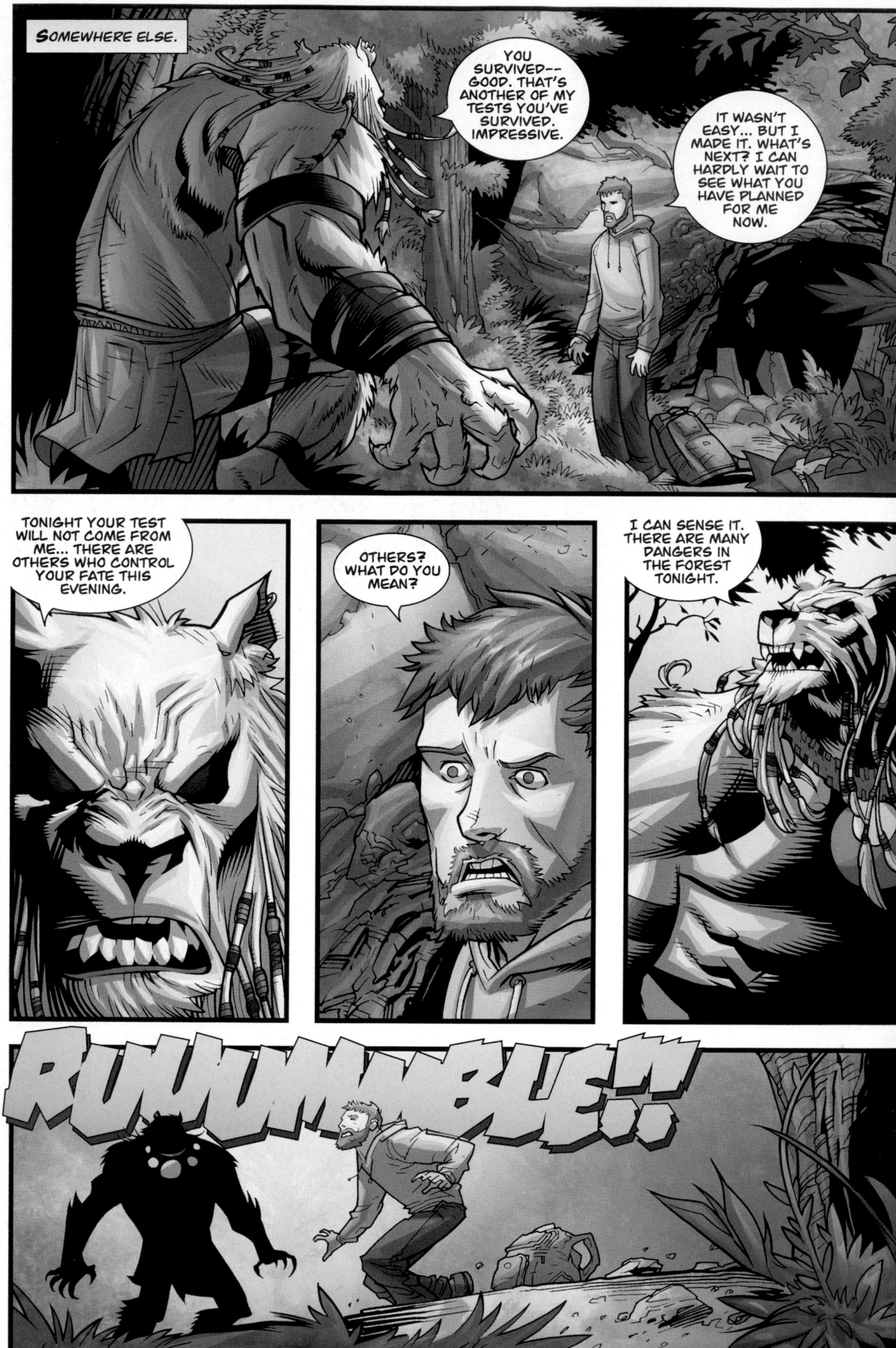
SOMEWHERE ELSE.
YOU SURVIVED-- GOOD. THAT'S ANOTHER OF MY TESTS YOU'VE SURVIVED. IMPRESSIVE.
IT WASN'T EASY... BUT I MADE IT. WHAT'S NEXT? I CAN HARDLY WAIT TO SEE WHAT YOU HAVE PLANNED FOR ME NOW.
TONIGHT YOUR TEST WILL NOT COME FROM ME... THERE ARE OTHERS WHO CONTROL YOUR FATE THIS EVENING.
OTHERS? WHAT DO YOU MEAN?
I CAN SENSE IT. THERE ARE MANY DANGERS IN THE FOREST TONIGHT.
RUUUMMBLE!!

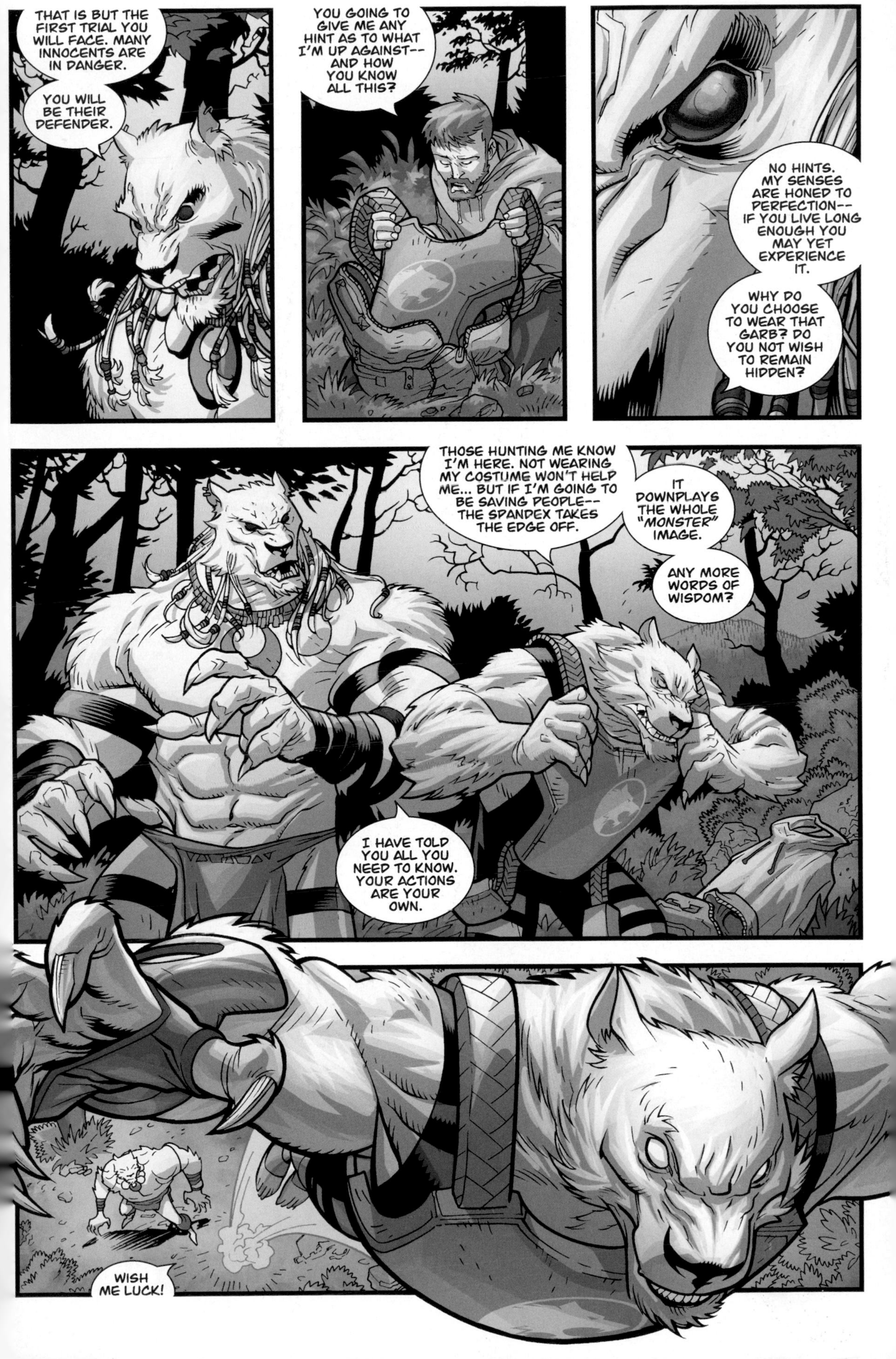
THAT IS BUT THE FIRST TRIAL YOU WILL FACE. MANY INNOCENTS ARE IN DANGER.
YOU WILL BE THEIR DEFENDER.
YOU GOING TO GIVE ME ANY HINT AS TO WHAT I'M UP AGAINST-- AND HOW YOU KNOW ALL THIS?
NO HINTS. MY SENSES ARE HONED TO PERFECTION-- IF YOU LIVE LONG ENOUGH YOU MAY YET EXPERIENCE IT.
WHY DO YOU CHOOSE TO WEAR THAT GARB? DO YOU NOT WISH TO REMAIN HIDDEN?
THOSE HUNTING ME KNOW I'M HERE. NOT WEARING MY COSTUME WON'T HELP ME... BUT IF I'M GOING TO BE SAVING PEOPLE-- THE SPANDEX TAKES THE EDGE OFF.
IT DOWNPLAYS THE WHOLE "MONSTER" IMAGE.
ANY MORE WORDS OF WISDOM?
I HAVE TOLD YOU ALL YOU NEED TO KNOW. YOUR ACTIONS ARE YOUR OWN.
WISH ME LUCK!

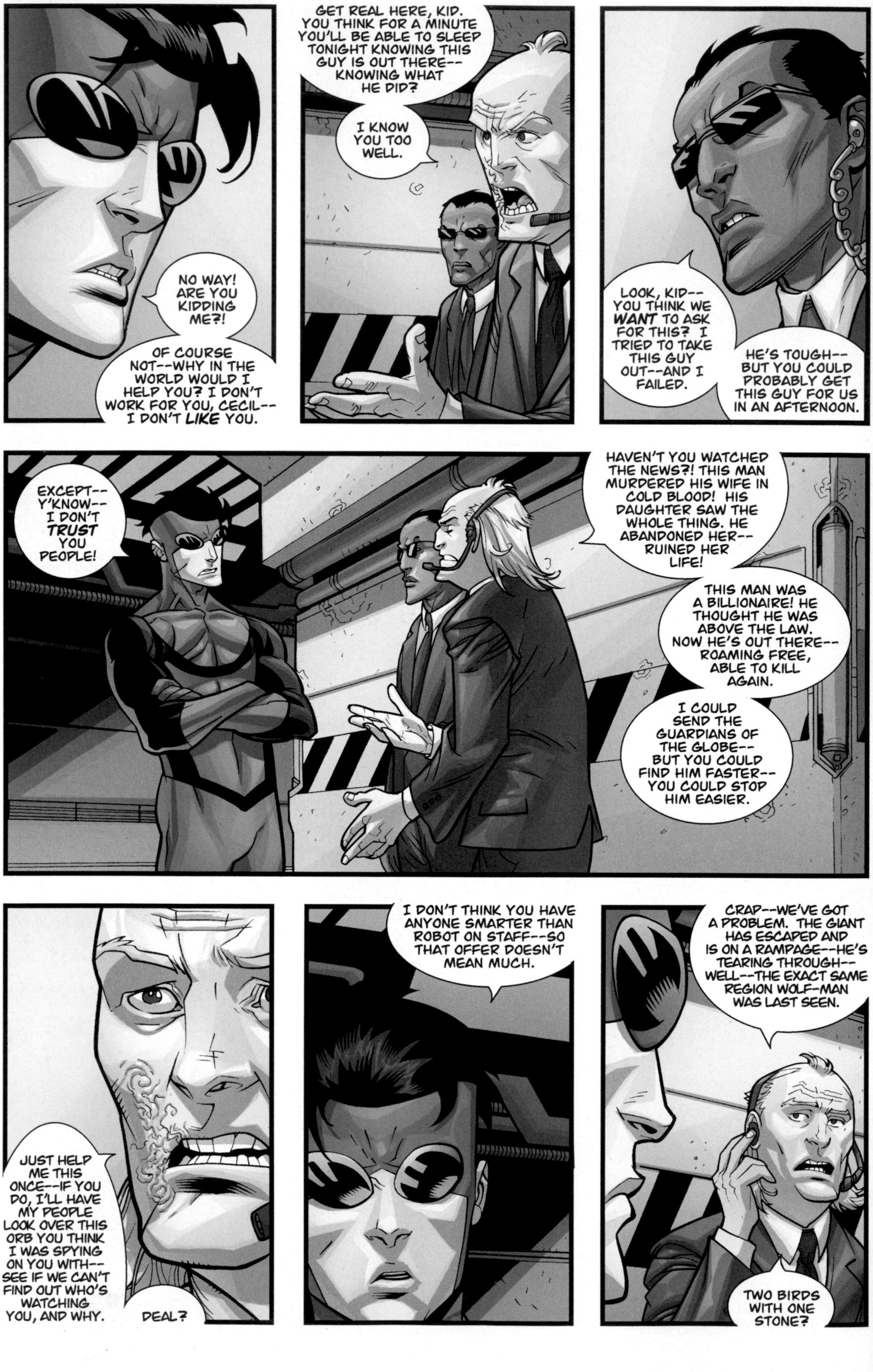
NO WAY! ARE YOU KIDDING ME?!
OF COURSE NOT--WHY IN THE WORLD WOULD I HELP YOU? I DON'T WORK FOR YOU, CECIL-- I DON'T LIKE YOU.
GET REAL HERE, KID. YOU THINK FOR A MINUTE YOU'LL BE ABLE TO SLEEP TONIGHT KNOWING THIS GUY IS OUT THERE-- KNOWING WHAT HE DID?
I KNOW YOU TOO WELL.
LOOK, KID-- YOU THINK WE WANT TO ASK FOR THIS? I TRIED TO TAKE THIS GUY OUT--AND I FAILED.
HE'S TOUGH-- BUT YOU COULD PROBABLY GET THIS GUY FOR US IN AN AFTERNOON.
EXCEPT-- Y'KNOW-- I DON'T TRUST YOU PEOPLE!
HAVEN'T YOU WATCHED THE NEWS?! THIS MAN MURDERED HIS WIFE IN COLD BLOOD! HIS DAUGHTER SAW THE WHOLE THING. HE ABANDONED HER-- RUINED HER LIFE!
THIS MAN WAS A BILLIONAIRE! HE THOUGHT HE WAS ABOVE THE LAW. NOW HE'S OUT THERE-- ROAMING FREE, ABLE TO KILL AGAIN.
I COULD SEND THE GUARDIANS OF THE GLOBE-- BUT YOU COULD FIND HIM FASTER-- YOU COULD STOP HIM EASIER.
JUST HELP ME THIS ONCE--IF YOU DO, I'LL HAVE MY PEOPLE LOOK OVER THIS ORB YOU THINK I WAS SPYING ON YOU WITH-- SEE IF WE CAN'T FIND OUT WHO'S WATCHING YOU, AND WHY.
DEAL?
I DON'T THINK YOU HAVE ANYONE SMARTER THAN ROBOT ON STAFF--SO THAT OFFER DOESN'T MEAN MUCH.
CRAP--WE'VE GOT A PROBLEM. THE GIANT HAS ESCAPED AND IS ON A RAMPAGE--HE'S TEARING THROUGH-- WELL--THE EXACT SAME REGION WOLF-MAN WAS LAST SEEN.
TWO BIRDS WITH ONE STONE?

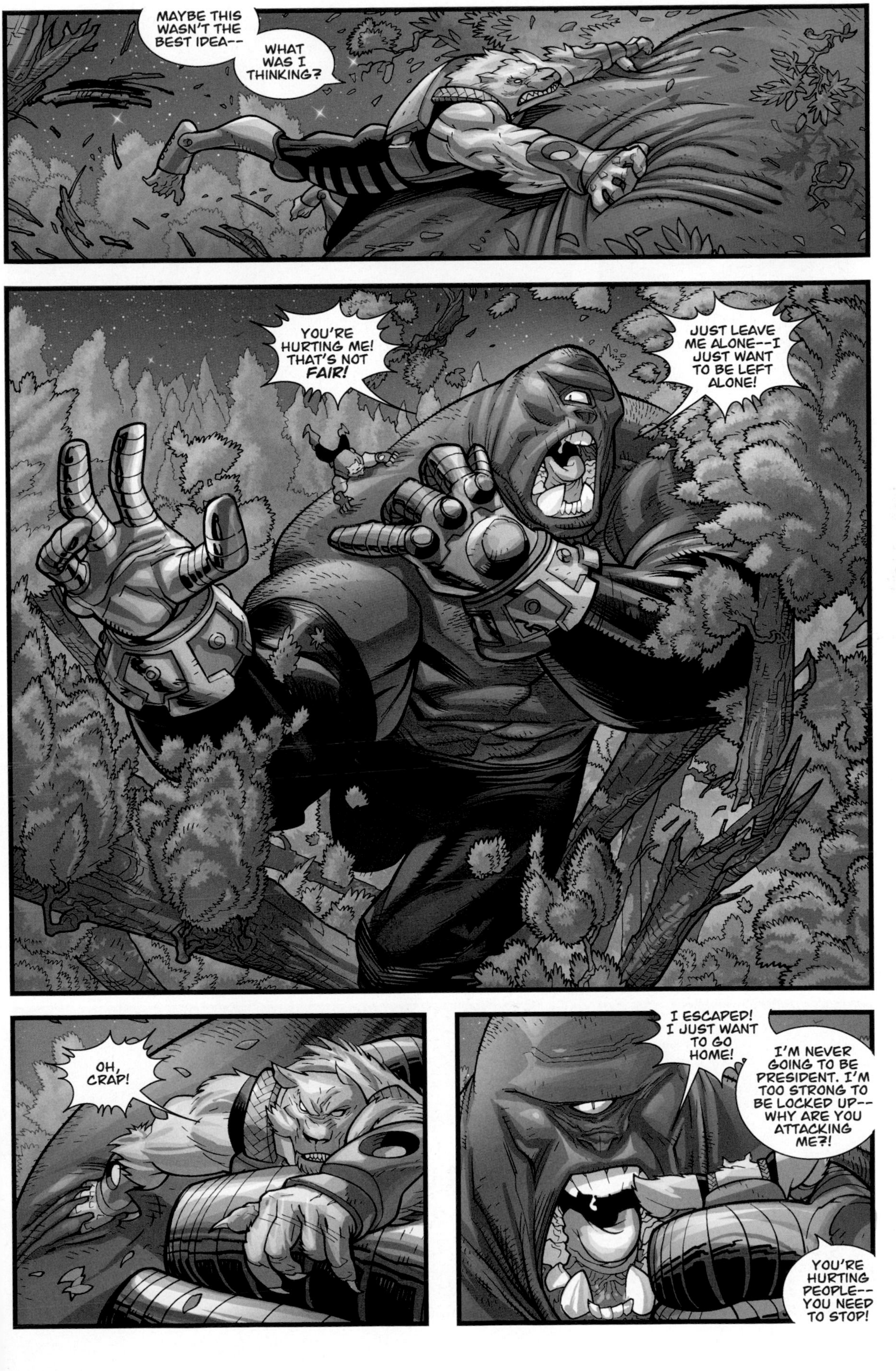
MAYBE THIS WASN'T THE BEST IDEA--
WHAT WAS I THINKING?
YOU'RE HURTING ME! THAT'S NOT **FAIR!**
JUST LEAVE ME ALONE--I JUST WANT TO BE LEFT ALONE!
OH, CRAP!
I ESCAPED! I JUST WANT TO GO HOME!
I'M NEVER GOING TO BE PRESIDENT. I'M TOO STRONG TO BE LOCKED UP--WHY ARE YOU ATTACKING ME?!
YOU'RE HURTING PEOPLE--YOU NEED TO STOP!

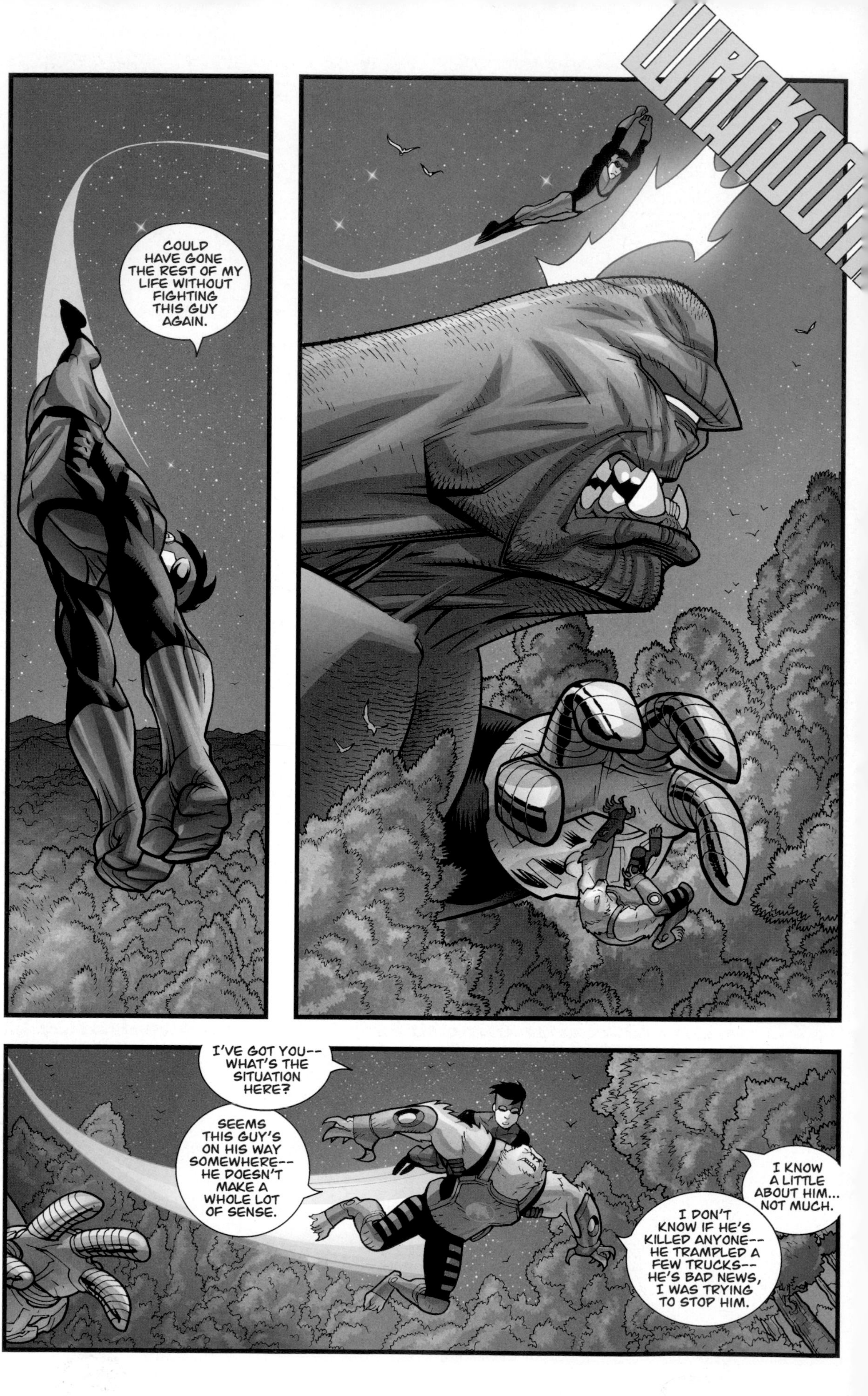
COULD HAVE GONE THE REST OF MY LIFE WITHOUT FIGHTING THIS GUY AGAIN.
I'VE GOT YOU-- WHAT'S THE SITUATION HERE?
SEEMS THIS GUY'S ON HIS WAY SOMEWHERE-- HE DOESN'T MAKE A WHOLE LOT OF SENSE.
I KNOW A LITTLE ABOUT HIM... NOT MUCH.
I DON'T KNOW IF HE'S KILLED ANYONE-- HE TRAMPLED A FEW TRUCKS-- HE'S BAD NEWS, I WAS TRYING TO STOP HIM.

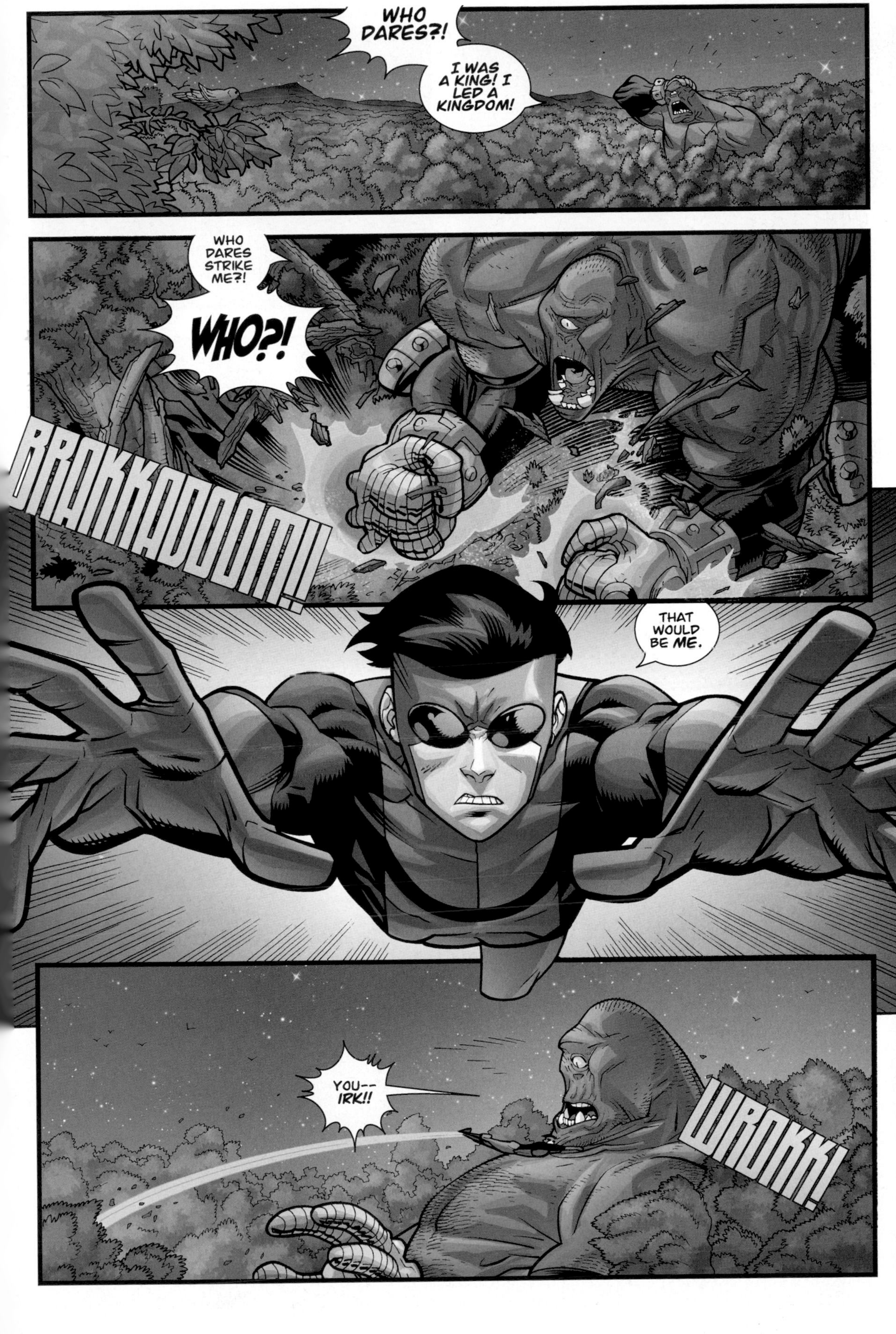
WHO DARES?!
I WAS A KING! I LED A KINGDOM!
WHO DARES STRIKE ME?!
WHO?!
BRAKKADOOOM!!
THAT WOULD BE ME.
YOU-- IRK!!
WRAKK!

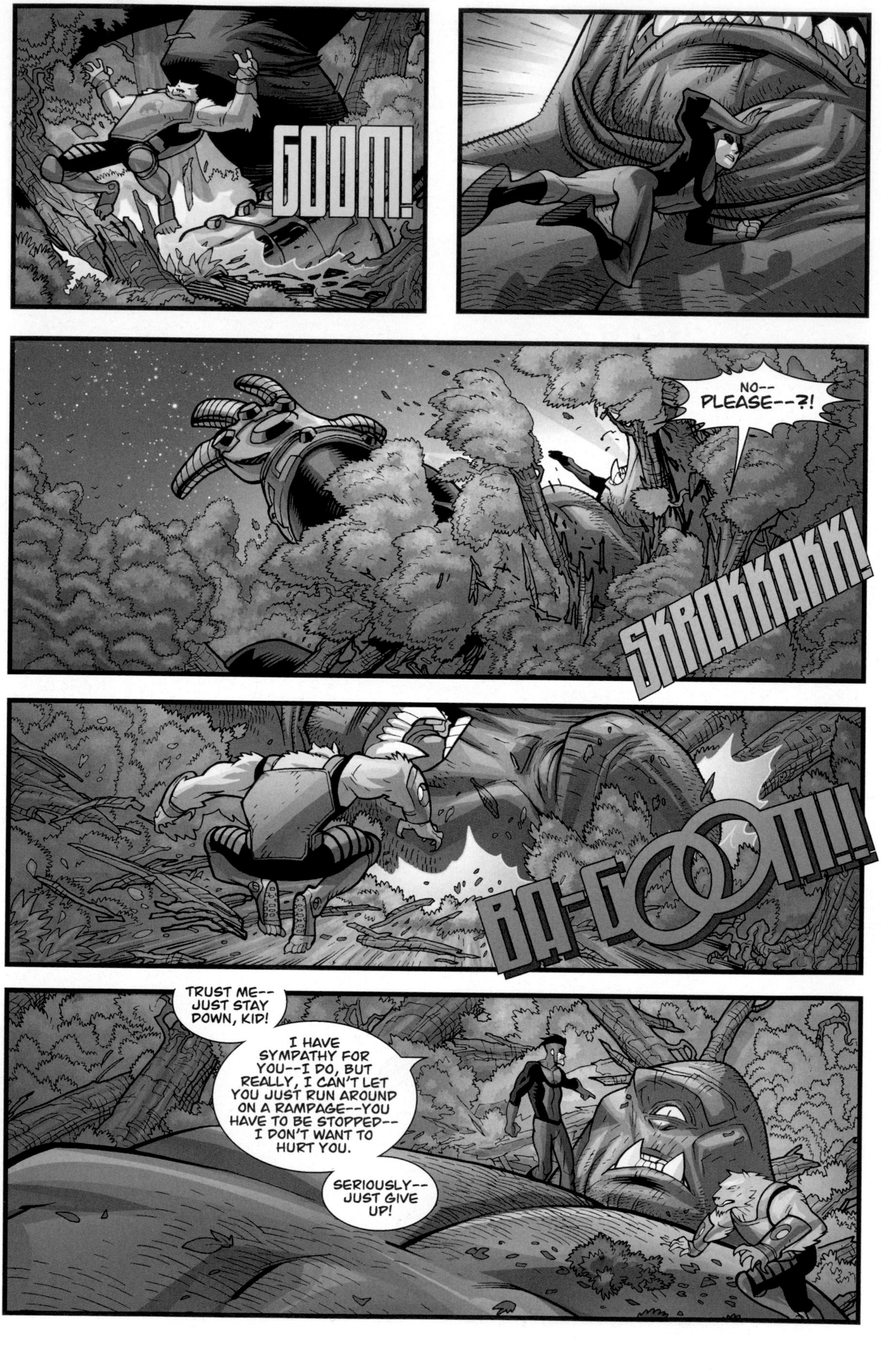
GOOM!
NO-- PLEASE--?!
SKRAKKAKK!
BA-GOOM!!
TRUST ME-- JUST STAY DOWN, KID!
I HAVE SYMPATHY FOR YOU--I DO, BUT REALLY, I CAN'T LET YOU JUST RUN AROUND ON A RAMPAGE--YOU HAVE TO BE STOPPED-- I DON'T WANT TO HURT YOU.
SERIOUSLY-- JUST GIVE UP!

WHAT--

WHAT DO YOU WANT ME TO DO?

JUST--I DON'T KNOW--SIT HERE QUIETLY UNTIL SOMEONE COMES ALONG TO TAKE YOU INTO CUSTODY.

THEY'RE JUST GOING TO TRY AND HELP YOU.

LET THEM.

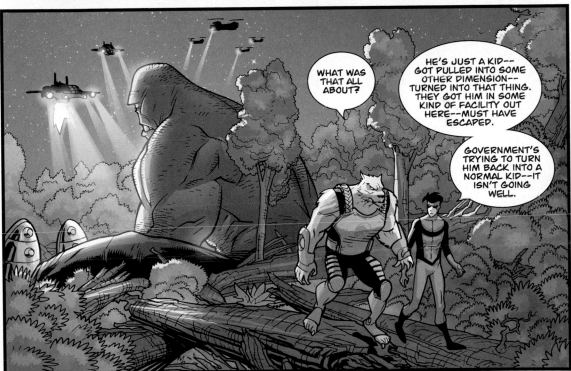

WHAT WAS THAT ALL ABOUT?

HE'S JUST A KID-- GOT PULLED INTO SOME OTHER DIMENSION-- TURNED INTO THAT THING. THEY GOT HIM IN SOME KIND OF FACILITY OUT HERE--MUST HAVE ESCAPED.

GOVERNMENT'S TRYING TO TURN HIM BACK INTO A NORMAL KID--IT ISN'T GOING WELL.

WELL, THANKS. I DON'T THINK I COULD HAVE HANDLED HIM ON MY OWN.

I OWE YOU FOR HELPING ME OUT WITH DOC SEISMIC A FEW WEEKS BACK.

STILL THOUGH-- I'M GOING TO HAVE TO TURN YOU IN.

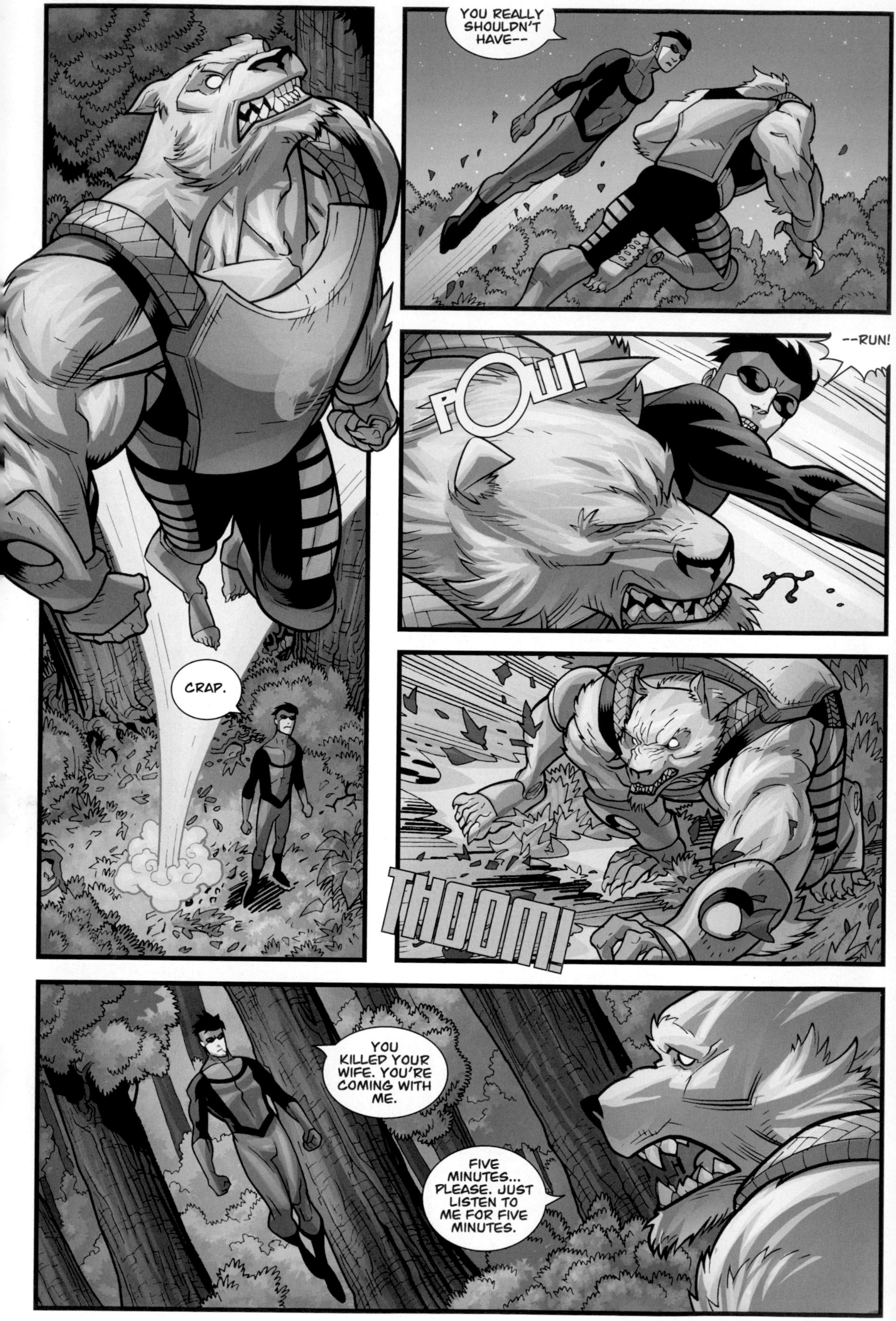
YOU REALLY SHOULDN'T HAVE--
--RUN!
POW!
CRAP.
THOOM!
YOU KILLED YOUR WIFE. YOU'RE COMING WITH ME.
FIVE MINUTES... PLEASE. JUST LISTEN TO ME FOR FIVE MINUTES.

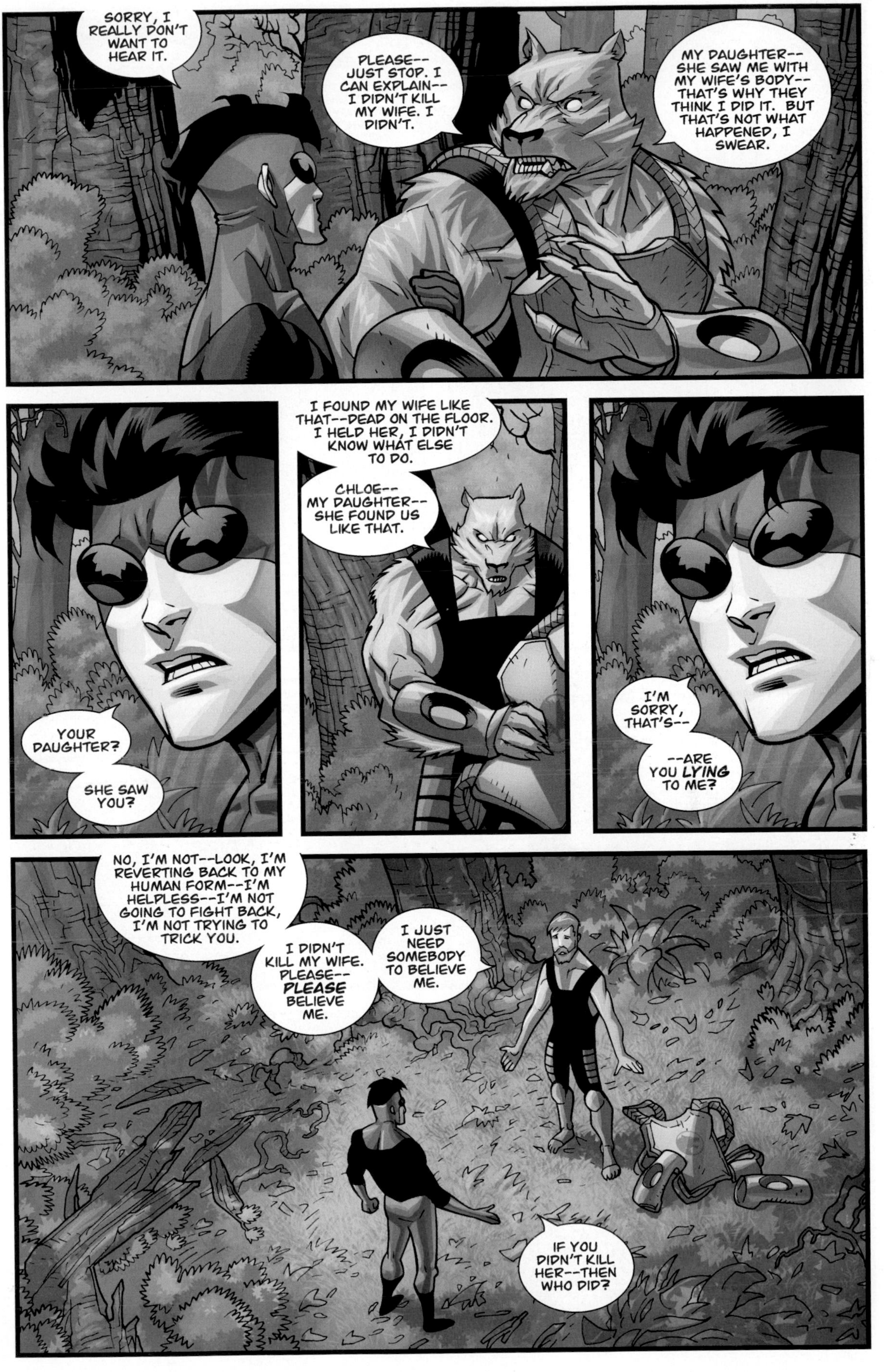
SORRY, I REALLY DON'T WANT TO HEAR IT.
PLEASE-- JUST STOP. I CAN EXPLAIN-- I DIDN'T KILL MY WIFE. I DIDN'T.
MY DAUGHTER-- SHE SAW ME WITH MY WIFE'S BODY-- THAT'S WHY THEY THINK I DID IT. BUT THAT'S NOT WHAT HAPPENED, I SWEAR.
YOUR DAUGHTER?
SHE SAW YOU?
I FOUND MY WIFE LIKE THAT--DEAD ON THE FLOOR. I HELD HER, I DIDN'T KNOW WHAT ELSE TO DO.
CHLOE-- MY DAUGHTER-- SHE FOUND US LIKE THAT.
I'M SORRY, THAT'S--
--ARE YOU LYING TO ME?
NO, I'M NOT--LOOK, I'M REVERTING BACK TO MY HUMAN FORM--I'M HELPLESS--I'M NOT GOING TO FIGHT BACK, I'M NOT TRYING TO TRICK YOU.
I DIDN'T KILL MY WIFE. PLEASE-- PLEASE BELIEVE ME.
I JUST NEED SOMEBODY TO BELIEVE ME.
IF YOU DIDN'T KILL HER--THEN WHO DID?

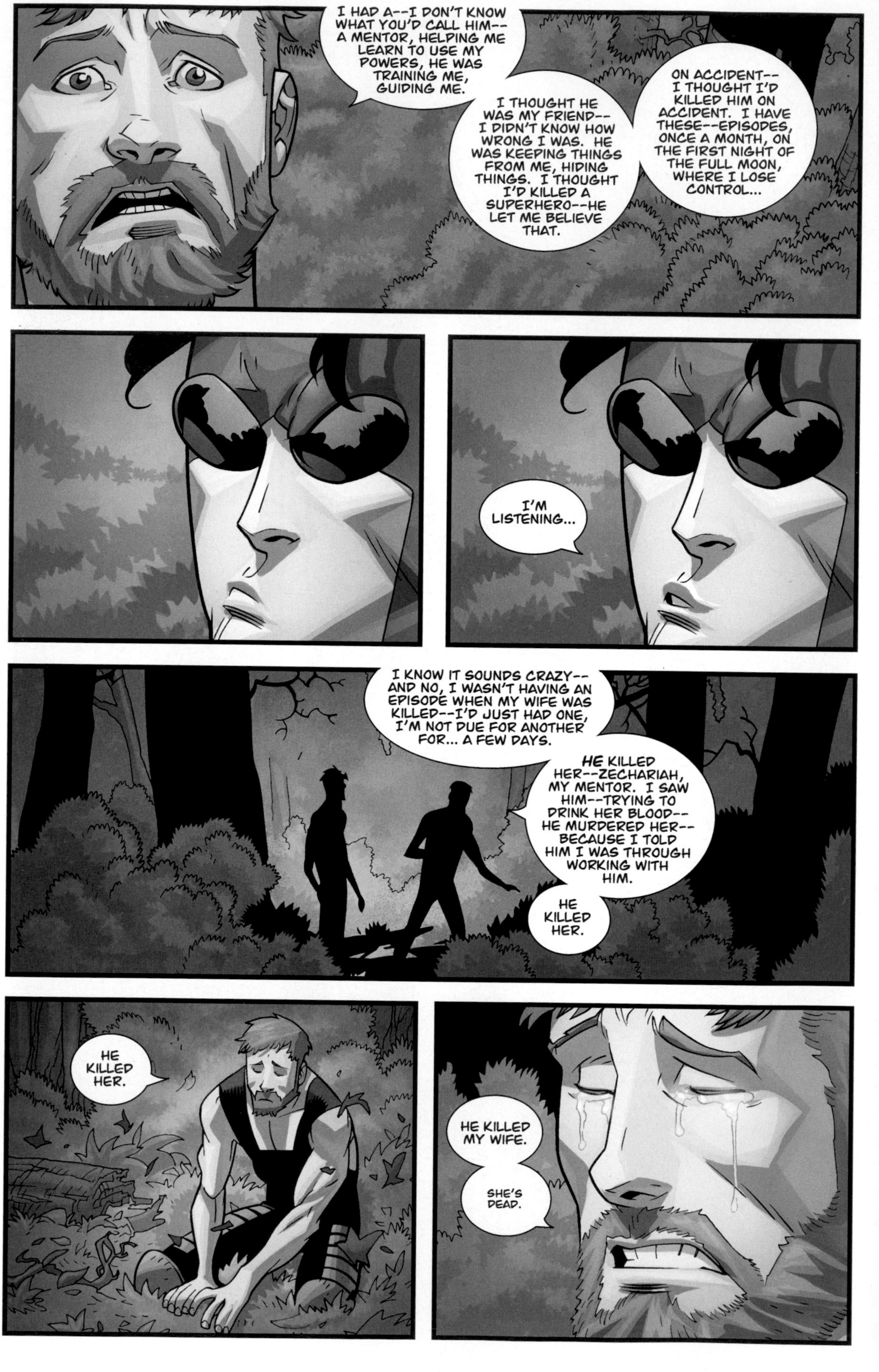
I HAD A--I DON'T KNOW WHAT YOU'D CALL HIM--A MENTOR, HELPING ME LEARN TO USE MY POWERS, HE WAS TRAINING ME, GUIDING ME.
I THOUGHT HE WAS MY FRIEND--I DIDN'T KNOW HOW WRONG I WAS. HE WAS KEEPING THINGS FROM ME, HIDING THINGS. I THOUGHT I'D KILLED A SUPERHERO--HE LET ME BELIEVE THAT.
ON ACCIDENT--I THOUGHT I'D KILLED HIM ON ACCIDENT. I HAVE THESE--EPISODES, ONCE A MONTH, ON THE FIRST NIGHT OF THE FULL MOON, WHERE I LOSE CONTROL...
I'M LISTENING...
I KNOW IT SOUNDS CRAZY--AND NO, I WASN'T HAVING AN EPISODE WHEN MY WIFE WAS KILLED--I'D JUST HAD ONE, I'M NOT DUE FOR ANOTHER FOR... A FEW DAYS.
HE KILLED HER--ZECHARIAH, MY MENTOR. I SAW HIM--TRYING TO DRINK HER BLOOD--HE MURDERED HER--BECAUSE I TOLD HIM I WAS THROUGH WORKING WITH HIM.
HE KILLED HER.
HE KILLED HER.
HE KILLED MY WIFE.
SHE'S DEAD.

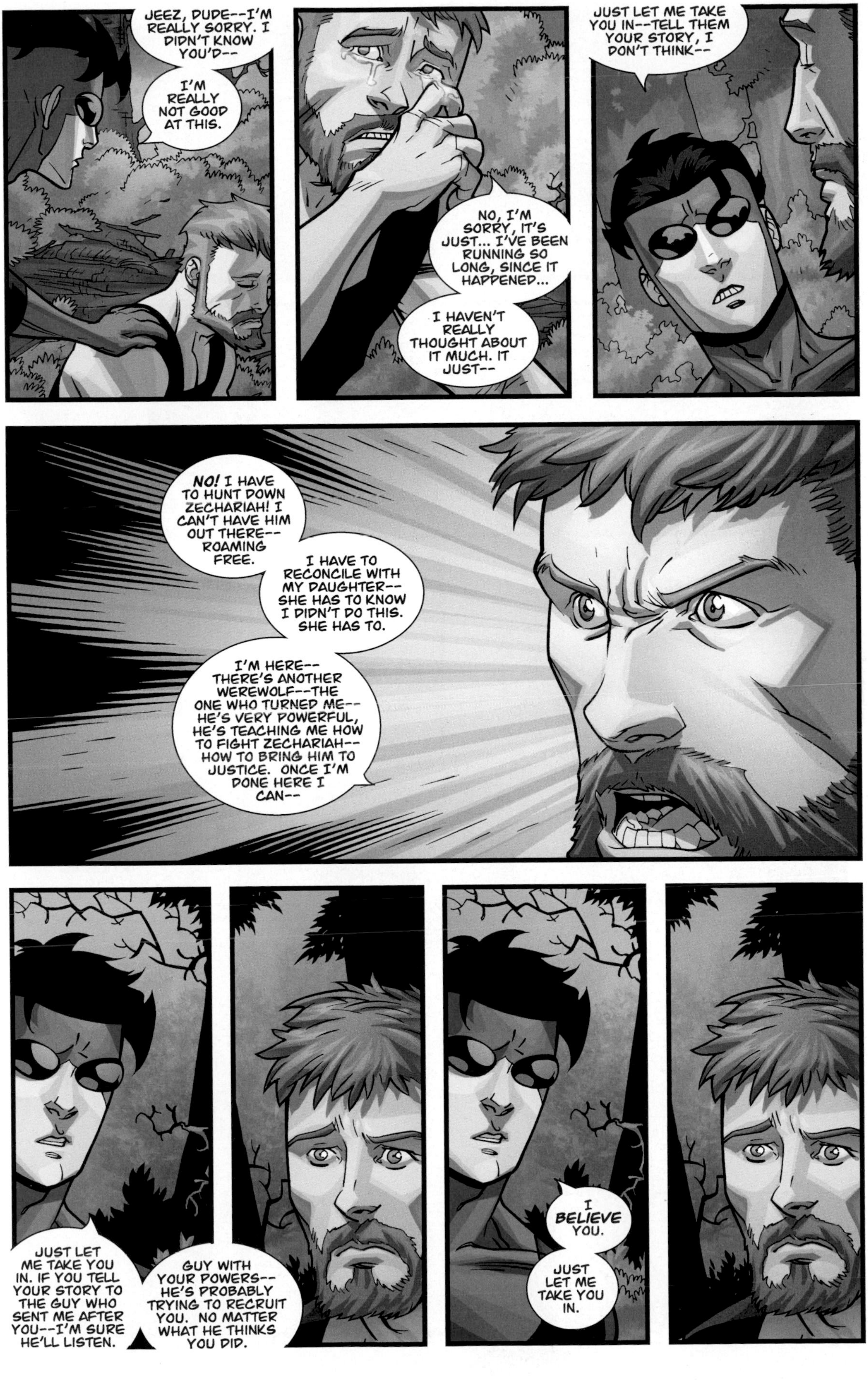
JEEZ, DUDE--I'M REALLY SORRY. I DIDN'T KNOW YOU'D--
I'M REALLY NOT GOOD AT THIS.
NO, I'M SORRY, IT'S JUST... I'VE BEEN RUNNING SO LONG, SINCE IT HAPPENED...
I HAVEN'T REALLY THOUGHT ABOUT IT MUCH. IT JUST--
JUST LET ME TAKE YOU IN--TELL THEM YOUR STORY, I DON'T THINK--
NO! I HAVE TO HUNT DOWN ZECHARIAH! I CAN'T HAVE HIM OUT THERE--ROAMING FREE.
I HAVE TO RECONCILE WITH MY DAUGHTER--SHE HAS TO KNOW I DIDN'T DO THIS. SHE HAS TO.
I'M HERE--THERE'S ANOTHER WEREWOLF--THE ONE WHO TURNED ME--HE'S VERY POWERFUL, HE'S TEACHING ME HOW TO FIGHT ZECHARIAH--HOW TO BRING HIM TO JUSTICE. ONCE I'M DONE HERE I CAN--
JUST LET ME TAKE YOU IN. IF YOU TELL YOUR STORY TO THE GUY WHO SENT ME AFTER YOU--I'M SURE HE'LL LISTEN.
GUY WITH YOUR POWERS--HE'S PROBABLY TRYING TO RECRUIT YOU. NO MATTER WHAT HE THINKS YOU DID.
I BELIEVE YOU.
JUST LET ME TAKE YOU IN.

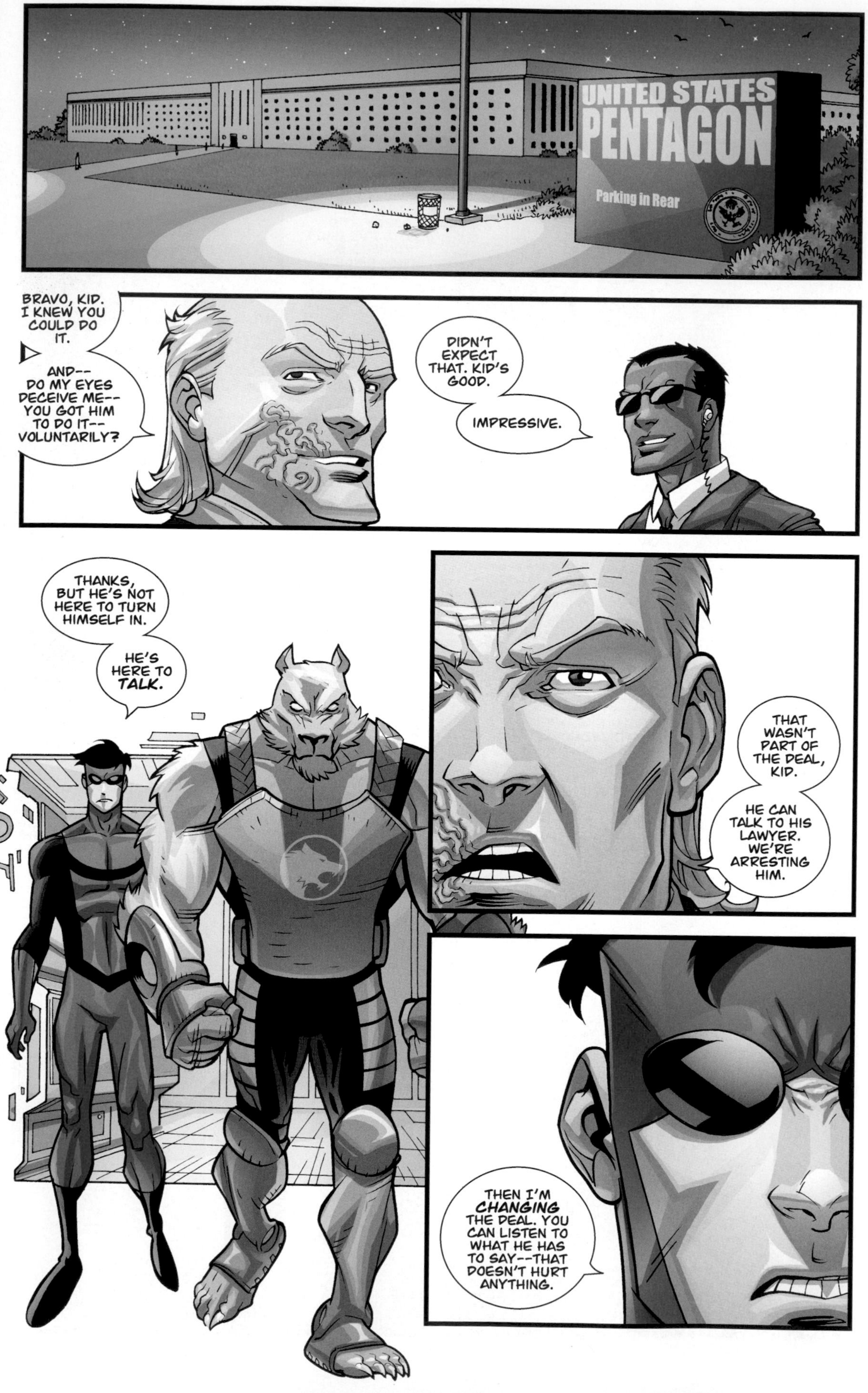
UNITED STATES PENTAGON
Parking in Rear
BRAVO, KID. I KNEW YOU COULD DO IT.
AND-- DO MY EYES DECEIVE ME-- YOU GOT HIM TO DO IT-- VOLUNTARILY?
DIDN'T EXPECT THAT. KID'S GOOD.
IMPRESSIVE.
THANKS, BUT HE'S NOT HERE TO TURN HIMSELF IN.
HE'S HERE TO TALK.
THAT WASN'T PART OF THE DEAL, KID.
HE CAN TALK TO HIS LAWYER. WE'RE ARRESTING HIM.
THEN I'M CHANGING THE DEAL. YOU CAN LISTEN TO WHAT HE HAS TO SAY--THAT DOESN'T HURT ANYTHING.

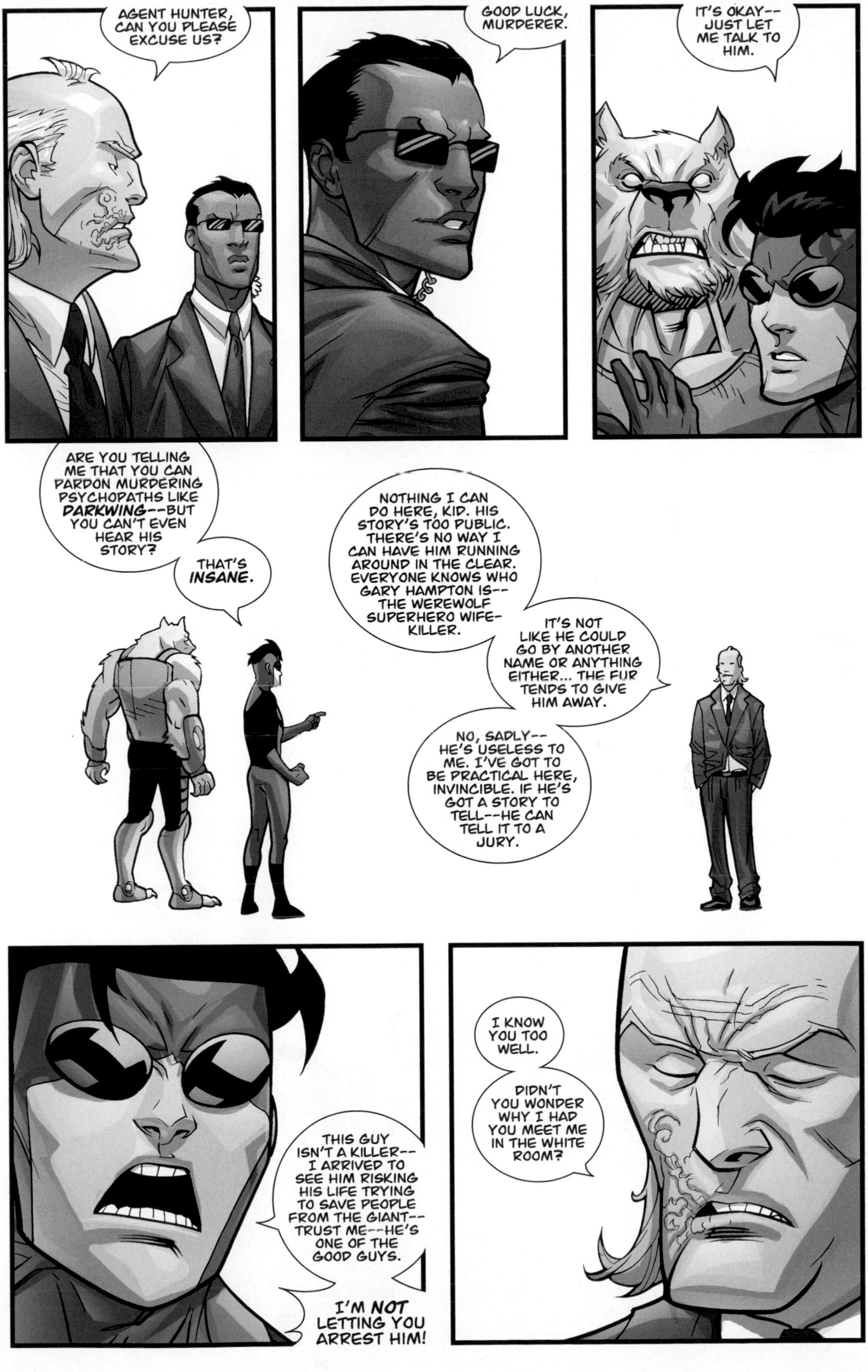
AGENT HUNTER, CAN YOU PLEASE EXCUSE US?
GOOD LUCK, MURDERER.
IT'S OKAY--JUST LET ME TALK TO HIM.
ARE YOU TELLING ME THAT YOU CAN PARDON MURDERING PSYCHOPATHS LIKE DARKWING--BUT YOU CAN'T EVEN HEAR HIS STORY?
THAT'S INSANE.
NOTHING I CAN DO HERE, KID. HIS STORY'S TOO PUBLIC. THERE'S NO WAY I CAN HAVE HIM RUNNING AROUND IN THE CLEAR. EVERYONE KNOWS WHO GARY HAMPTON IS--THE WEREWOLF SUPERHERO WIFE-KILLER.
IT'S NOT LIKE HE COULD GO BY ANOTHER NAME OR ANYTHING EITHER... THE FUR TENDS TO GIVE HIM AWAY.
NO, SADLY--HE'S USELESS TO ME. I'VE GOT TO BE PRACTICAL HERE, INVINCIBLE. IF HE'S GOT A STORY TO TELL--HE CAN TELL IT TO A JURY.
THIS GUY ISN'T A KILLER--I ARRIVED TO SEE HIM RISKING HIS LIFE TRYING TO SAVE PEOPLE FROM THE GIANT--TRUST ME--HE'S ONE OF THE GOOD GUYS.
I'M NOT LETTING YOU ARREST HIM!
I KNOW YOU TOO WELL.
DIDN'T YOU WONDER WHY I HAD YOU MEET ME IN THE WHITE ROOM?

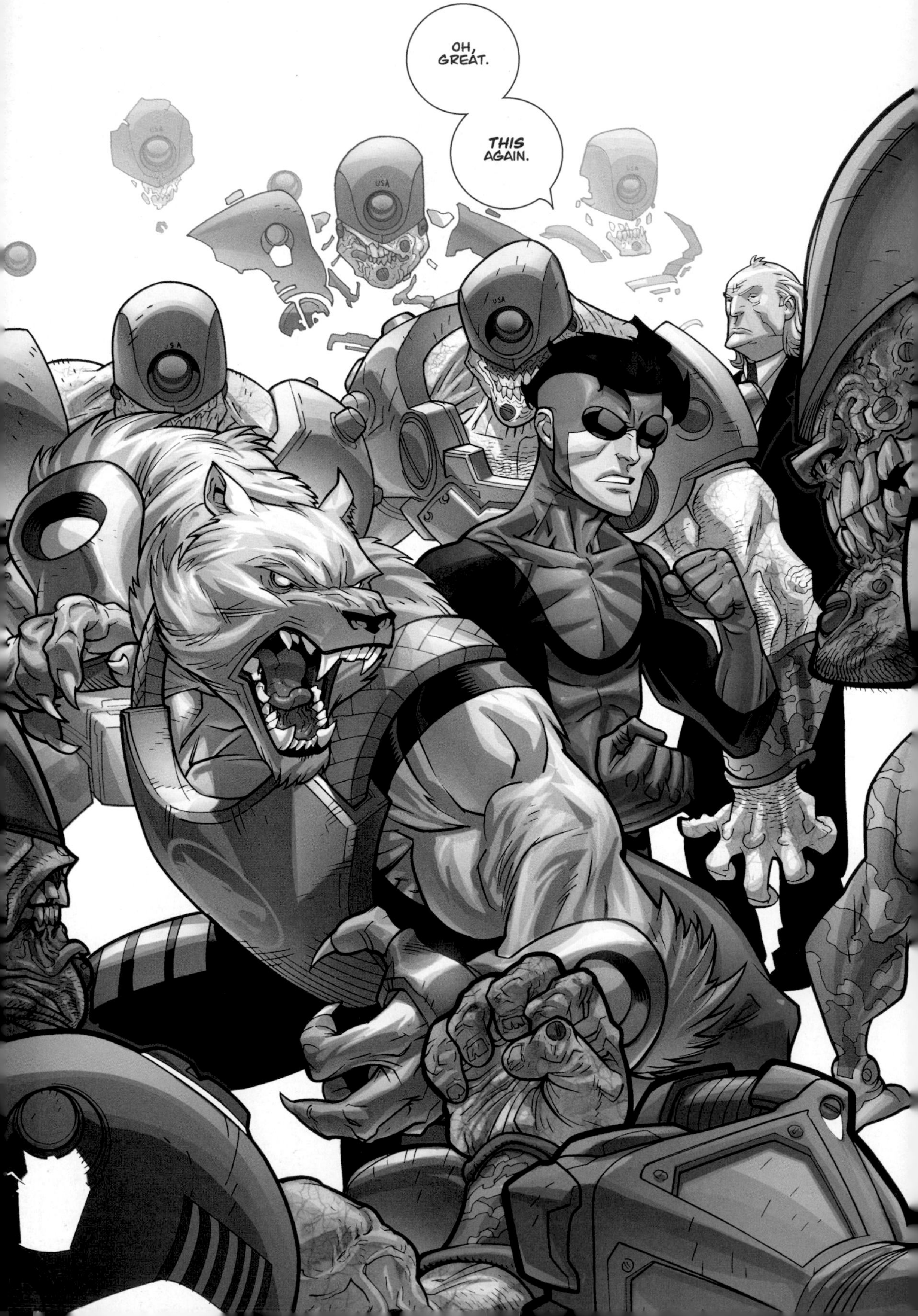
OH, GREAT.
THIS AGAIN.

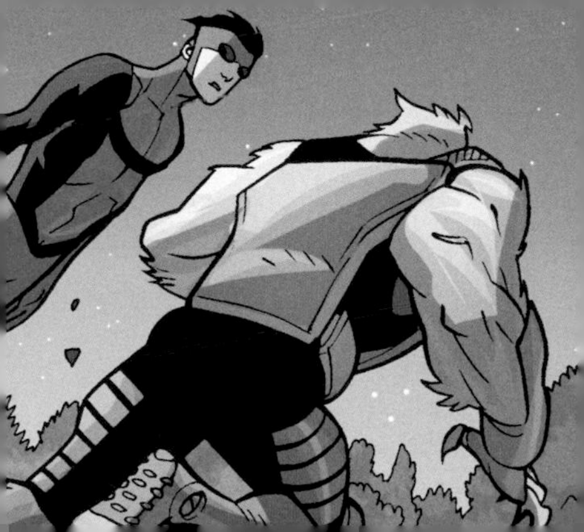

11
PART TWO

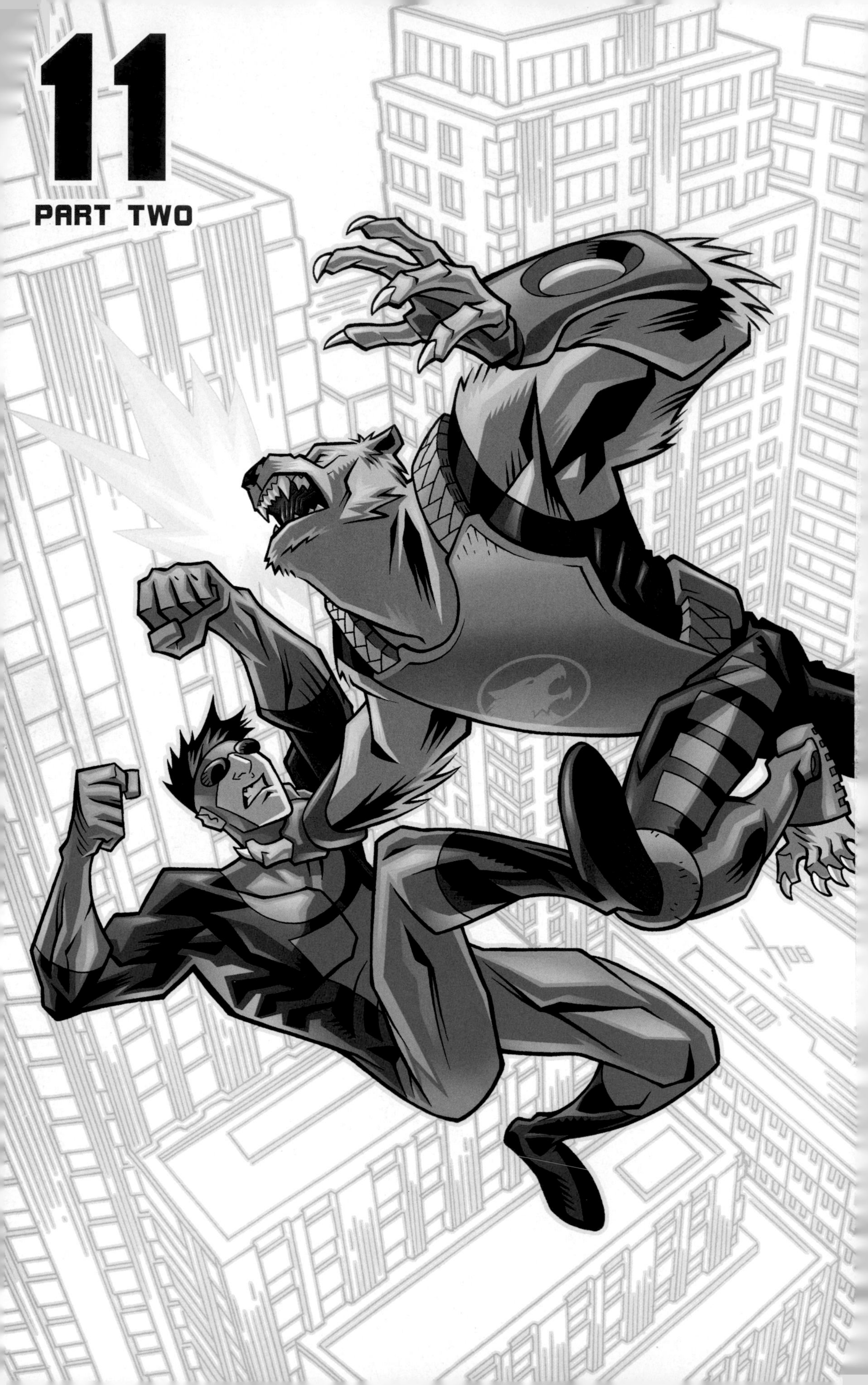

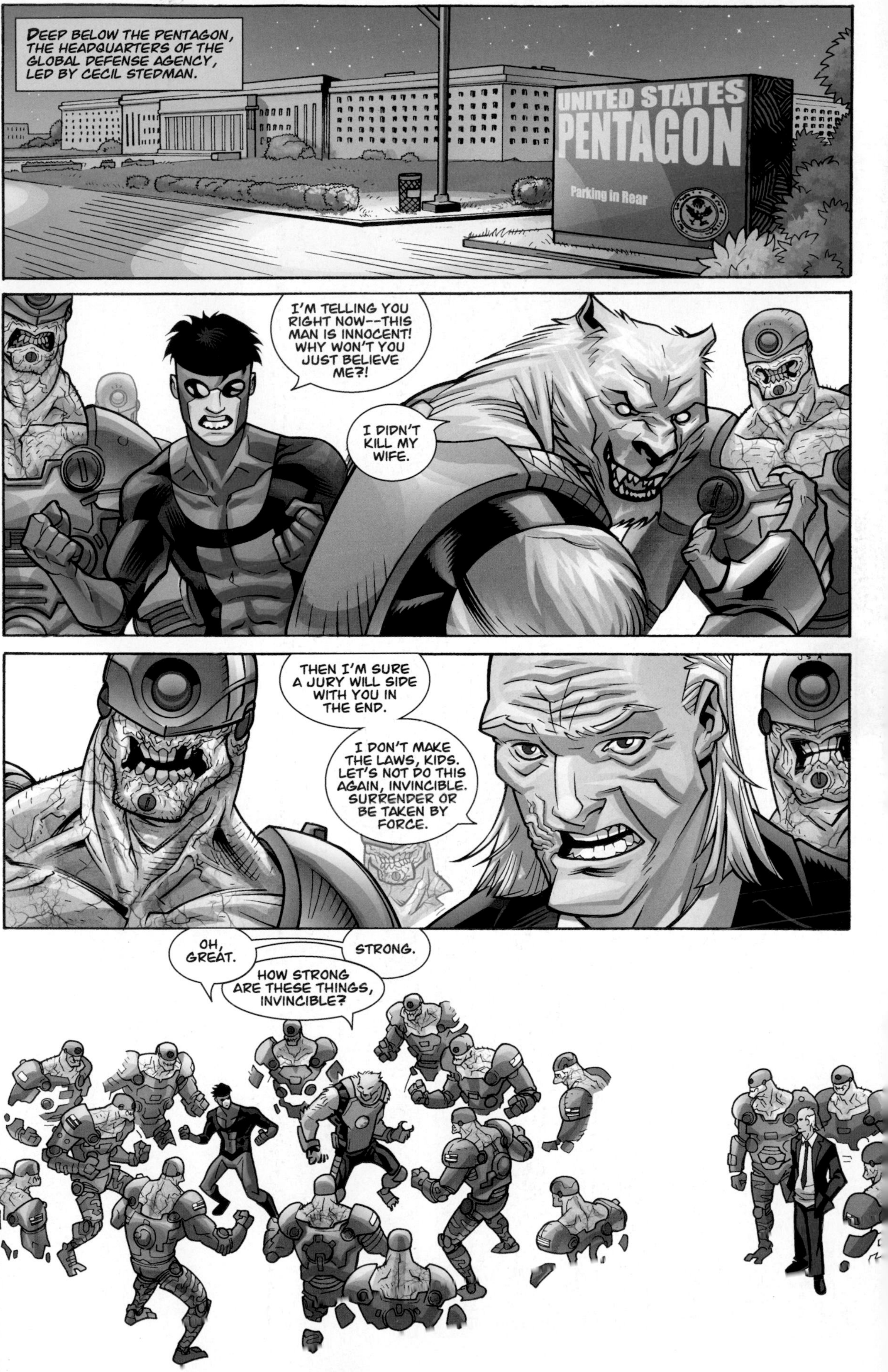
DEEP BELOW THE PENTAGON, THE HEADQUARTERS OF THE GLOBAL DEFENSE AGENCY, LED BY CECIL STEDMAN.
UNITED STATES PENTAGON
Parking in Rear
I'M TELLING YOU RIGHT NOW--THIS MAN IS INNOCENT! WHY WON'T YOU JUST BELIEVE ME?!
I DIDN'T KILL MY WIFE.
THEN I'M SURE A JURY WILL SIDE WITH YOU IN THE END.
I DON'T MAKE THE LAWS, KIDS. LET'S NOT DO THIS AGAIN, INVINCIBLE. SURRENDER OR BE TAKEN BY FORCE.
OH, GREAT.
HOW STRONG ARE THESE THINGS, INVINCIBLE?
STRONG.

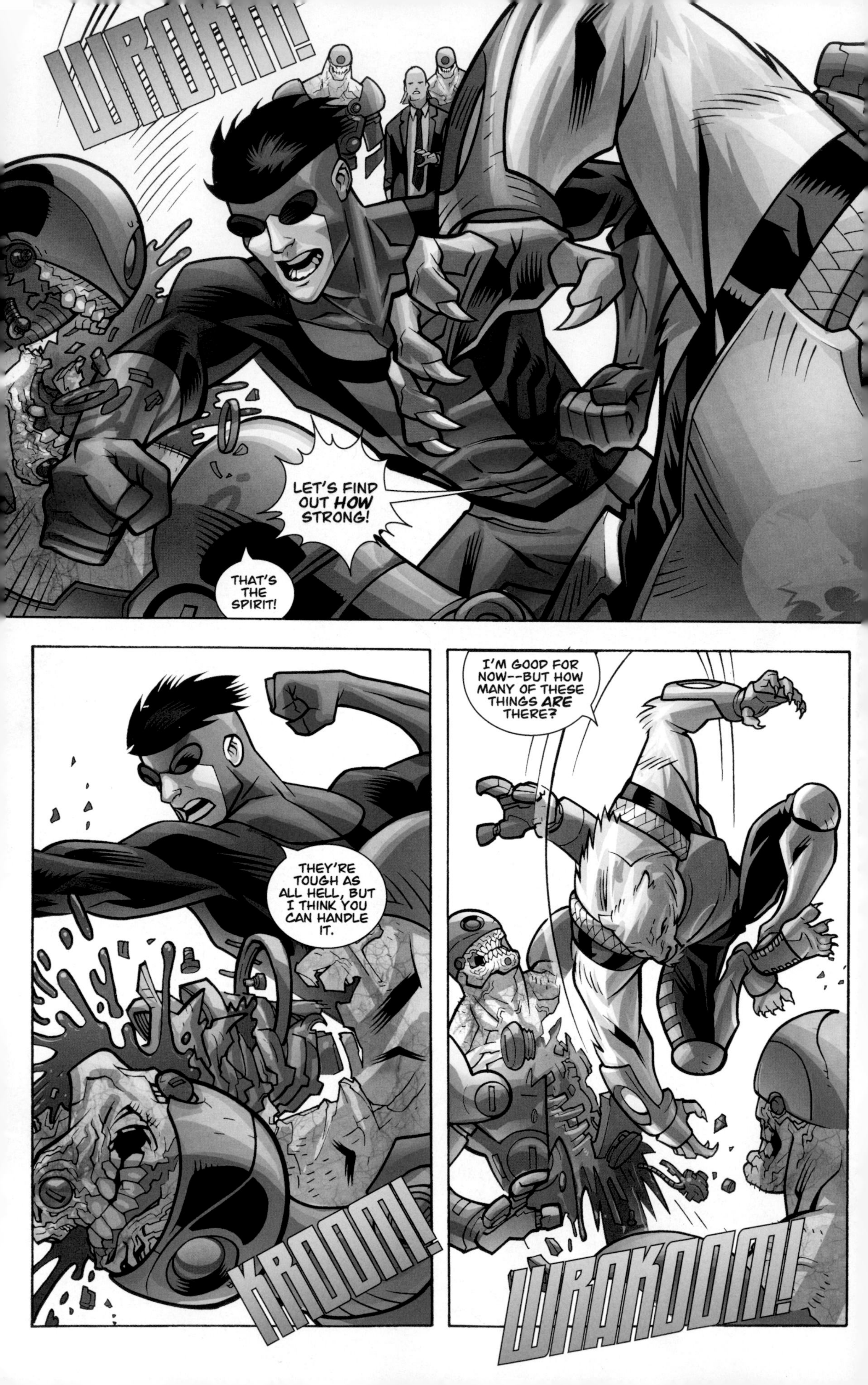
WROOM!
LET'S FIND OUT HOW STRONG!
THAT'S THE SPIRIT!
THEY'RE TOUGH AS ALL HELL, BUT I THINK YOU CAN HANDLE IT.
KROOM!
I'M GOOD FOR NOW--BUT HOW MANY OF THESE THINGS ARE THERE?
WRAKOOM!

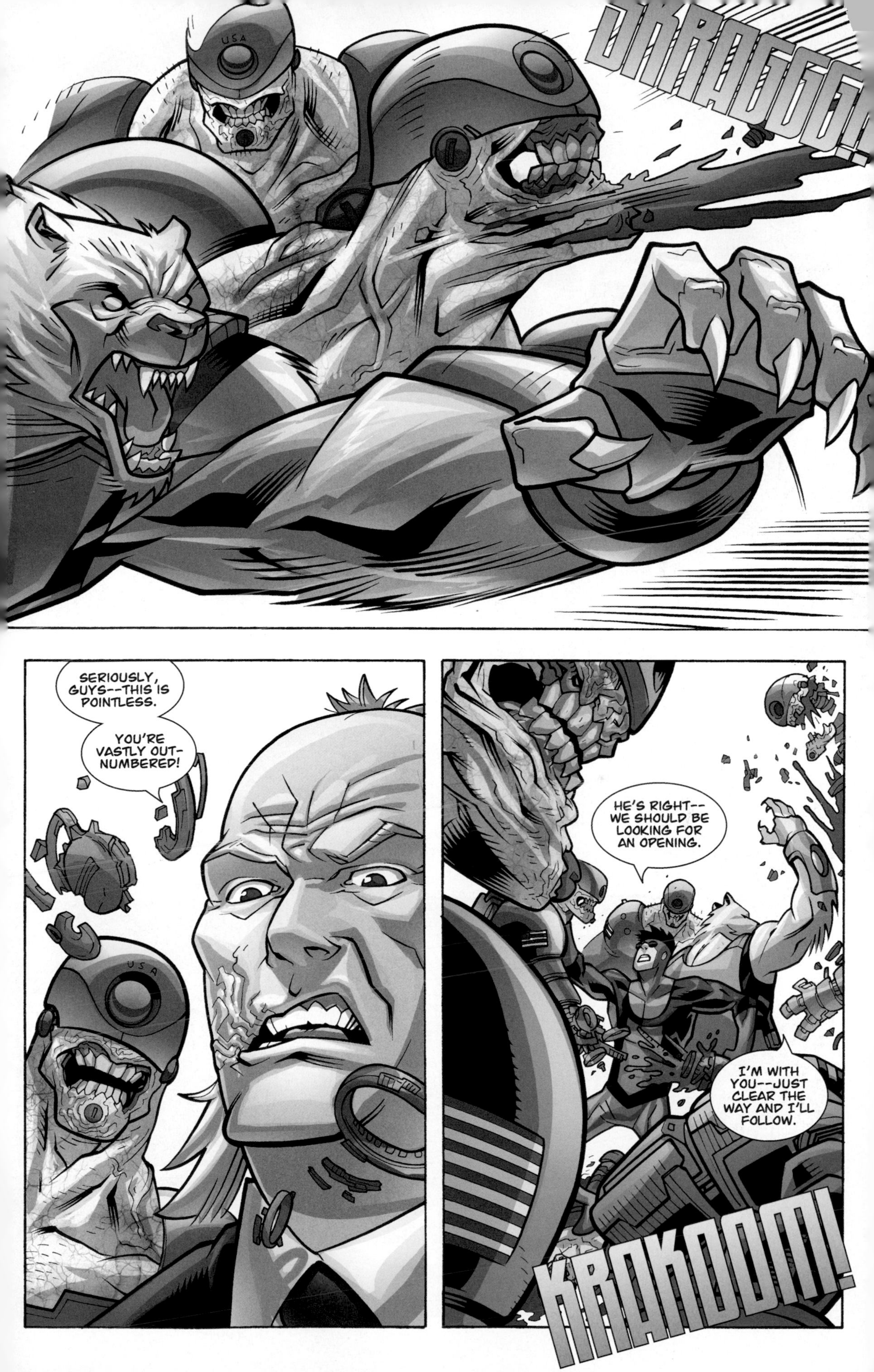
DRAGGG!
SERIOUSLY, GUYS--THIS IS POINTLESS.
YOU'RE VASTLY OUT-NUMBERED!
HE'S RIGHT--WE SHOULD BE LOOKING FOR AN OPENING.
I'M WITH YOU--JUST CLEAR THE WAY AND I'LL FOLLOW.
KRAKOOM!

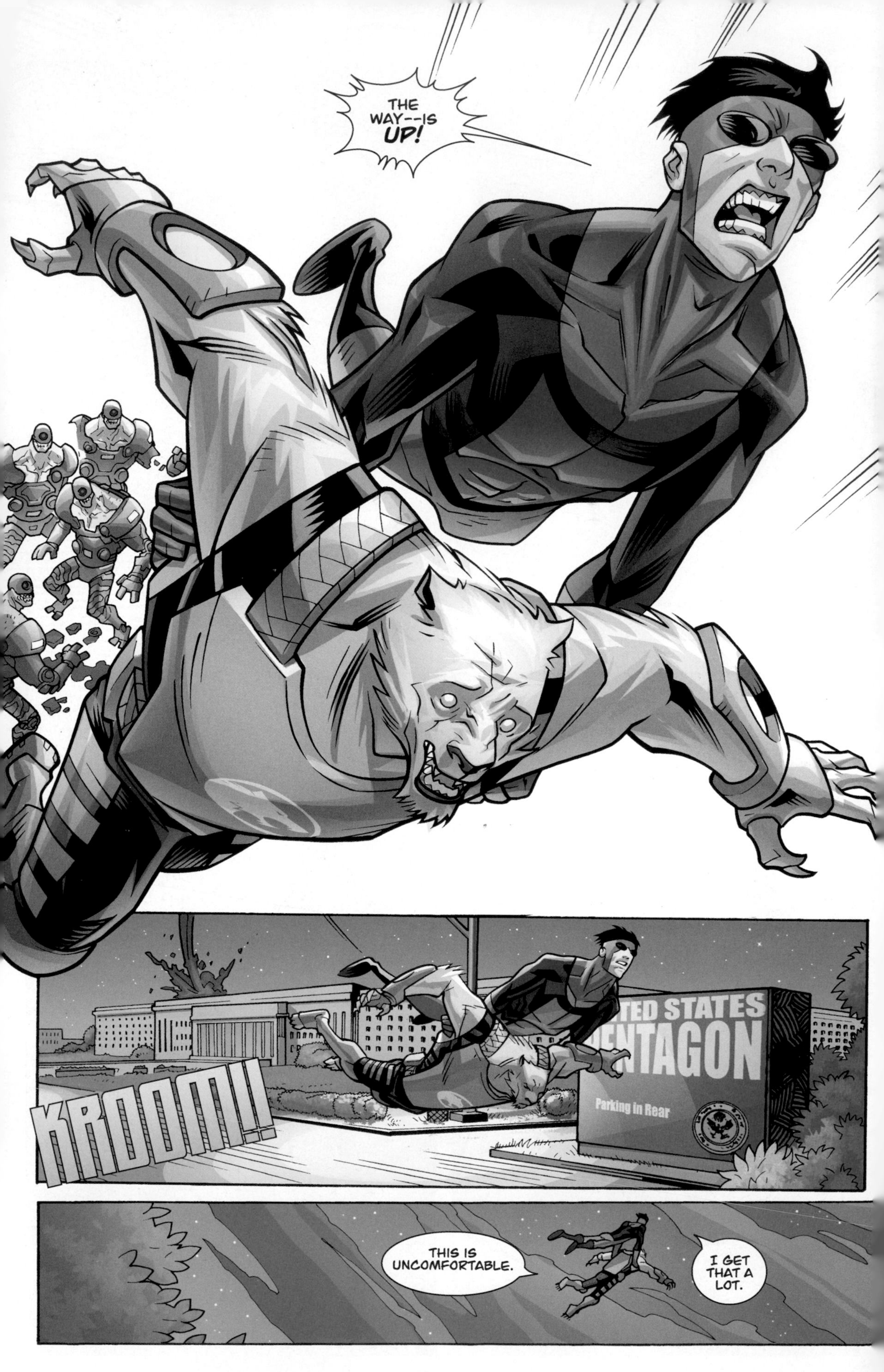
THE WAY--IS UP!
KROOM!!
...TED STATES
...ENTAGON
Parking in Rear
THIS IS UNCOMFORTABLE.
I GET THAT A LOT.

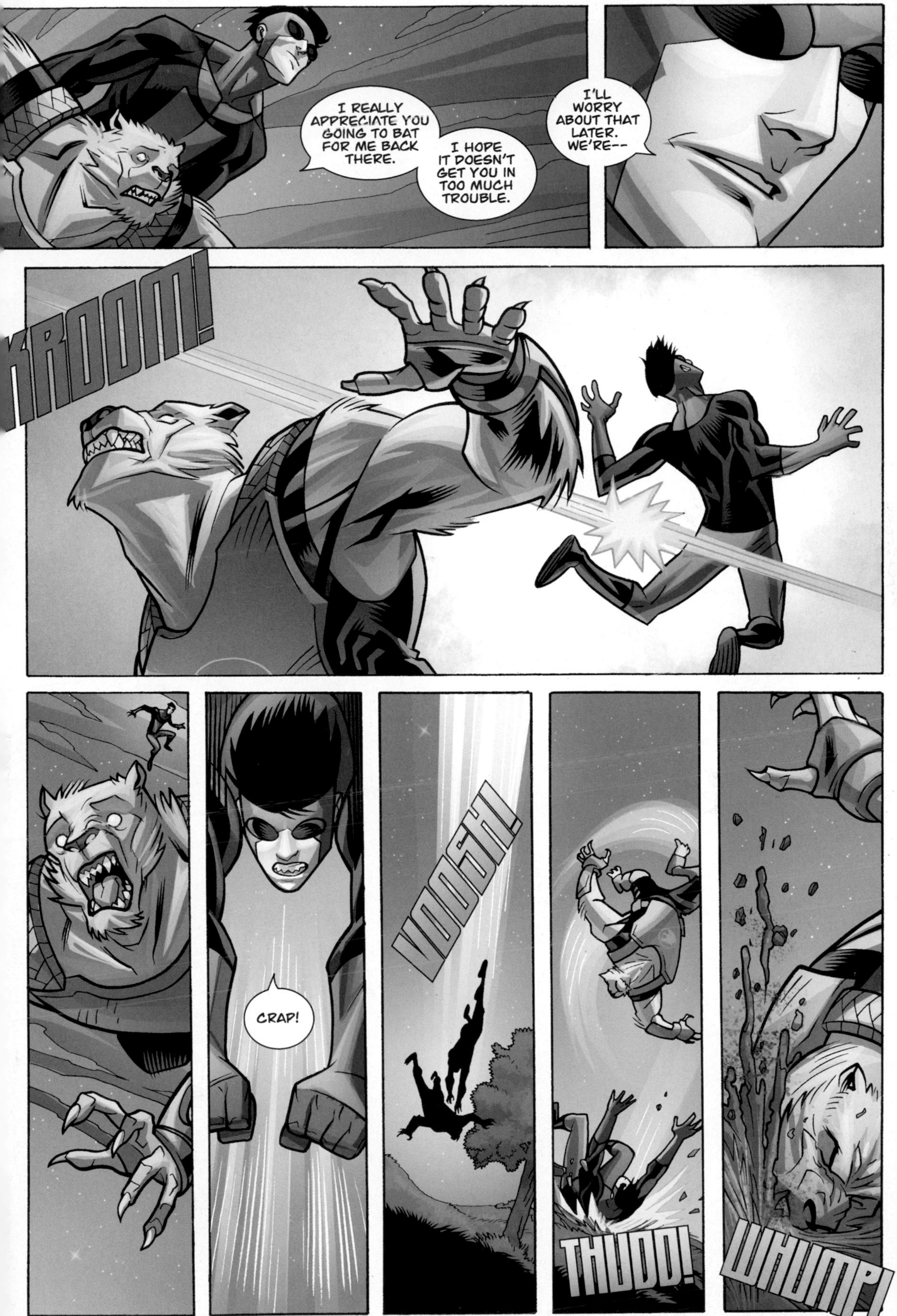
I REALLY APPRECIATE YOU GOING TO BAT FOR ME BACK THERE.
I HOPE IT DOESN'T GET YOU IN TOO MUCH TROUBLE.
I'LL WORRY ABOUT THAT LATER. WE'RE--
KROOM!
CRAP!
VOOSH!
THUDD!
WHUMP!

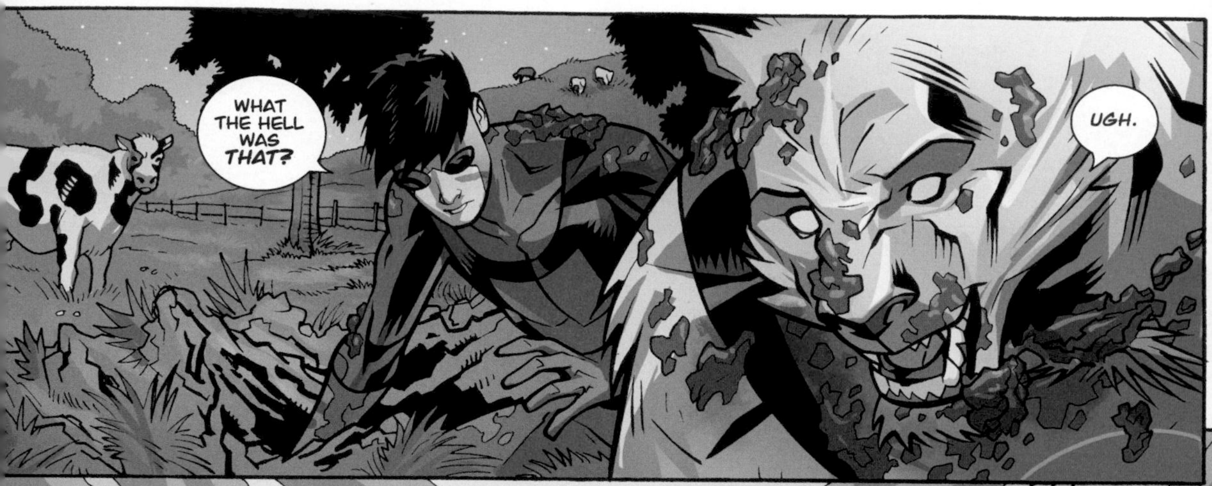
WHAT THE HELL WAS THAT?
UGH.

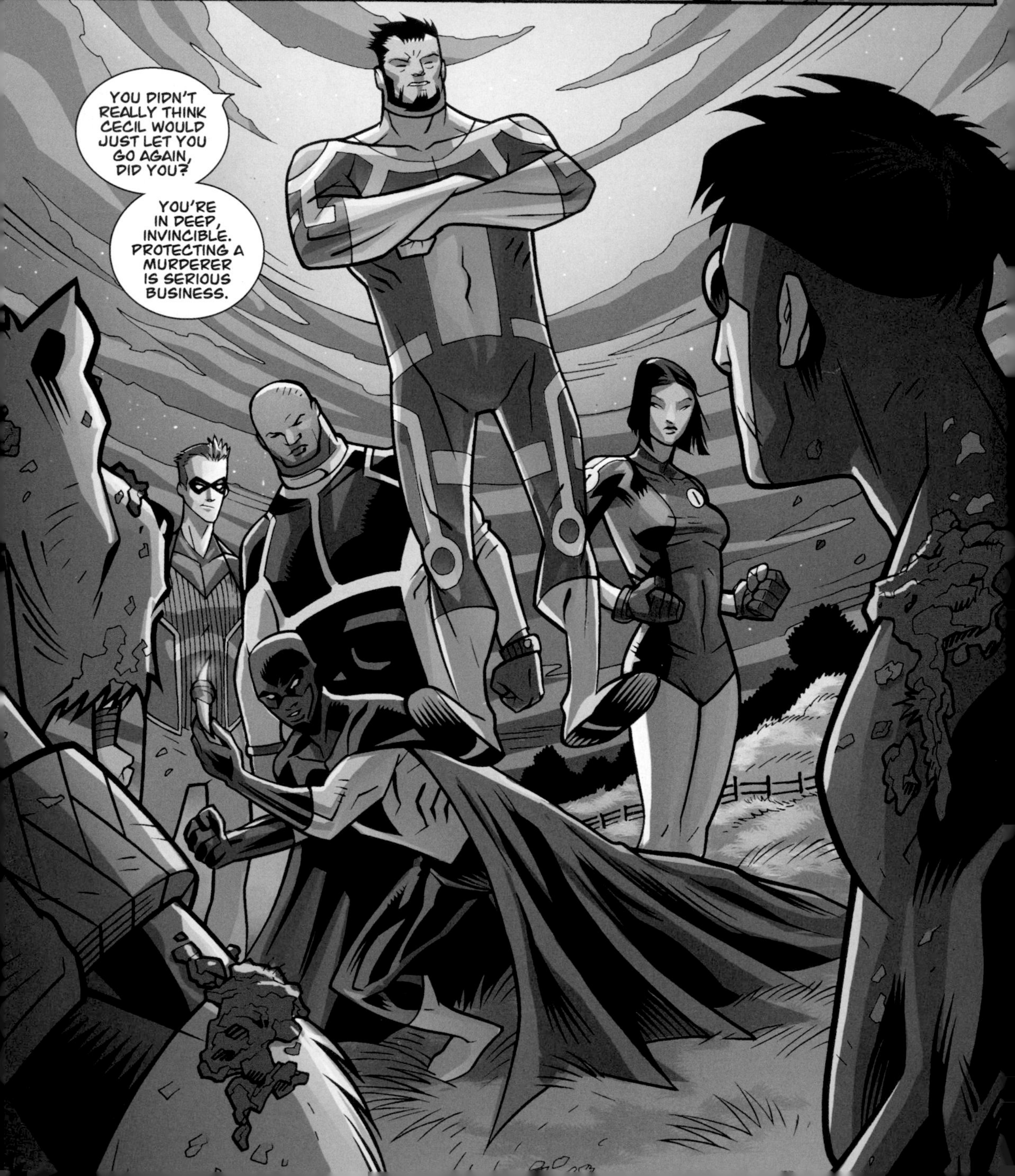
YOU DIDN'T REALLY THINK CECIL WOULD JUST LET YOU GO AGAIN, DID YOU?
YOU'RE IN DEEP, INVINCIBLE. PROTECTING A MURDERER IS SERIOUS BUSINESS.

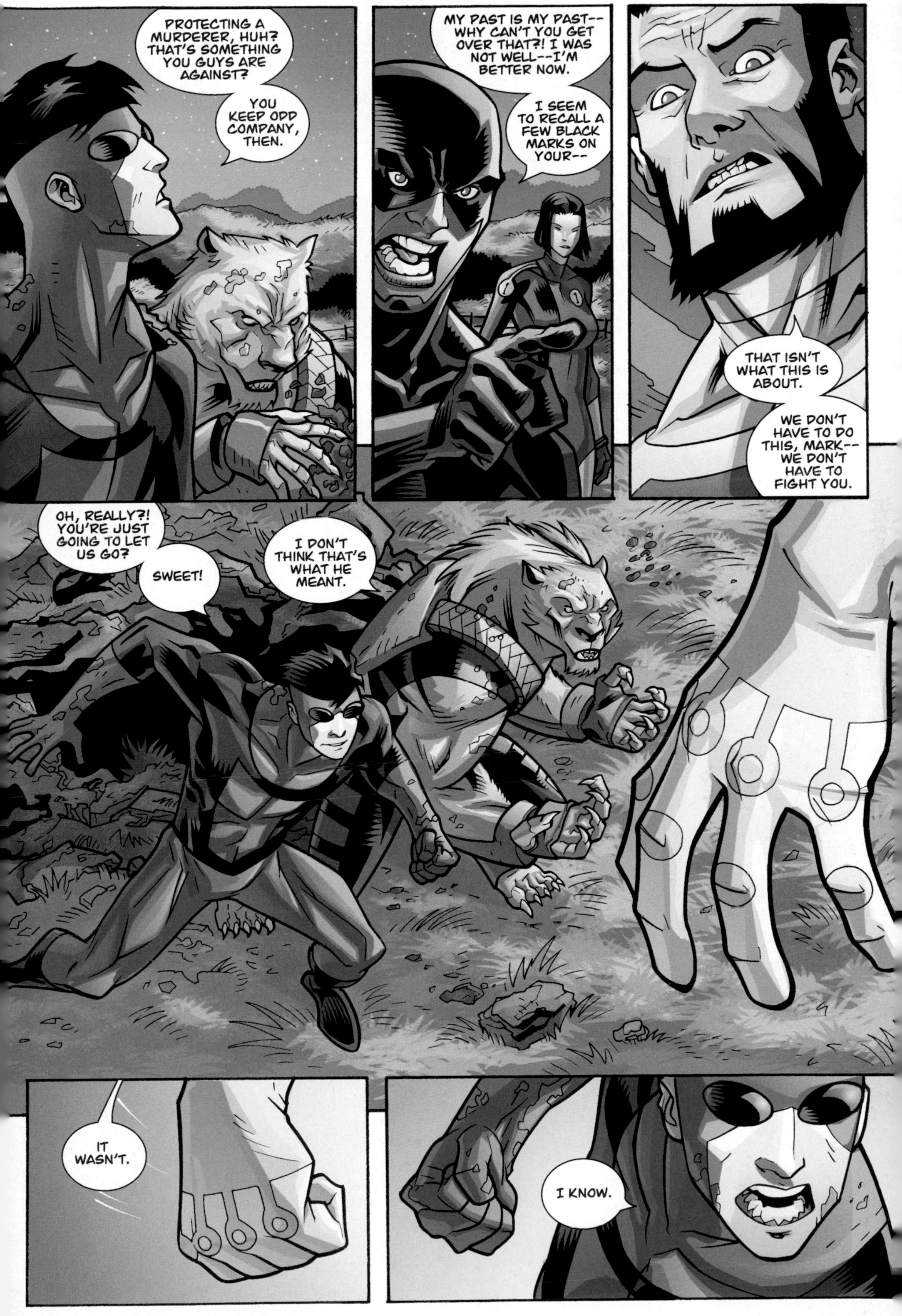
PROTECTING A MURDERER, HUH? THAT'S SOMETHING YOU GUYS ARE AGAINST?
YOU KEEP ODD COMPANY, THEN.
MY PAST IS MY PAST--WHY CAN'T YOU GET OVER THAT?! I WAS NOT WELL--I'M BETTER NOW.
I SEEM TO RECALL A FEW BLACK MARKS ON YOUR--
THAT ISN'T WHAT THIS IS ABOUT.
WE DON'T HAVE TO DO THIS, MARK--WE DON'T HAVE TO FIGHT YOU.
OH, REALLY?! YOU'RE JUST GOING TO LET US GO?
SWEET!
I DON'T THINK THAT'S WHAT HE MEANT.
IT WASN'T.
I KNOW.

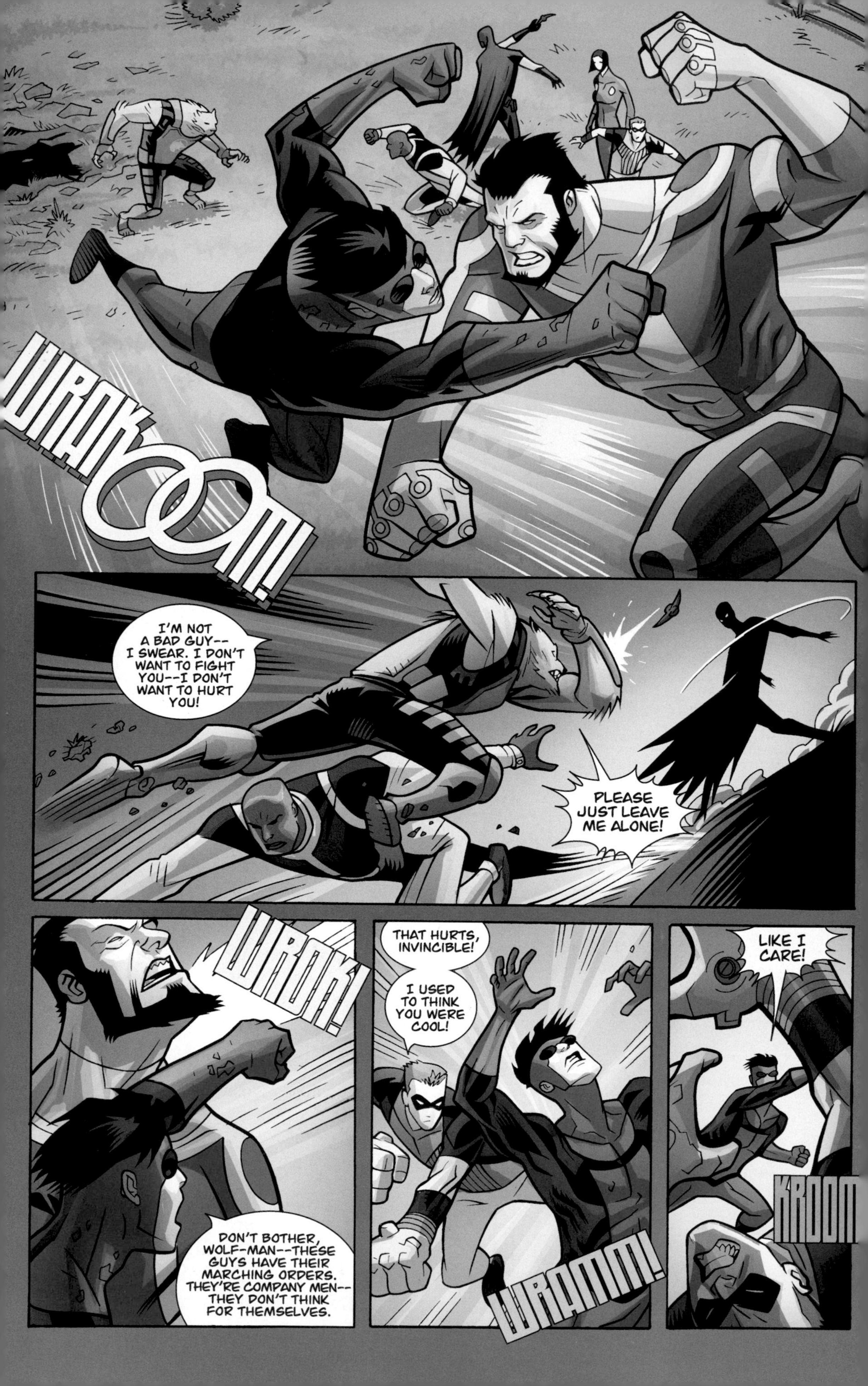
WRAKOOM!
I'M NOT A BAD GUY-- I SWEAR. I DON'T WANT TO FIGHT YOU--I DON'T WANT TO HURT YOU!
PLEASE JUST LEAVE ME ALONE!
WRAK!
DON'T BOTHER, WOLF-MAN--THESE GUYS HAVE THEIR MARCHING ORDERS. THEY'RE COMPANY MEN-- THEY DON'T THINK FOR THEMSELVES.
THAT HURTS, INVINCIBLE!
I USED TO THINK YOU WERE COOL!
WRAMM!
LIKE I CARE!
KROOM

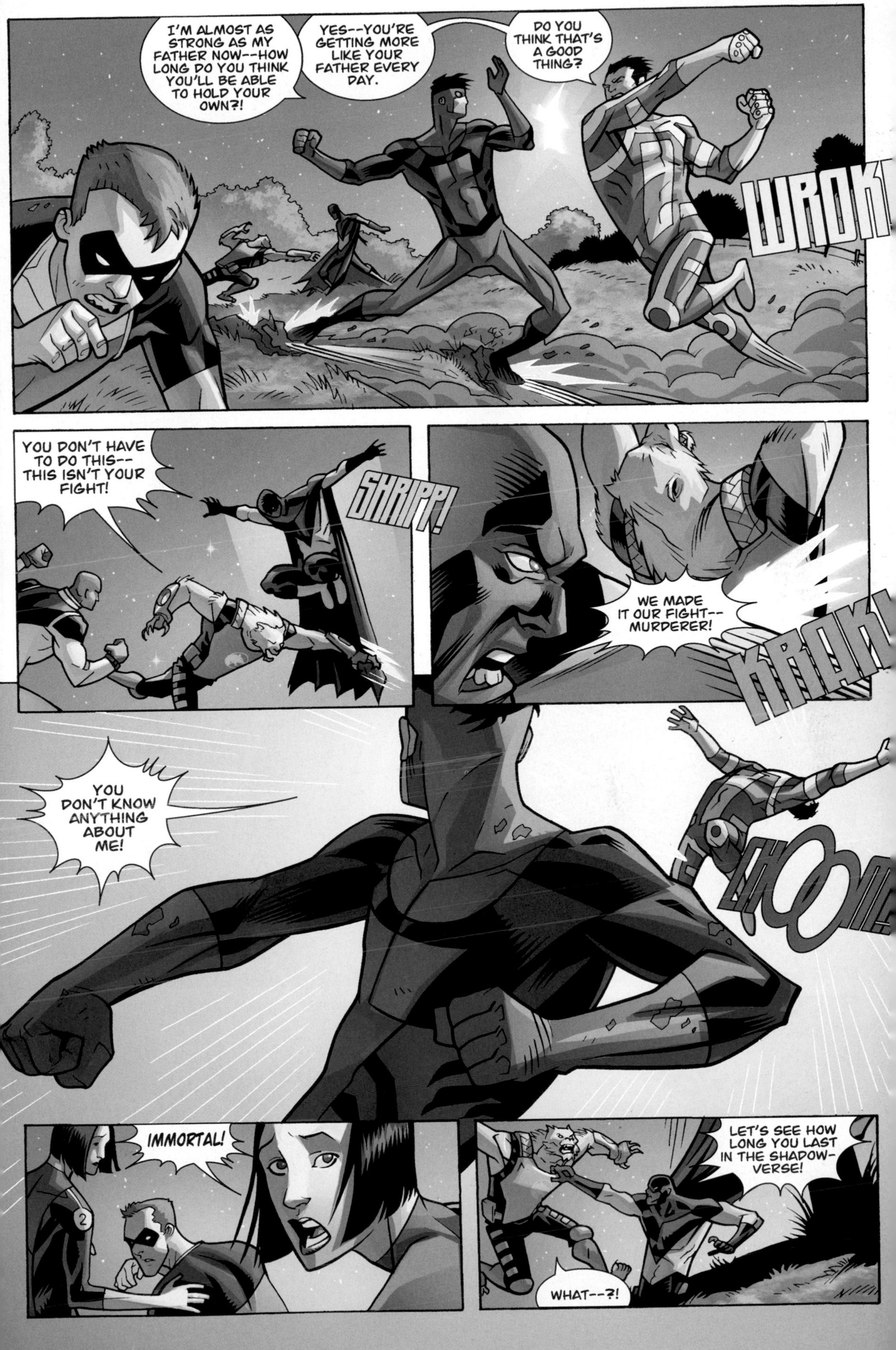
I'M ALMOST AS STRONG AS MY FATHER NOW--HOW LONG DO YOU THINK YOU'LL BE ABLE TO HOLD YOUR OWN?!
YES--YOU'RE GETTING MORE LIKE YOUR FATHER EVERY DAY.
DO YOU THINK THAT'S A GOOD THING?
WROK!
YOU DON'T HAVE TO DO THIS-- THIS ISN'T YOUR FIGHT!
SHRIPP!
WE MADE IT OUR FIGHT-- MURDERER!
YOU DON'T KNOW ANYTHING ABOUT ME!
IMMORTAL!
LET'S SEE HOW LONG YOU LAST IN THE SHADOW-VERSE!
WHAT--?!

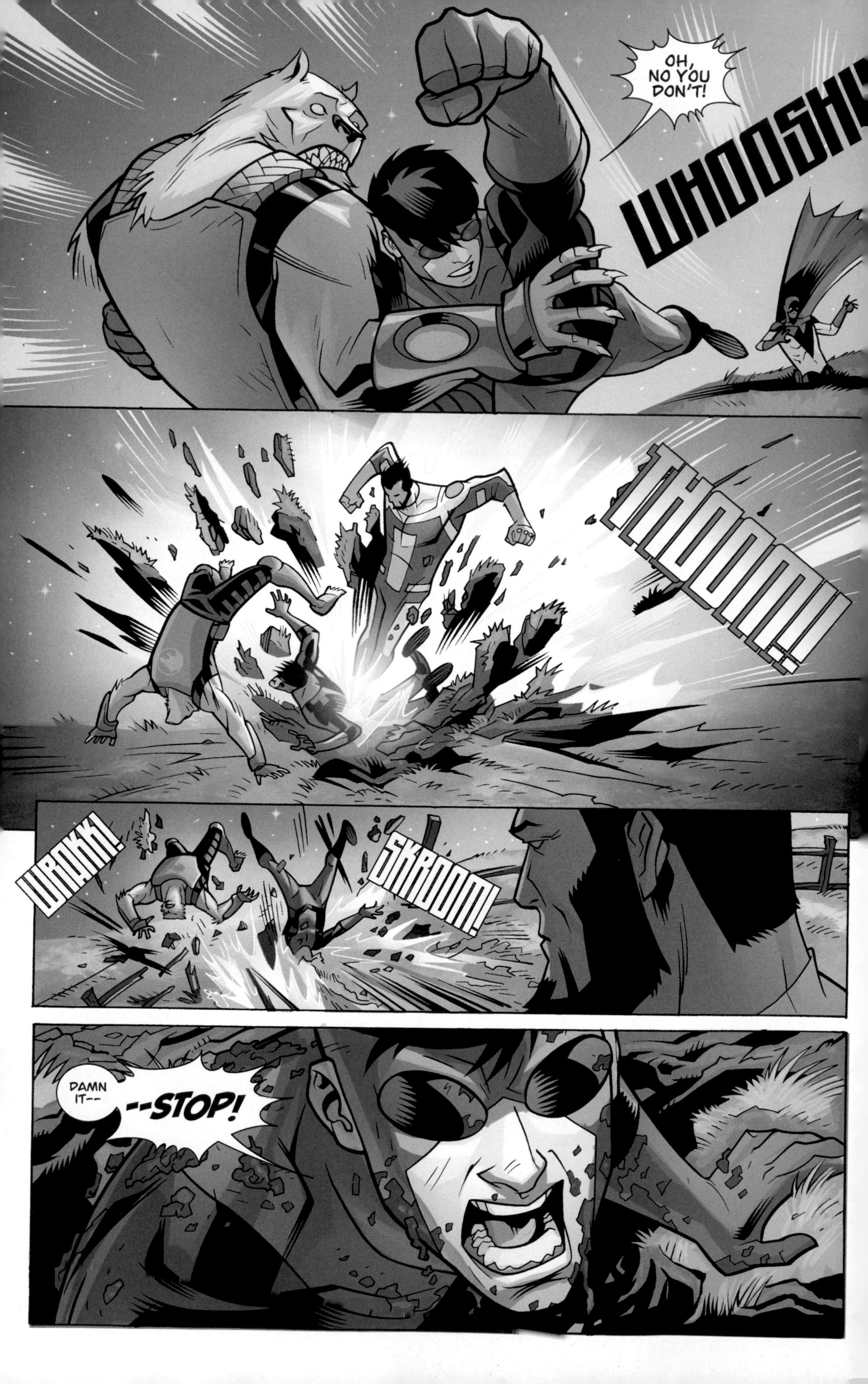

OH, NO YOU DON'T!
WHOOSH!
THOOM!
URKK!
SKROOM!
DAMN IT--
--STOP!

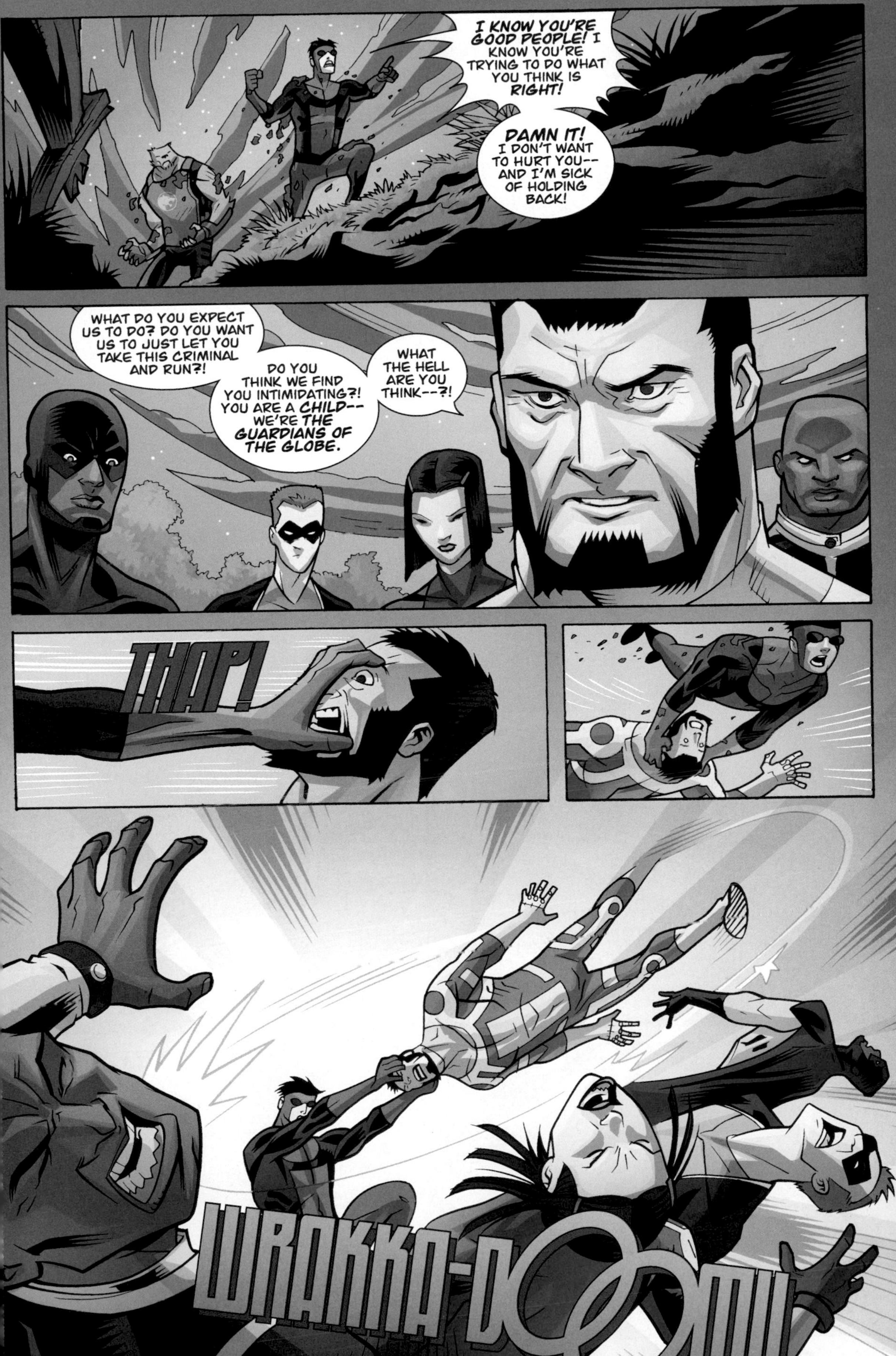
I KNOW YOU'RE GOOD PEOPLE! I KNOW YOU'RE TRYING TO DO WHAT YOU THINK IS RIGHT!
DAMN IT! I DON'T WANT TO HURT YOU-- AND I'M SICK OF HOLDING BACK!
WHAT DO YOU EXPECT US TO DO? DO YOU WANT US TO JUST LET YOU TAKE THIS CRIMINAL AND RUN?!
DO YOU THINK WE FIND YOU INTIMIDATING?! YOU ARE A CHILD-- WE'RE THE GUARDIANS OF THE GLOBE.
WHAT THE HELL ARE YOU THINK--?!
THAP!
WRAKKA-DOOM!!

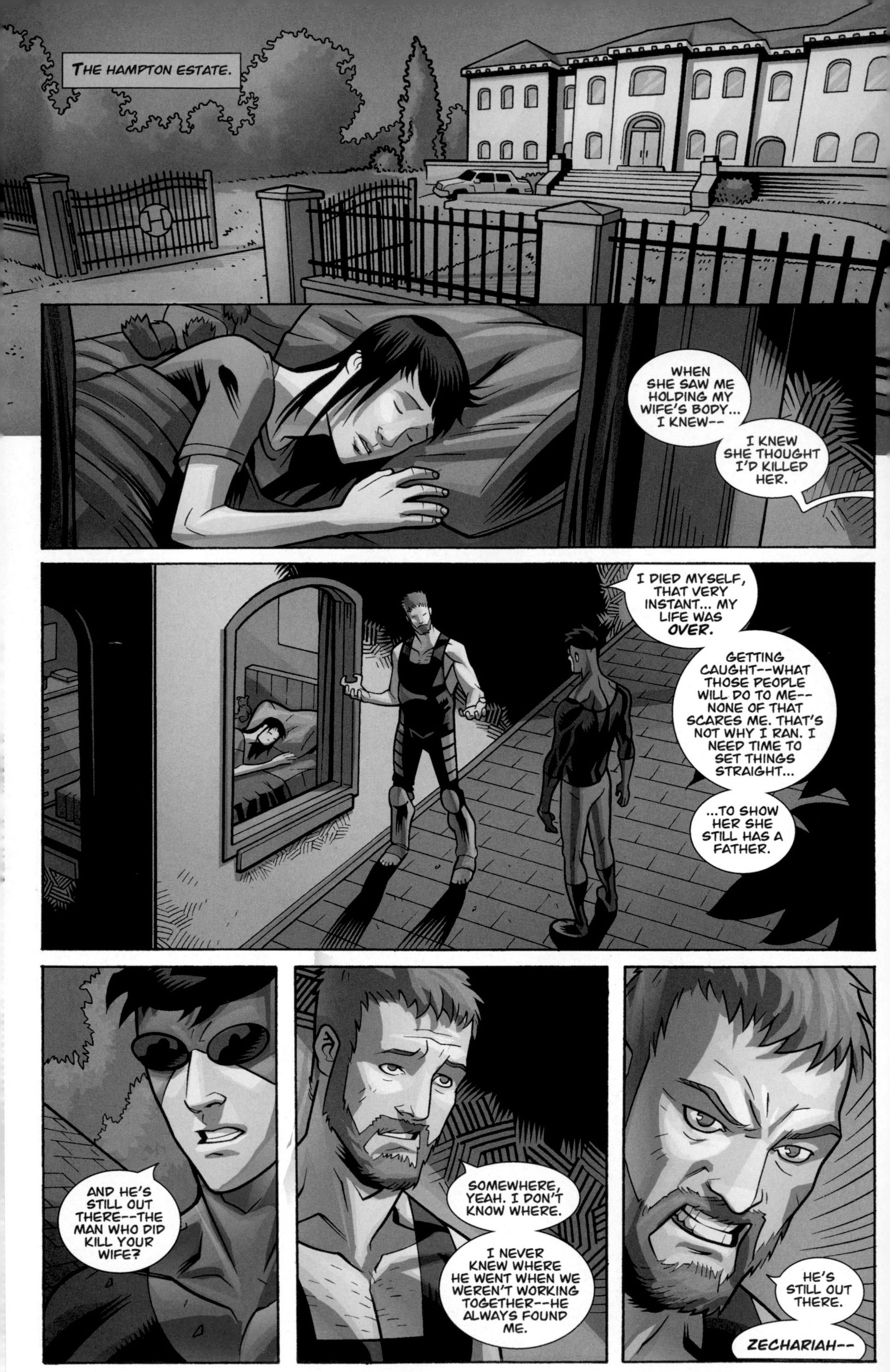
THE HAMPTON ESTATE.
WHEN SHE SAW ME HOLDING MY WIFE'S BODY... I KNEW--
I KNEW SHE THOUGHT I'D KILLED HER.
I DIED MYSELF, THAT VERY INSTANT... MY LIFE WAS OVER.
GETTING CAUGHT--WHAT THOSE PEOPLE WILL DO TO ME--NONE OF THAT SCARES ME. THAT'S NOT WHY I RAN. I NEED TIME TO SET THINGS STRAIGHT...
...TO SHOW HER SHE STILL HAS A FATHER.
AND HE'S STILL OUT THERE--THE MAN WHO DID KILL YOUR WIFE?
SOMEWHERE, YEAH. I DON'T KNOW WHERE.
I NEVER KNEW WHERE HE WENT WHEN WE WEREN'T WORKING TOGETHER--HE ALWAYS FOUND ME.
HE'S STILL OUT THERE.
ZECHARIAH--

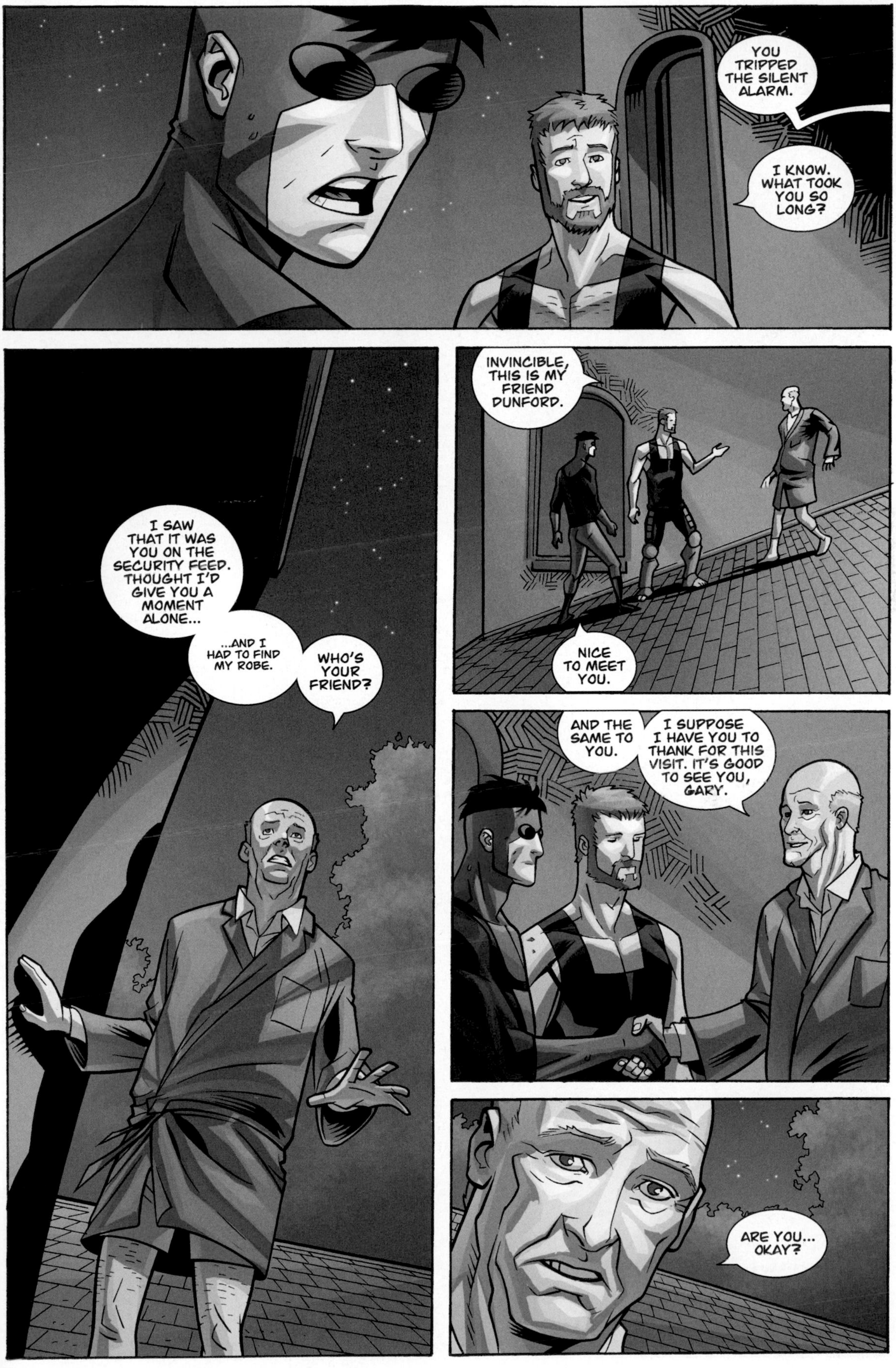
YOU TRIPPED THE SILENT ALARM.
I KNOW. WHAT TOOK YOU SO LONG?
I SAW THAT IT WAS YOU ON THE SECURITY FEED. THOUGHT I'D GIVE YOU A MOMENT ALONE...
...AND I HAD TO FIND MY ROBE.
WHO'S YOUR FRIEND?
INVINCIBLE, THIS IS MY FRIEND DUNFORD.
NICE TO MEET YOU.
AND THE SAME TO YOU.
I SUPPOSE I HAVE YOU TO THANK FOR THIS VISIT. IT'S GOOD TO SEE YOU, GARY.
ARE YOU... OKAY?

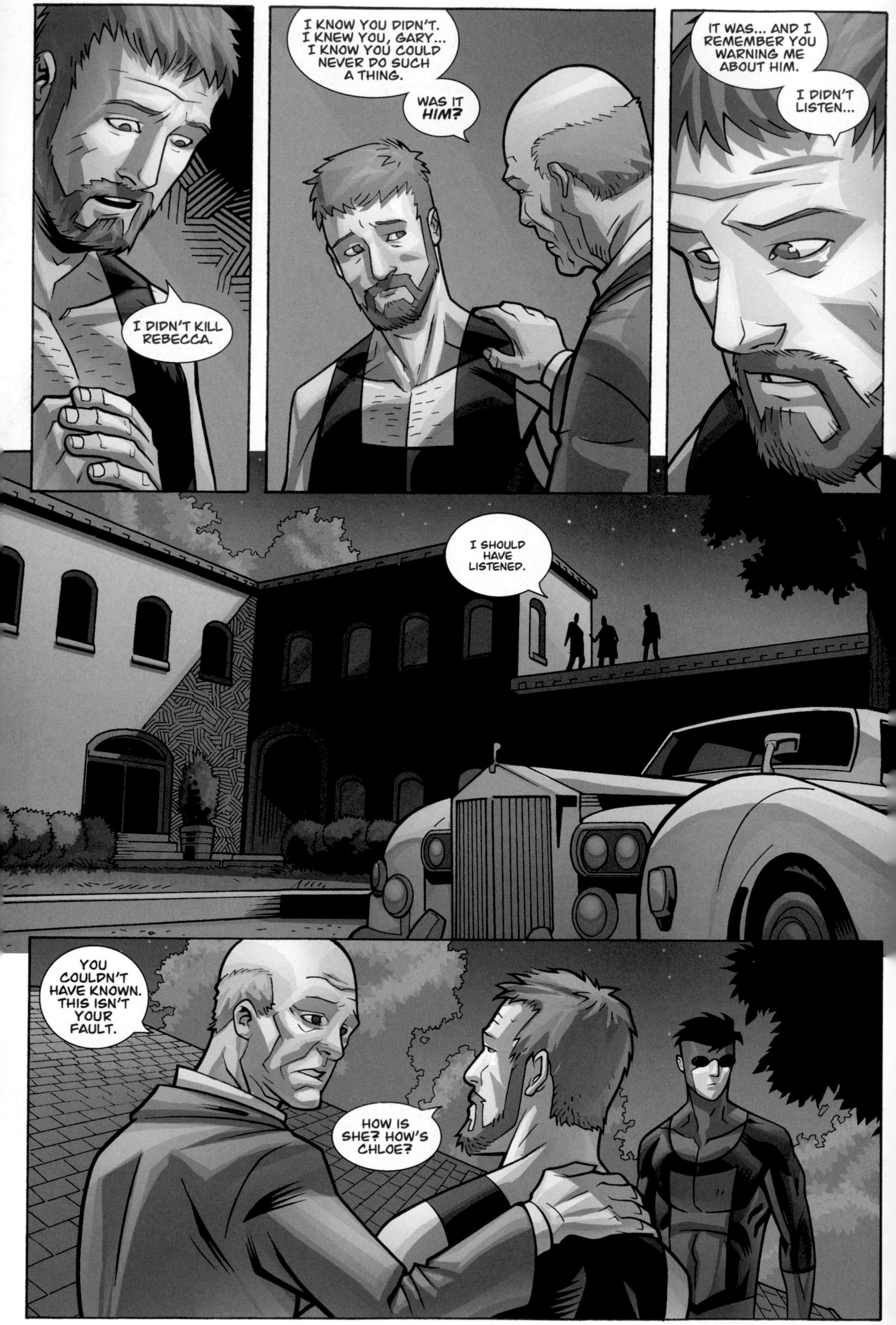
I DIDN'T KILL REBECCA.
I KNOW YOU DIDN'T. I KNEW YOU, GARY... I KNOW YOU COULD NEVER DO SUCH A THING.
WAS IT HIM?
IT WAS... AND I REMEMBER YOU WARNING ME ABOUT HIM.
I DIDN'T LISTEN...
I SHOULD HAVE LISTENED.
YOU COULDN'T HAVE KNOWN. THIS ISN'T YOUR FAULT.
HOW IS SHE? HOW'S CHLOE?

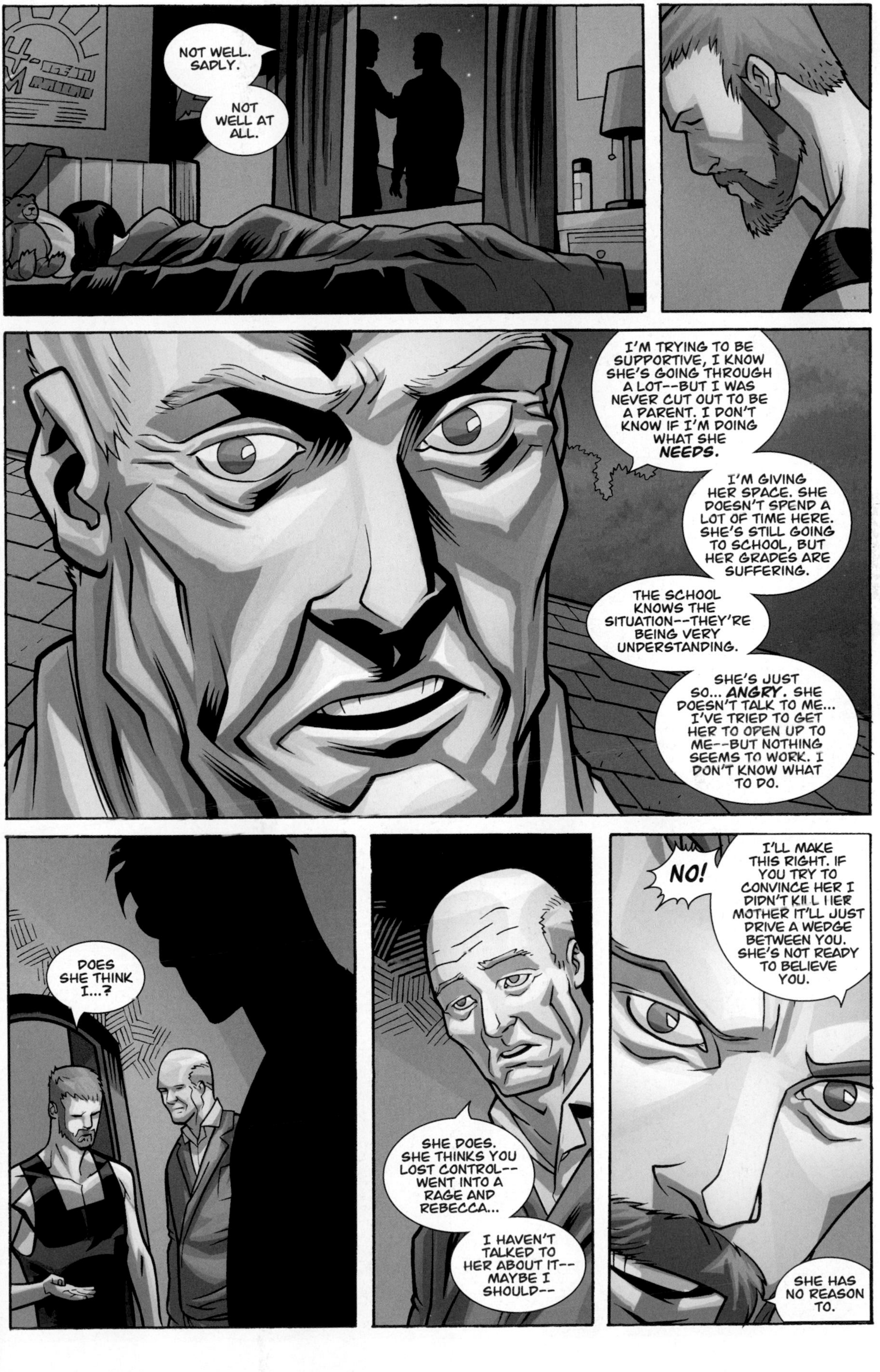
NOT WELL. SADLY.
NOT WELL AT ALL.
I'M TRYING TO BE SUPPORTIVE, I KNOW SHE'S GOING THROUGH A LOT--BUT I WAS NEVER CUT OUT TO BE A PARENT. I DON'T KNOW IF I'M DOING WHAT SHE NEEDS.
I'M GIVING HER SPACE. SHE DOESN'T SPEND A LOT OF TIME HERE. SHE'S STILL GOING TO SCHOOL, BUT HER GRADES ARE SUFFERING.
THE SCHOOL KNOWS THE SITUATION--THEY'RE BEING VERY UNDERSTANDING.
SHE'S JUST SO... ANGRY. SHE DOESN'T TALK TO ME... I'VE TRIED TO GET HER TO OPEN UP TO ME--BUT NOTHING SEEMS TO WORK. I DON'T KNOW WHAT TO DO.
DOES SHE THINK I...?
SHE DOES. SHE THINKS YOU LOST CONTROL--WENT INTO A RAGE AND REBECCA...
I HAVEN'T TALKED TO HER ABOUT IT--MAYBE I SHOULD--
NO!
I'LL MAKE THIS RIGHT. IF YOU TRY TO CONVINCE HER I DIDN'T KILL HER MOTHER IT'LL JUST DRIVE A WEDGE BETWEEN YOU. SHE'S NOT READY TO BELIEVE YOU.
SHE HAS NO REASON TO.

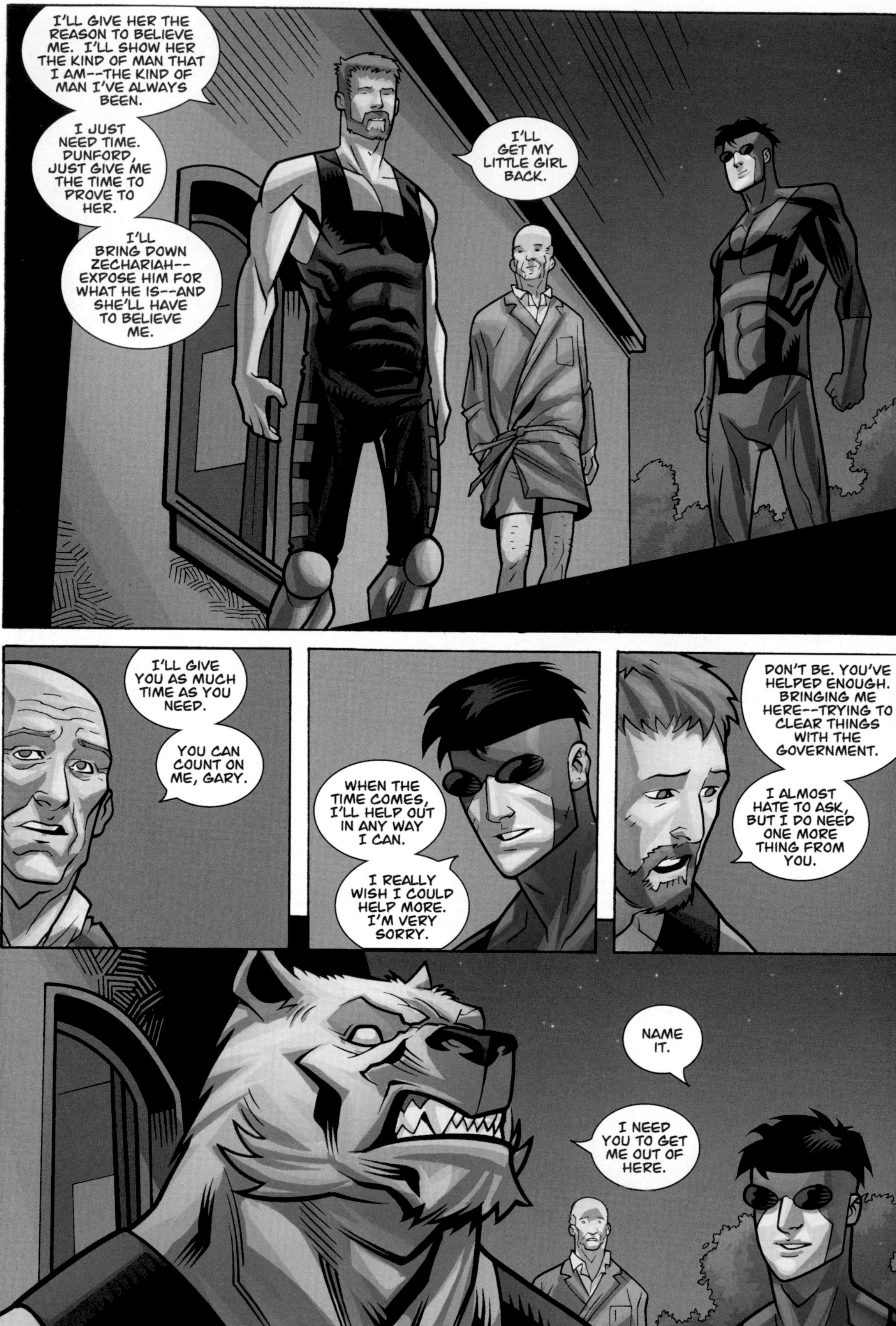
I'LL GIVE HER THE REASON TO BELIEVE ME. I'LL SHOW HER THE KIND OF MAN THAT I AM--THE KIND OF MAN I'VE ALWAYS BEEN.
I JUST NEED TIME. DUNFORD, JUST GIVE ME THE TIME TO PROVE TO HER.
I'LL BRING DOWN ZECHARIAH--EXPOSE HIM FOR WHAT HE IS--AND SHE'LL HAVE TO BELIEVE ME.
I'LL GET MY LITTLE GIRL BACK.
I'LL GIVE YOU AS MUCH TIME AS YOU NEED.
YOU CAN COUNT ON ME, GARY.
WHEN THE TIME COMES, I'LL HELP OUT IN ANY WAY I CAN.
I REALLY WISH I COULD HELP MORE. I'M VERY SORRY.
DON'T BE. YOU'VE HELPED ENOUGH. BRINGING ME HERE--TRYING TO CLEAR THINGS WITH THE GOVERNMENT.
I ALMOST HATE TO ASK, BUT I DO NEED ONE MORE THING FROM YOU.
NAME IT.
I NEED YOU TO GET ME OUT OF HERE.

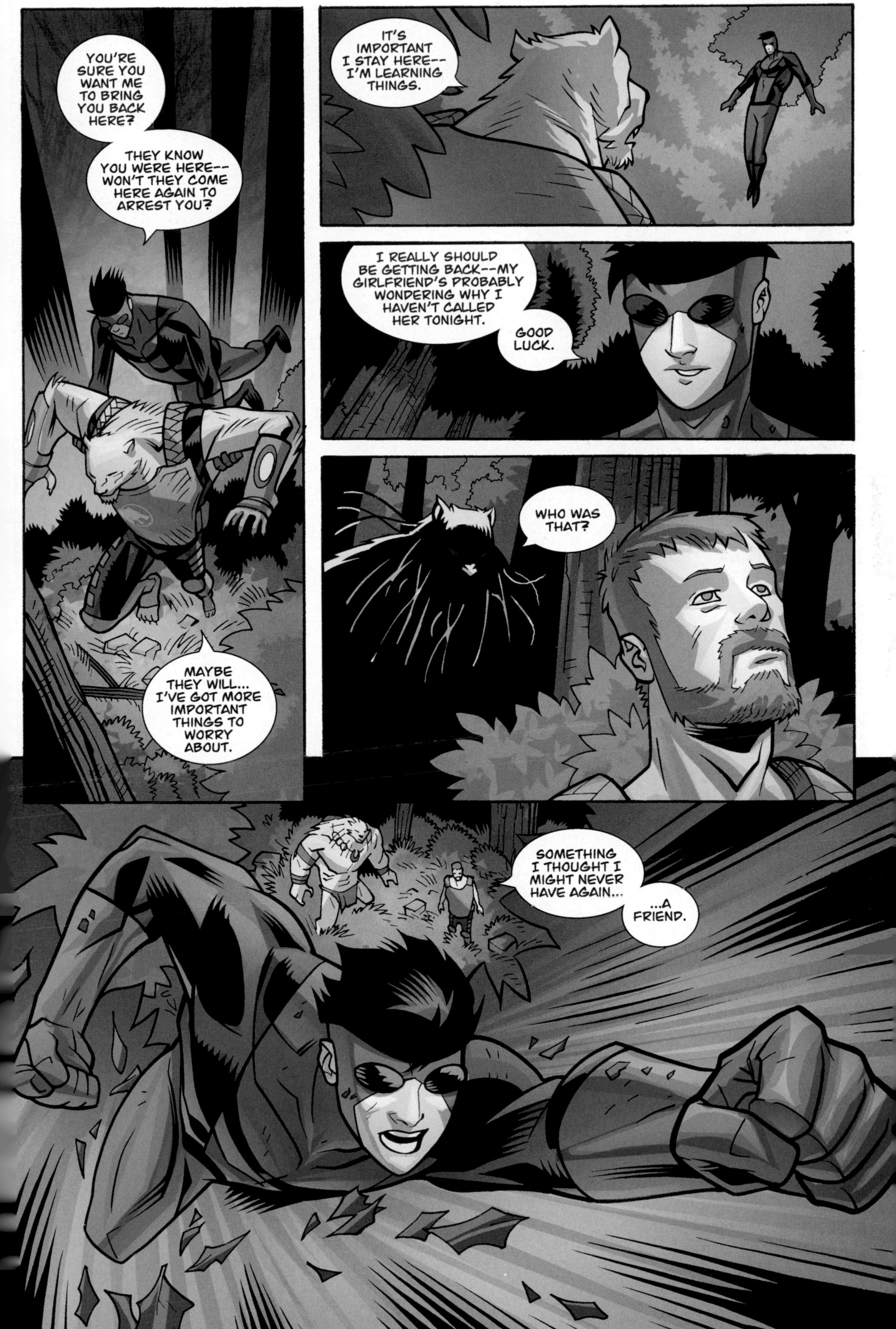
YOU'RE SURE YOU WANT ME TO BRING YOU BACK HERE?
THEY KNOW YOU WERE HERE--WON'T THEY COME HERE AGAIN TO ARREST YOU?
MAYBE THEY WILL... I'VE GOT MORE IMPORTANT THINGS TO WORRY ABOUT.
IT'S IMPORTANT I STAY HERE--I'M LEARNING THINGS.
I REALLY SHOULD BE GETTING BACK--MY GIRLFRIEND'S PROBABLY WONDERING WHY I HAVEN'T CALLED HER TONIGHT.
GOOD LUCK.
WHO WAS THAT?
SOMETHING I THOUGHT I MIGHT NEVER HAVE AGAIN...
...A FRIEND.

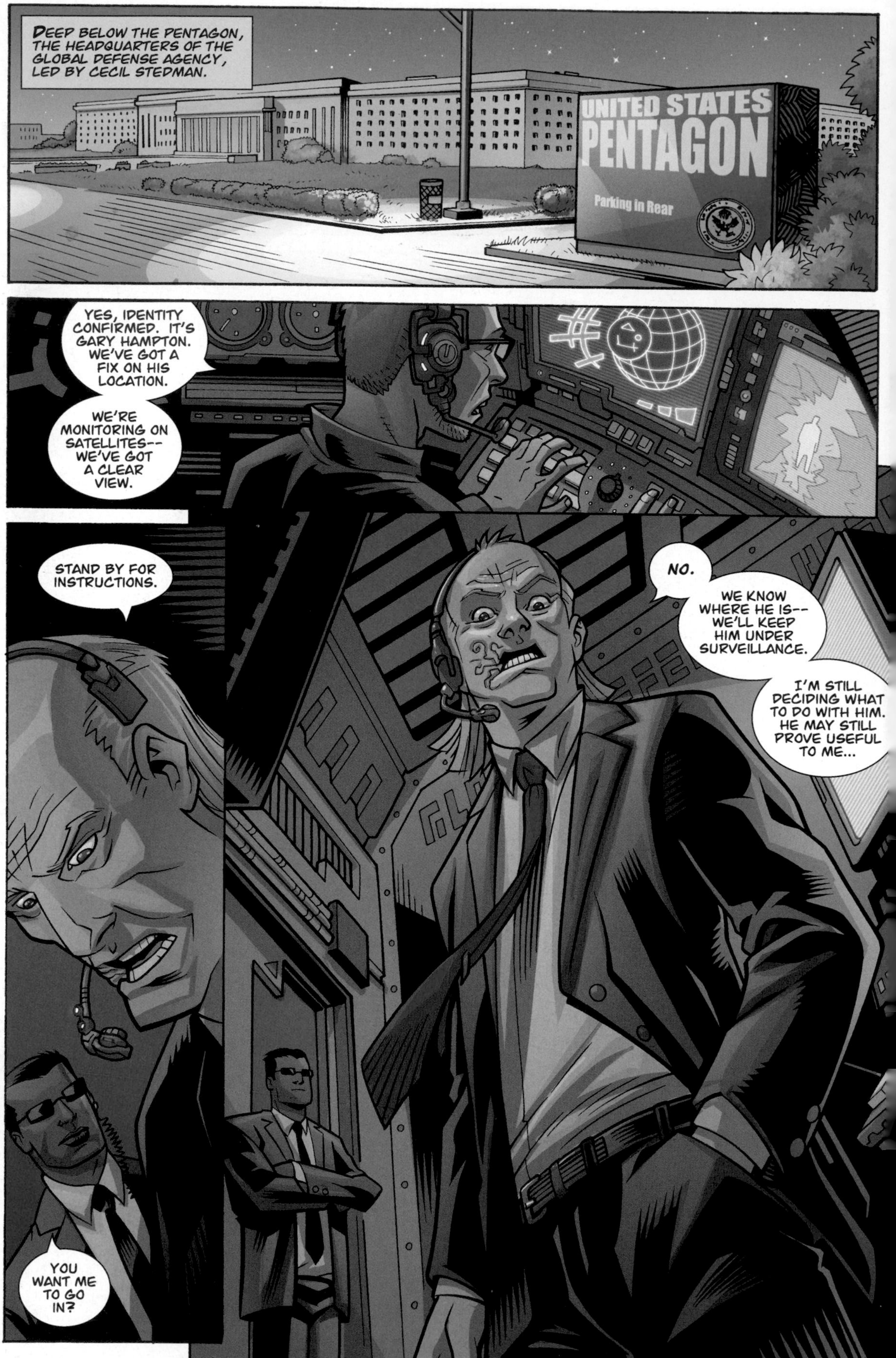
DEEP BELOW THE PENTAGON, THE HEADQUARTERS OF THE GLOBAL DEFENSE AGENCY, LED BY CECIL STEDMAN.
UNITED STATES PENTAGON
Parking in Rear
YES, IDENTITY CONFIRMED. IT'S GARY HAMPTON. WE'VE GOT A FIX ON HIS LOCATION.
WE'RE MONITORING ON SATELLITES-- WE'VE GOT A CLEAR VIEW.
STAND BY FOR INSTRUCTIONS.
YOU WANT ME TO GO IN?
NO.
WE KNOW WHERE HE IS-- WE'LL KEEP HIM UNDER SURVEILLANCE.
I'M STILL DECIDING WHAT TO DO WITH HIM. HE MAY STILL PROVE USEFUL TO ME...

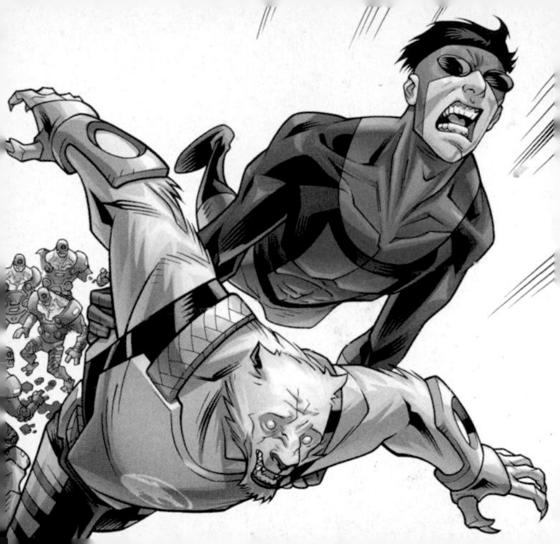

12

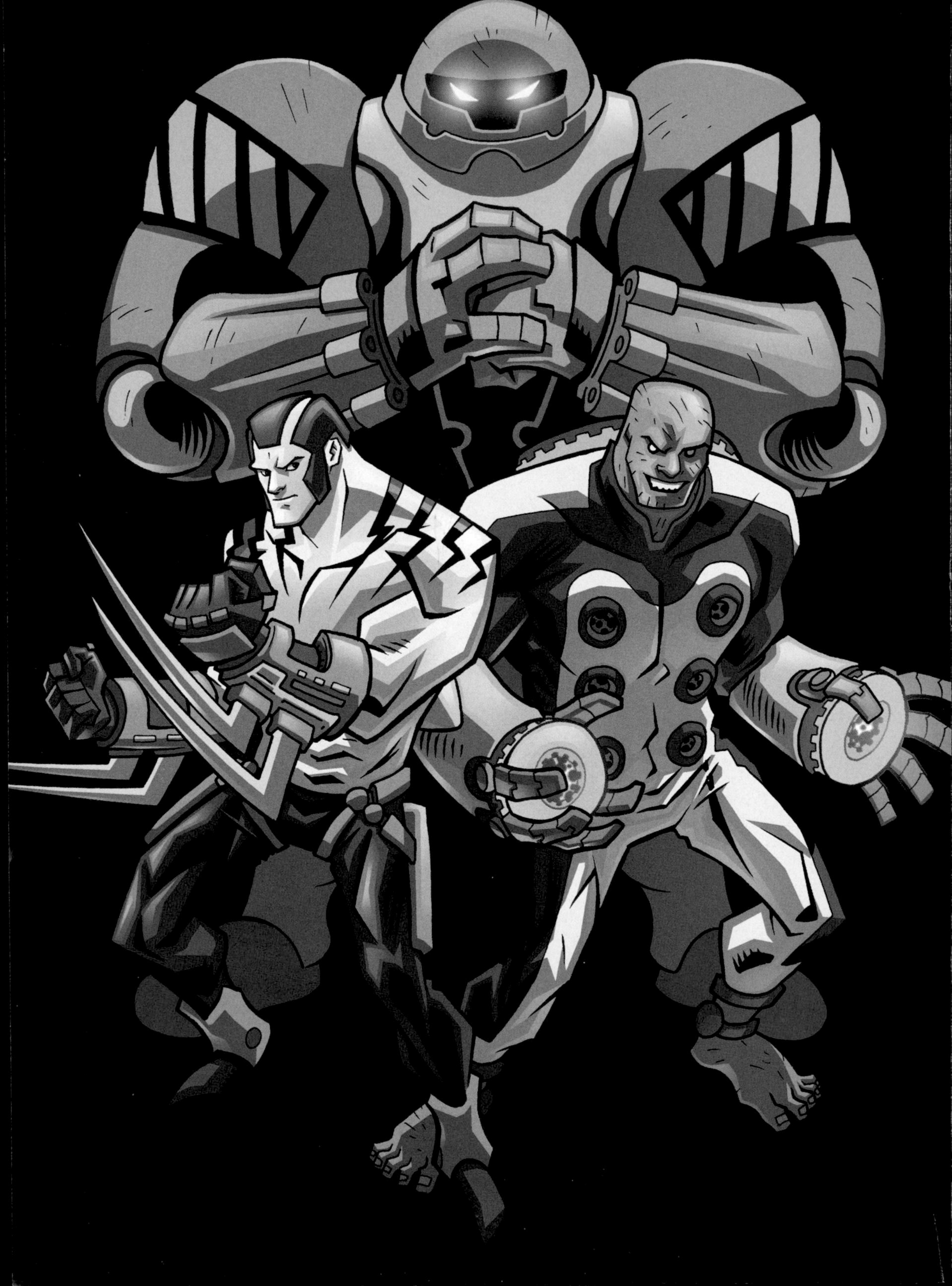

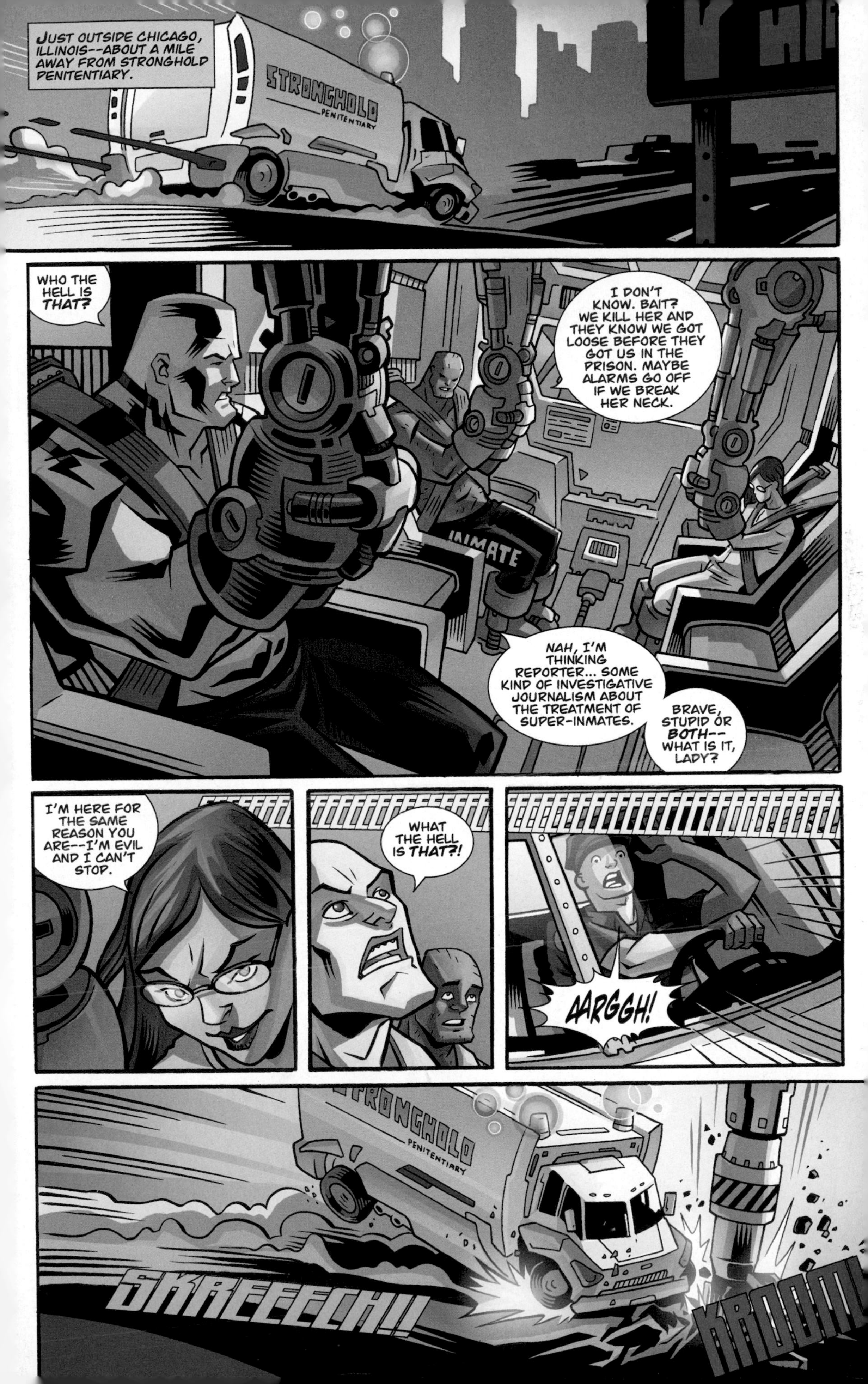
JUST OUTSIDE CHICAGO, ILLINOIS--ABOUT A MILE AWAY FROM STRONGHOLD PENITENTIARY.
STRONGHOLD PENITENTIARY
WHO THE HELL IS *THAT?*
I DON'T KNOW. BAIT? WE KILL HER AND THEY KNOW WE GOT LOOSE BEFORE THEY GOT US IN THE PRISON. MAYBE ALARMS GO OFF IF WE BREAK HER NECK.
INMATE
NAH, I'M THINKING REPORTER... SOME KIND OF INVESTIGATIVE JOURNALISM ABOUT THE TREATMENT OF SUPER-INMATES.
BRAVE, STUPID OR *BOTH*-- WHAT IS IT, LADY?
I'M HERE FOR THE SAME REASON YOU ARE--I'M EVIL AND I CAN'T STOP.
WHAT THE HELL IS *THAT?!*
AARGGH!
STRONGHOLD PENITENTIARY
SKREEEECH!!
KROOM

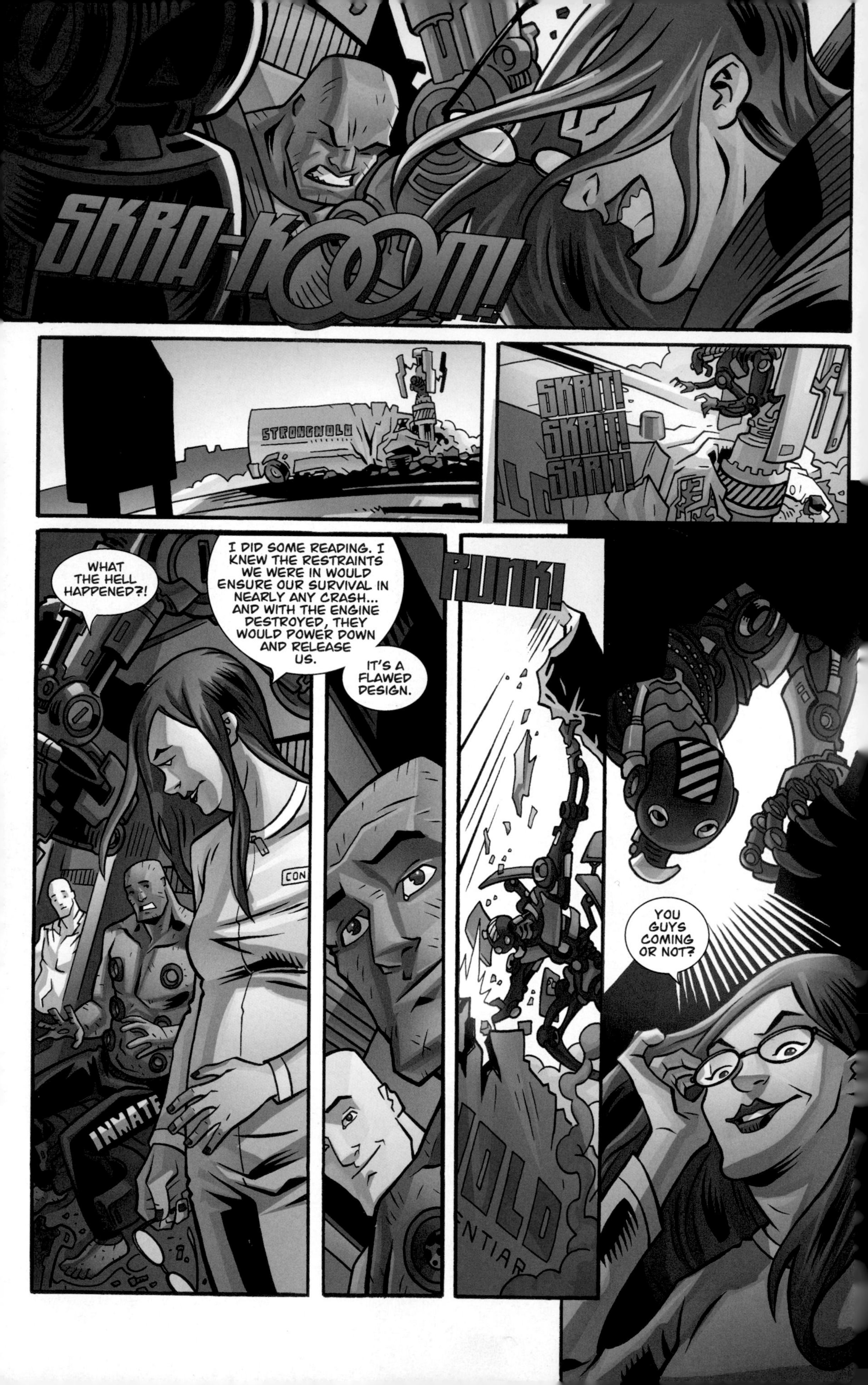
SKRO-KOOOM!
STRONGHOLD
SKRIT! SKRIT! SKRIT!
WHAT THE HELL HAPPENED?!
I DID SOME READING. I KNEW THE RESTRAINTS WE WERE IN WOULD ENSURE OUR SURVIVAL IN NEARLY ANY CRASH... AND WITH THE ENGINE DESTROYED, THEY WOULD POWER DOWN AND RELEASE US.
IT'S A FLAWED DESIGN.
INMATE
RUNK!
YOU GUYS COMING OR NOT?

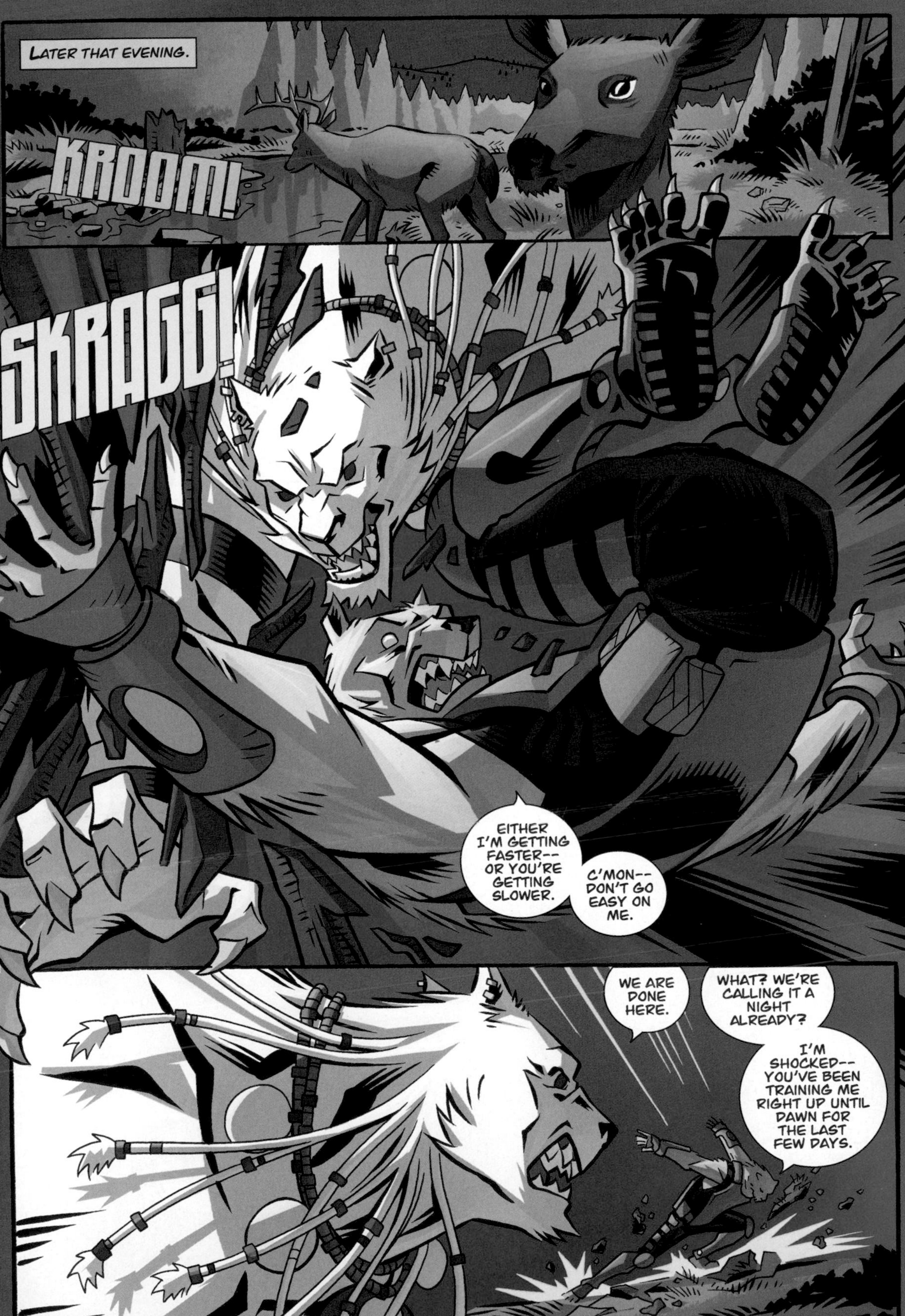
LATER THAT EVENING.
KROOM!
SKRAGG!
EITHER I'M GETTING FASTER-- OR YOU'RE GETTING SLOWER.
C'MON-- DON'T GO EASY ON ME.
WE ARE DONE HERE.
WHAT? WE'RE CALLING IT A NIGHT ALREADY?
I'M SHOCKED-- YOU'VE BEEN TRAINING ME RIGHT UP UNTIL DAWN FOR THE LAST FEW DAYS.

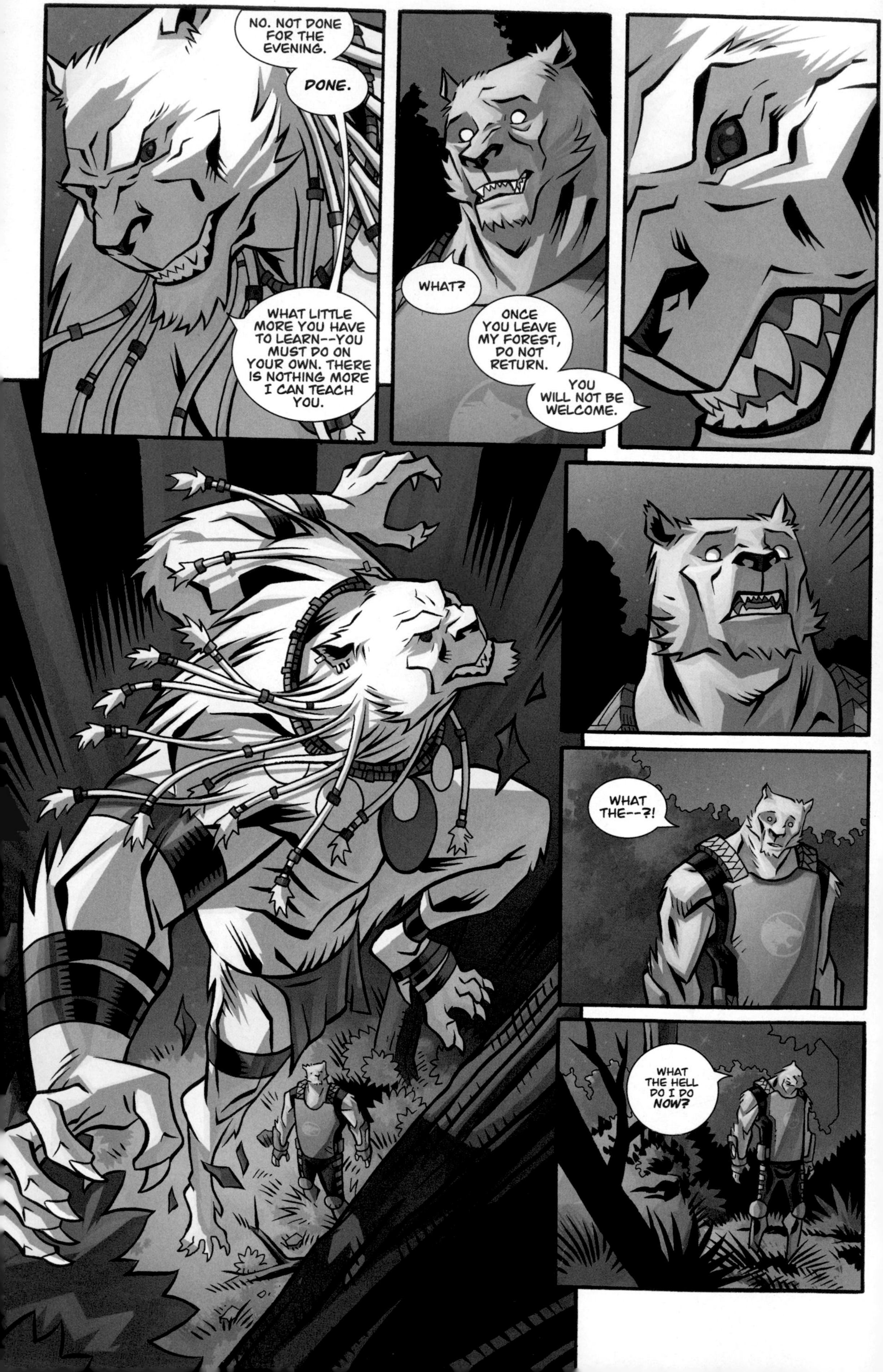
NO. NOT DONE FOR THE EVENING.
DONE.
WHAT LITTLE MORE YOU HAVE TO LEARN--YOU MUST DO ON YOUR OWN. THERE IS NOTHING MORE I CAN TEACH YOU.
WHAT?
ONCE YOU LEAVE MY FOREST, DO NOT RETURN.
YOU WILL NOT BE WELCOME.
WHAT THE--?!
WHAT THE HELL DO I DO NOW?

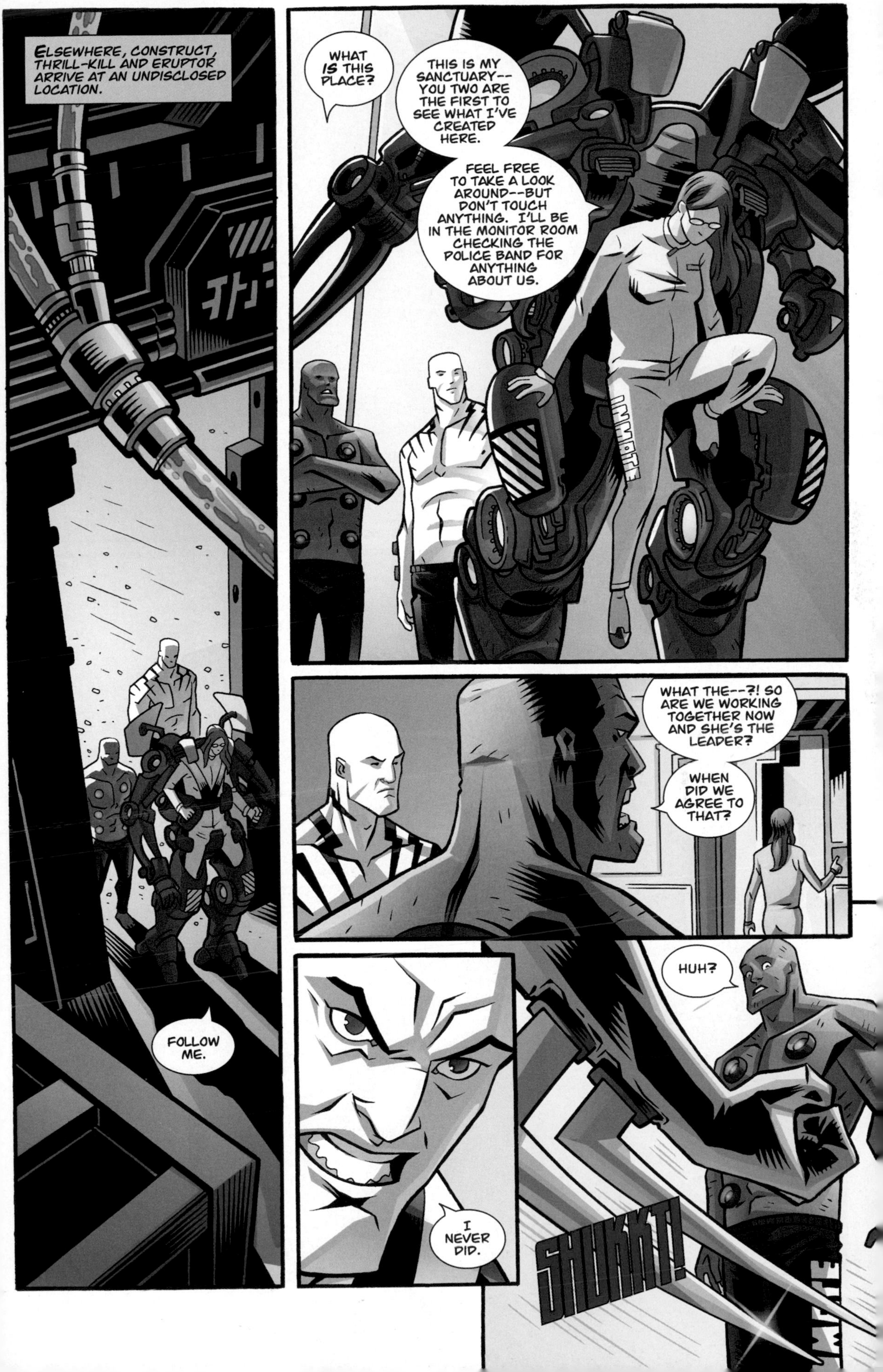
ELSEWHERE, CONSTRUCT, THRILL-KILL AND ERUPTOR ARRIVE AT AN UNDISCLOSED LOCATION.
FOLLOW ME.
WHAT IS THIS PLACE?
THIS IS MY SANCTUARY-- YOU TWO ARE THE FIRST TO SEE WHAT I'VE CREATED HERE.
FEEL FREE TO TAKE A LOOK AROUND--BUT DON'T TOUCH ANYTHING. I'LL BE IN THE MONITOR ROOM CHECKING THE POLICE BAND FOR ANYTHING ABOUT US.
WHAT THE--?! SO ARE WE WORKING TOGETHER NOW AND SHE'S THE LEADER?
WHEN DID WE AGREE TO THAT?
I NEVER DID.
HUH?
SHUKKT!

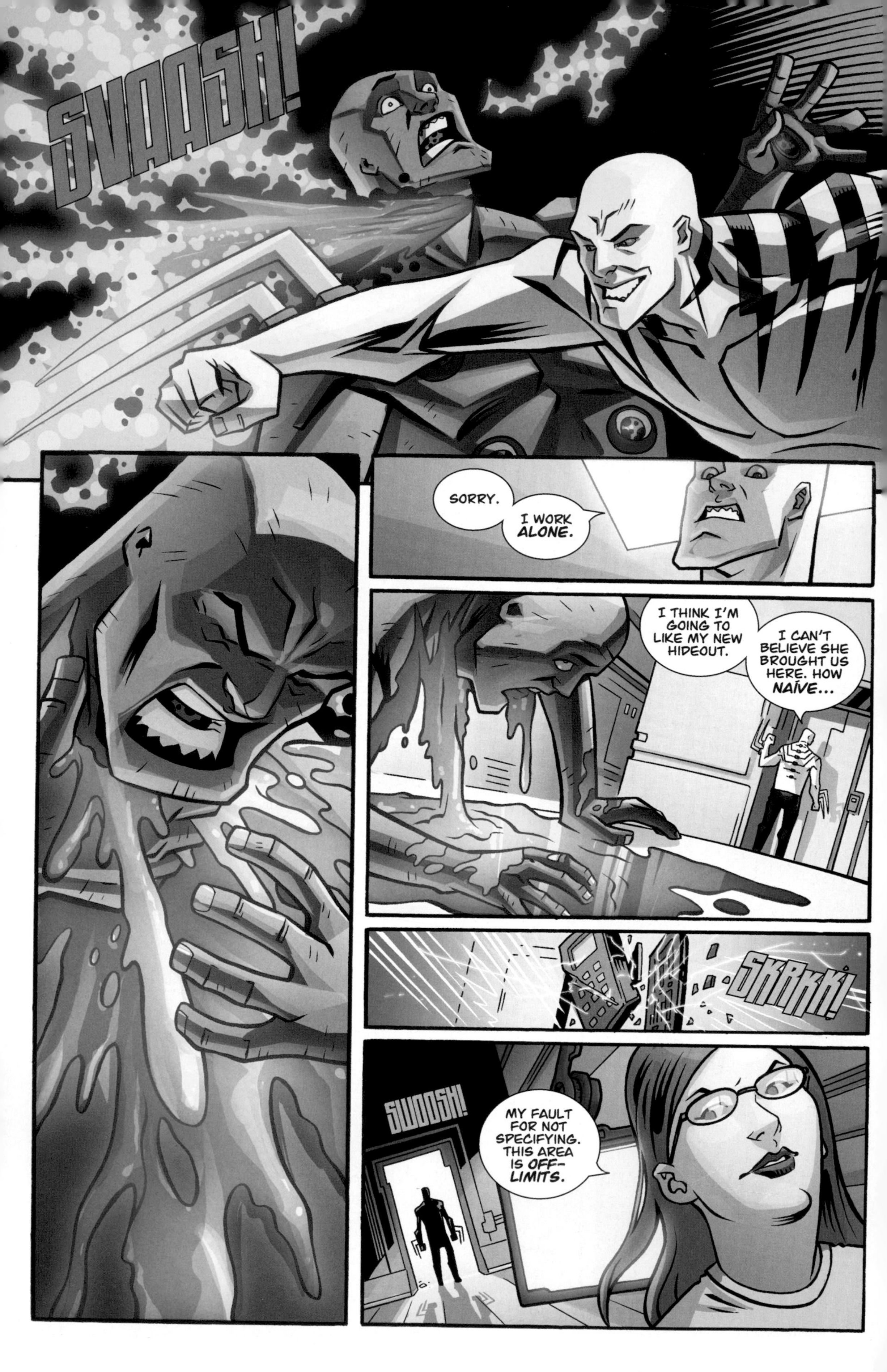
SVAASH!
SORRY.
I WORK ALONE.
I THINK I'M GOING TO LIKE MY NEW HIDEOUT.
I CAN'T BELIEVE SHE BROUGHT US HERE. HOW NAÏVE...
SKRKK!
SWOOSH!
MY FAULT FOR NOT SPECIFYING. THIS AREA IS OFF-LIMITS.

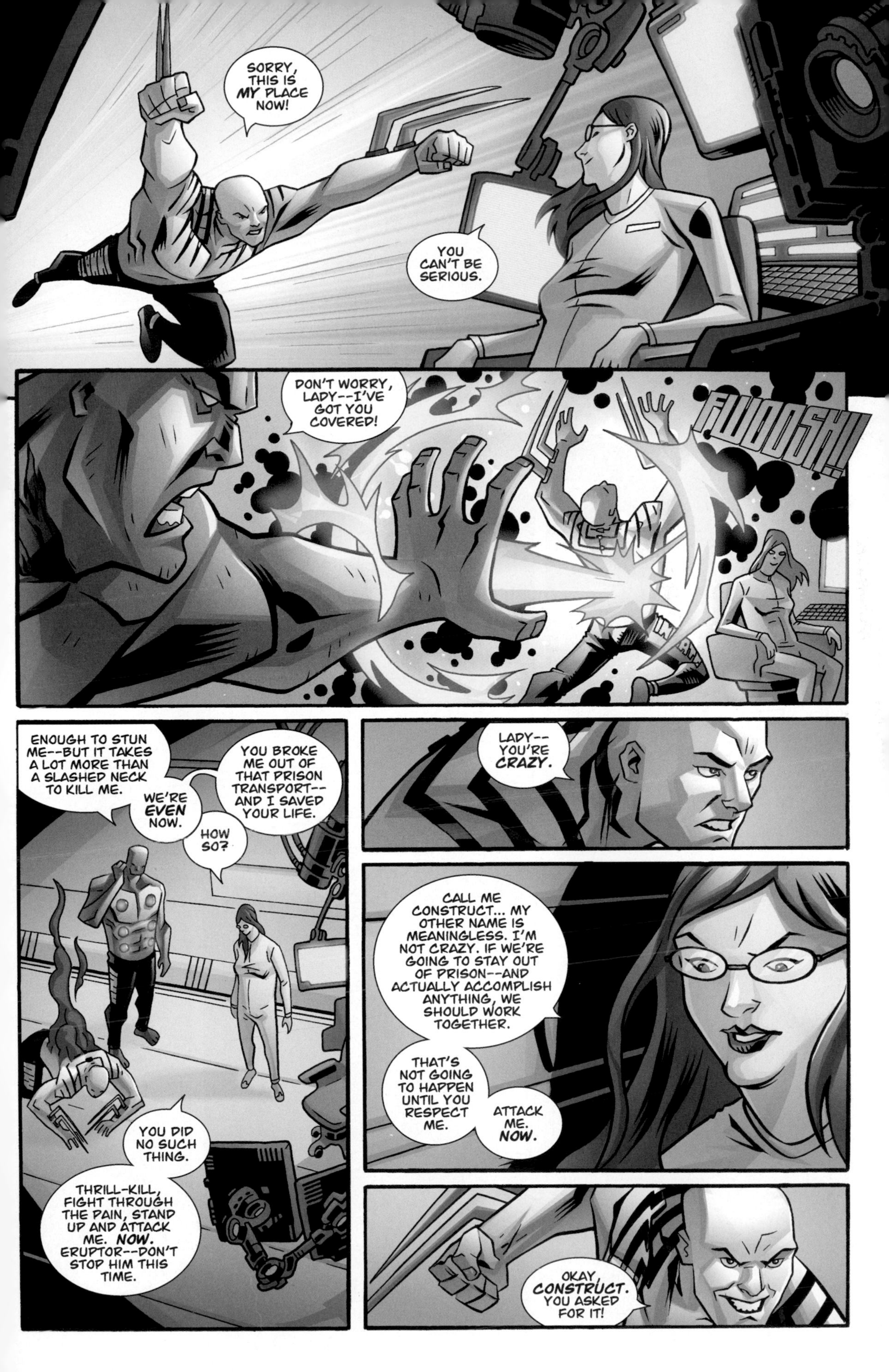
SORRY, THIS IS MY PLACE NOW!
YOU CAN'T BE SERIOUS.
DON'T WORRY, LADY--I'VE GOT YOU COVERED!
FWOOSH!!
ENOUGH TO STUN ME--BUT IT TAKES A LOT MORE THAN A SLASHED NECK TO KILL ME.
YOU BROKE ME OUT OF THAT PRISON TRANSPORT--AND I SAVED YOUR LIFE.
WE'RE EVEN NOW.
HOW SO?
YOU DID NO SUCH THING.
THRILL-KILL, FIGHT THROUGH THE PAIN, STAND UP AND ATTACK ME. NOW. ERUPTOR--DON'T STOP HIM THIS TIME.
LADY--YOU'RE CRAZY.
CALL ME CONSTRUCT... MY OTHER NAME IS MEANINGLESS. I'M NOT CRAZY. IF WE'RE GOING TO STAY OUT OF PRISON--AND ACTUALLY ACCOMPLISH ANYTHING, WE SHOULD WORK TOGETHER.
THAT'S NOT GOING TO HAPPEN UNTIL YOU RESPECT ME.
ATTACK ME. NOW.
OKAY, CONSTRUCT. YOU ASKED FOR IT!

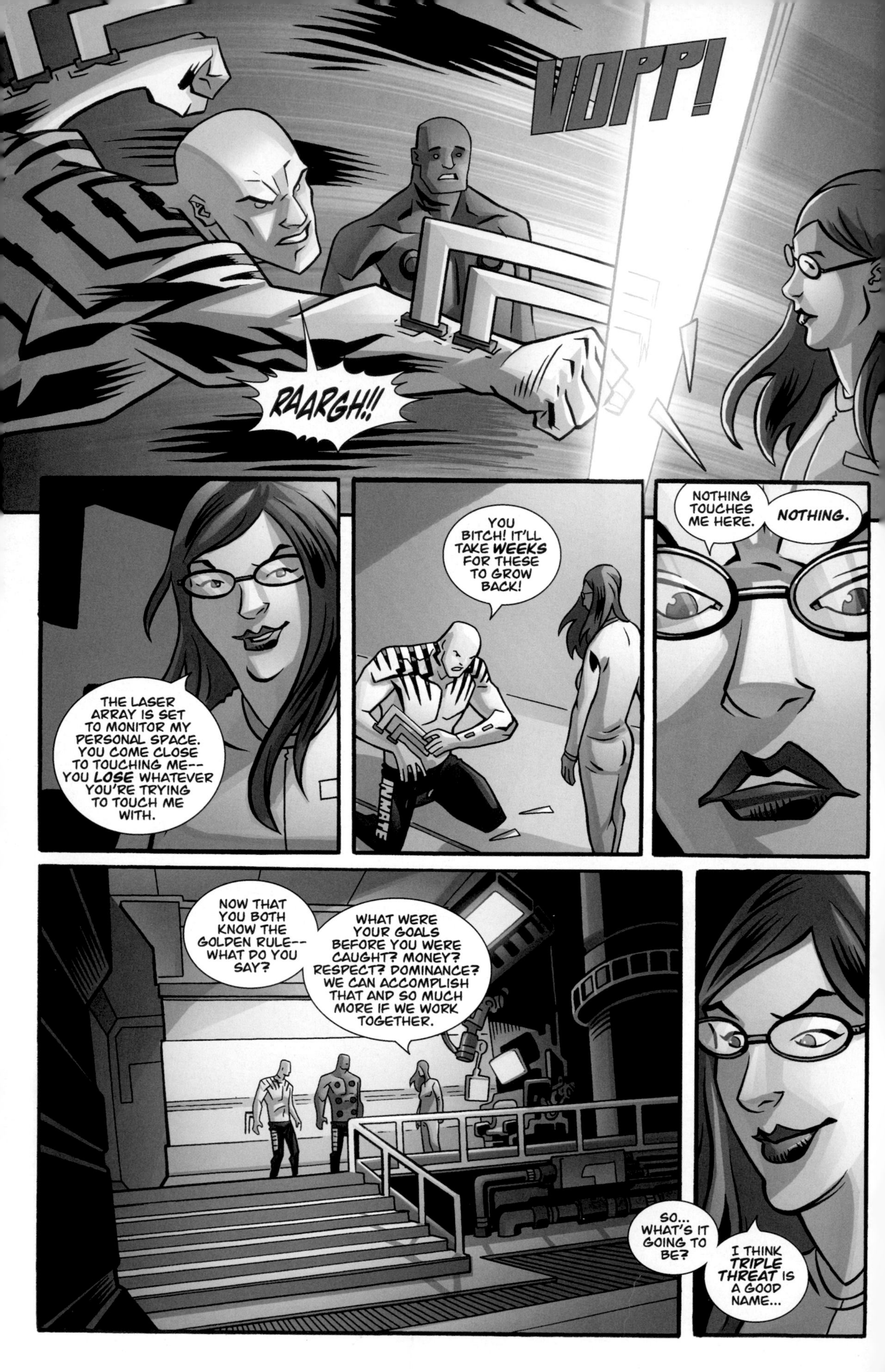
VOPP!
RAARGH!!
THE LASER ARRAY IS SET TO MONITOR MY PERSONAL SPACE. YOU COME CLOSE TO TOUCHING ME-- YOU LOSE WHATEVER YOU'RE TRYING TO TOUCH ME WITH.
YOU BITCH! IT'LL TAKE WEEKS FOR THESE TO GROW BACK!
INMATE
NOTHING TOUCHES ME HERE.
NOTHING.
NOW THAT YOU BOTH KNOW THE GOLDEN RULE-- WHAT DO YOU SAY?
WHAT WERE YOUR GOALS BEFORE YOU WERE CAUGHT? MONEY? RESPECT? DOMINANCE? WE CAN ACCOMPLISH THAT AND SO MUCH MORE IF WE WORK TOGETHER.
SO... WHAT'S IT GOING TO BE?
I THINK TRIPLE THREAT IS A GOOD NAME...

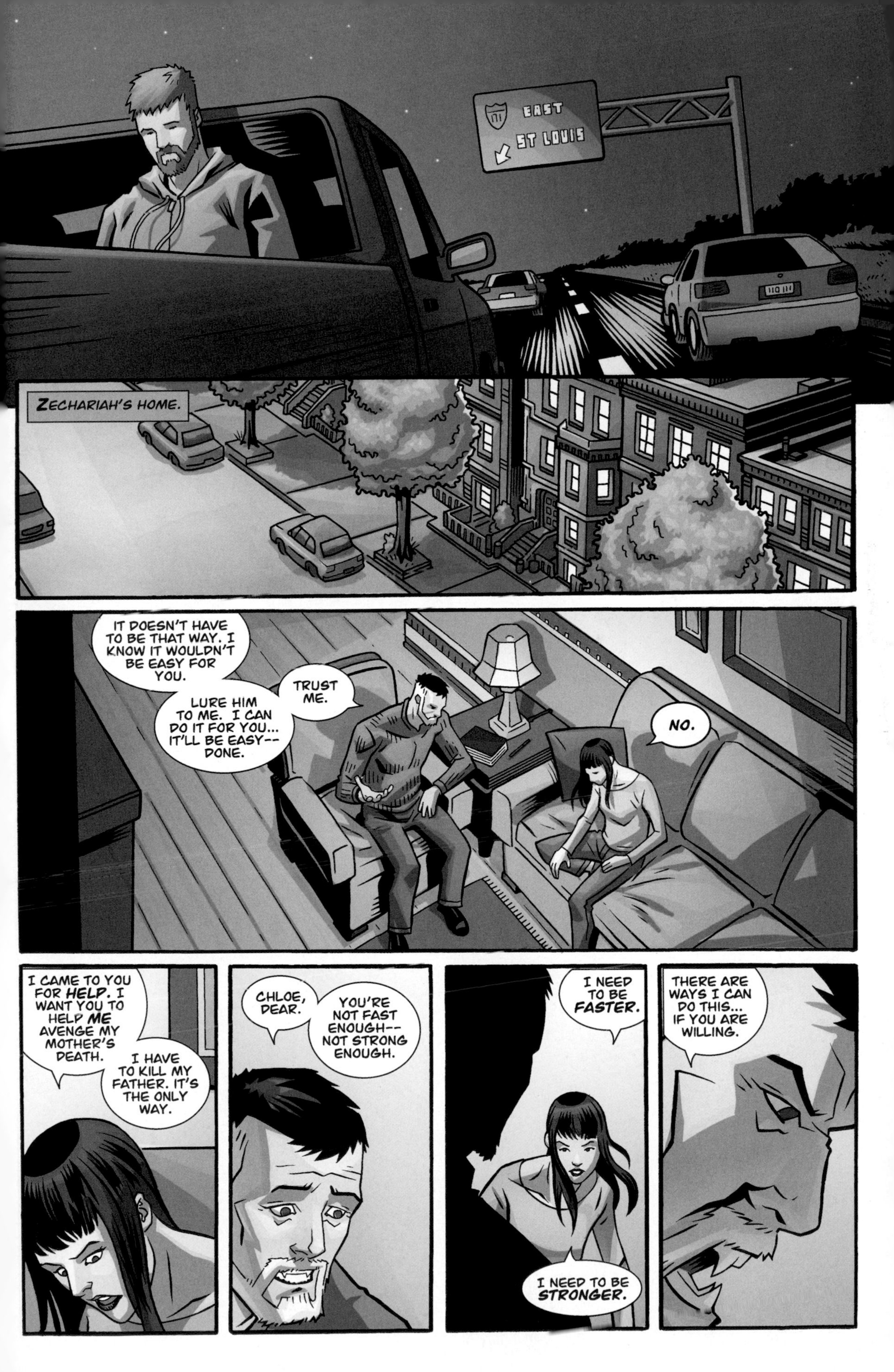
EAST
ST LOUIS
ZECHARIAH'S HOME.
IT DOESN'T HAVE TO BE THAT WAY. I KNOW IT WOULDN'T BE EASY FOR YOU.
LURE HIM TO ME. I CAN DO IT FOR YOU... IT'LL BE EASY-- DONE.
TRUST ME.
NO.
I CAME TO YOU FOR HELP. I WANT YOU TO HELP ME AVENGE MY MOTHER'S DEATH.
I HAVE TO KILL MY FATHER. IT'S THE ONLY WAY.
CHLOE, DEAR.
YOU'RE NOT FAST ENOUGH-- NOT STRONG ENOUGH.
I NEED TO BE FASTER.
I NEED TO BE STRONGER.
THERE ARE WAYS I CAN DO THIS... IF YOU ARE WILLING.

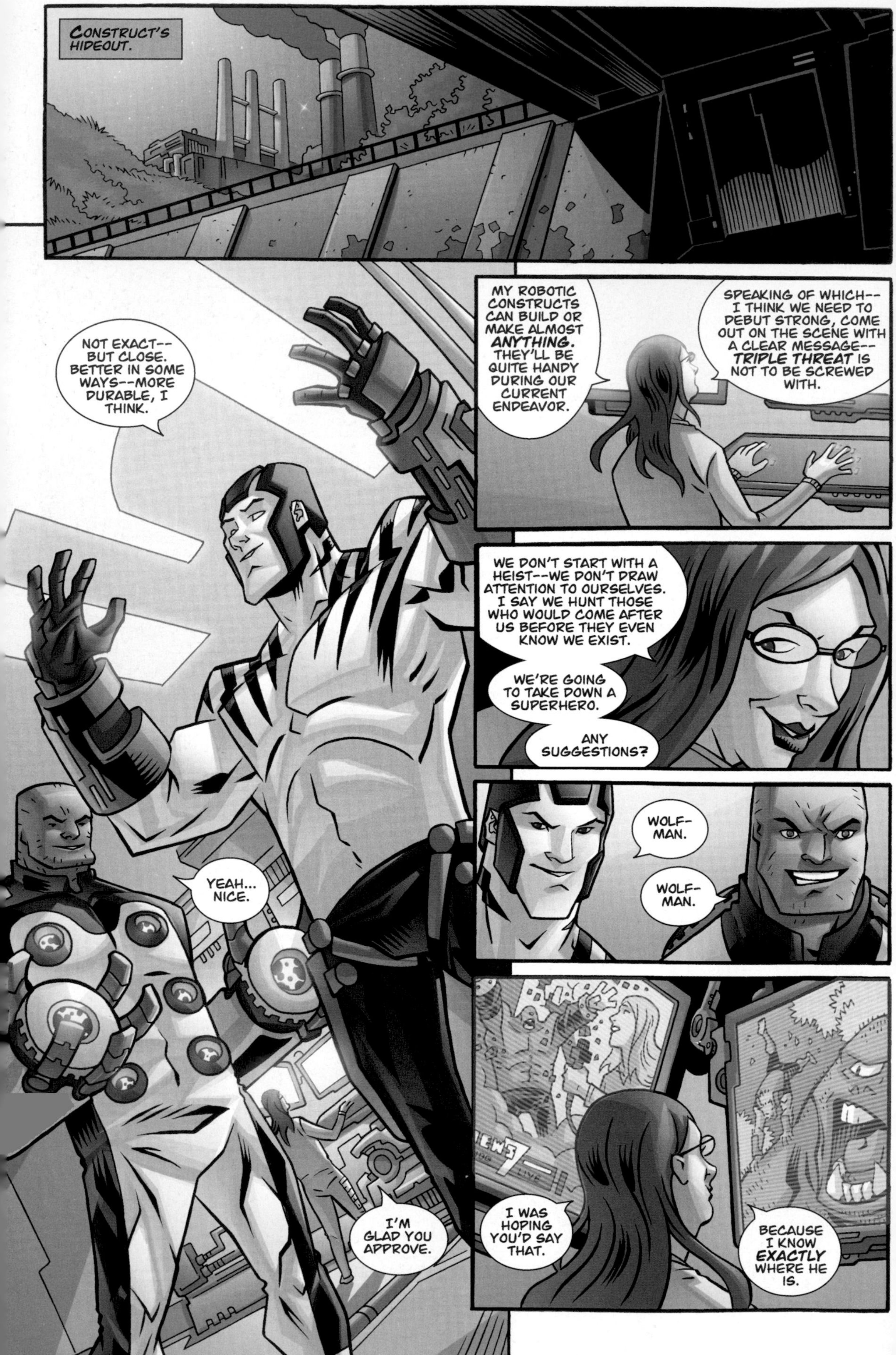
CONSTRUCT'S HIDEOUT.
NOT EXACT--BUT CLOSE. BETTER IN SOME WAYS--MORE DURABLE, I THINK.
MY ROBOTIC CONSTRUCTS CAN BUILD OR MAKE ALMOST ANYTHING. THEY'LL BE QUITE HANDY DURING OUR CURRENT ENDEAVOR.
SPEAKING OF WHICH--I THINK WE NEED TO DEBUT STRONG, COME OUT ON THE SCENE WITH A CLEAR MESSAGE--TRIPLE THREAT IS NOT TO BE SCREWED WITH.
WE DON'T START WITH A HEIST--WE DON'T DRAW ATTENTION TO OURSELVES. I SAY WE HUNT THOSE WHO WOULD COME AFTER US BEFORE THEY EVEN KNOW WE EXIST.
WE'RE GOING TO TAKE DOWN A SUPERHERO.
ANY SUGGESTIONS?
YEAH... NICE.
WOLF-MAN.
WOLF-MAN.
I'M GLAD YOU APPROVE.
I WAS HOPING YOU'D SAY THAT.
BECAUSE I KNOW EXACTLY WHERE HE IS.

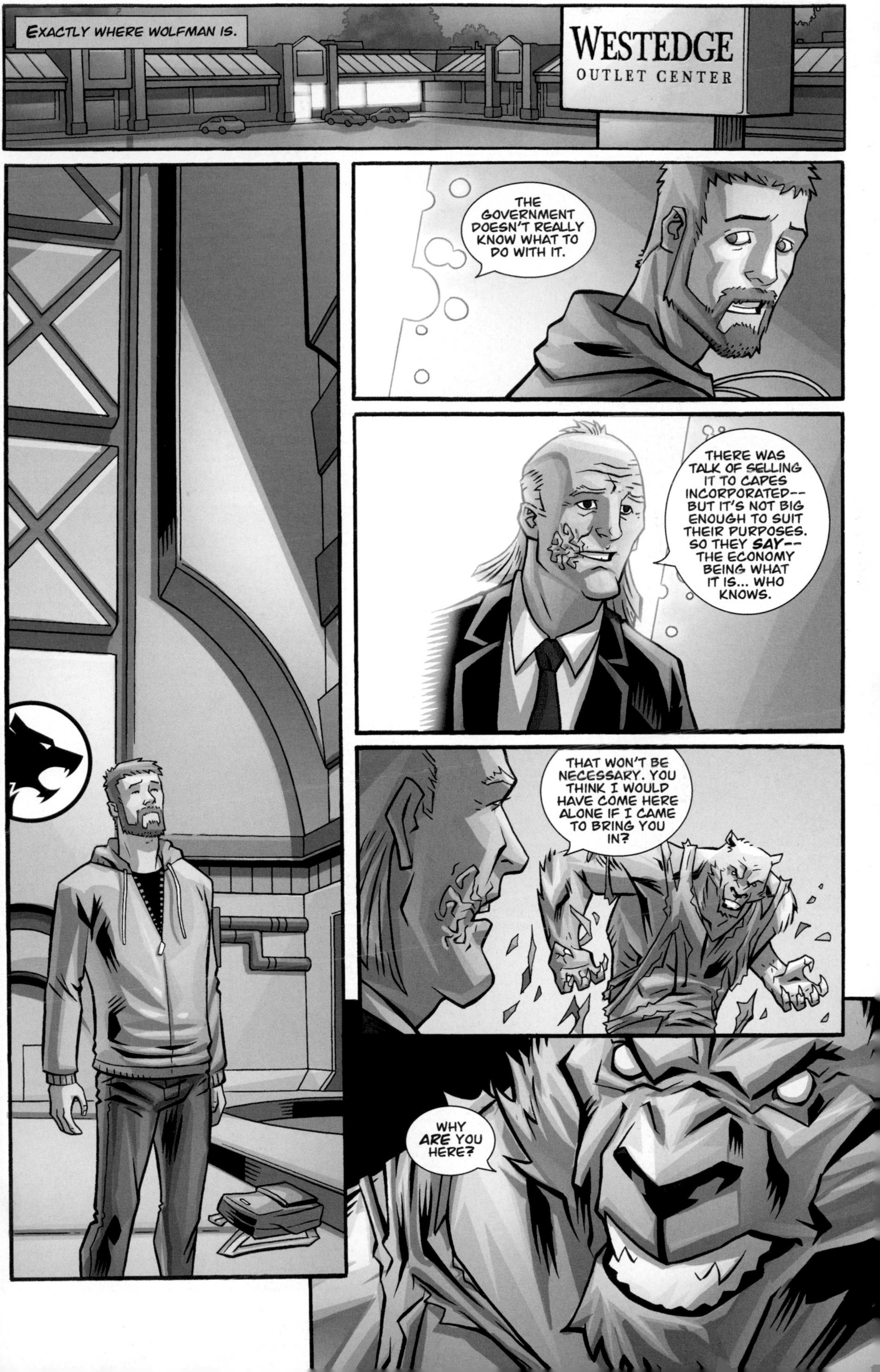
EXACTLY WHERE WOLFMAN IS.
WESTEDGE OUTLET CENTER
THE GOVERNMENT DOESN'T REALLY KNOW WHAT TO DO WITH IT.
THERE WAS TALK OF SELLING IT TO CAPES INCORPORATED-- BUT IT'S NOT BIG ENOUGH TO SUIT THEIR PURPOSES. SO THEY SAY-- THE ECONOMY BEING WHAT IT IS... WHO KNOWS.
THAT WON'T BE NECESSARY. YOU THINK I WOULD HAVE COME HERE ALONE IF I CAME TO BRING YOU IN?
WHY ARE YOU HERE?

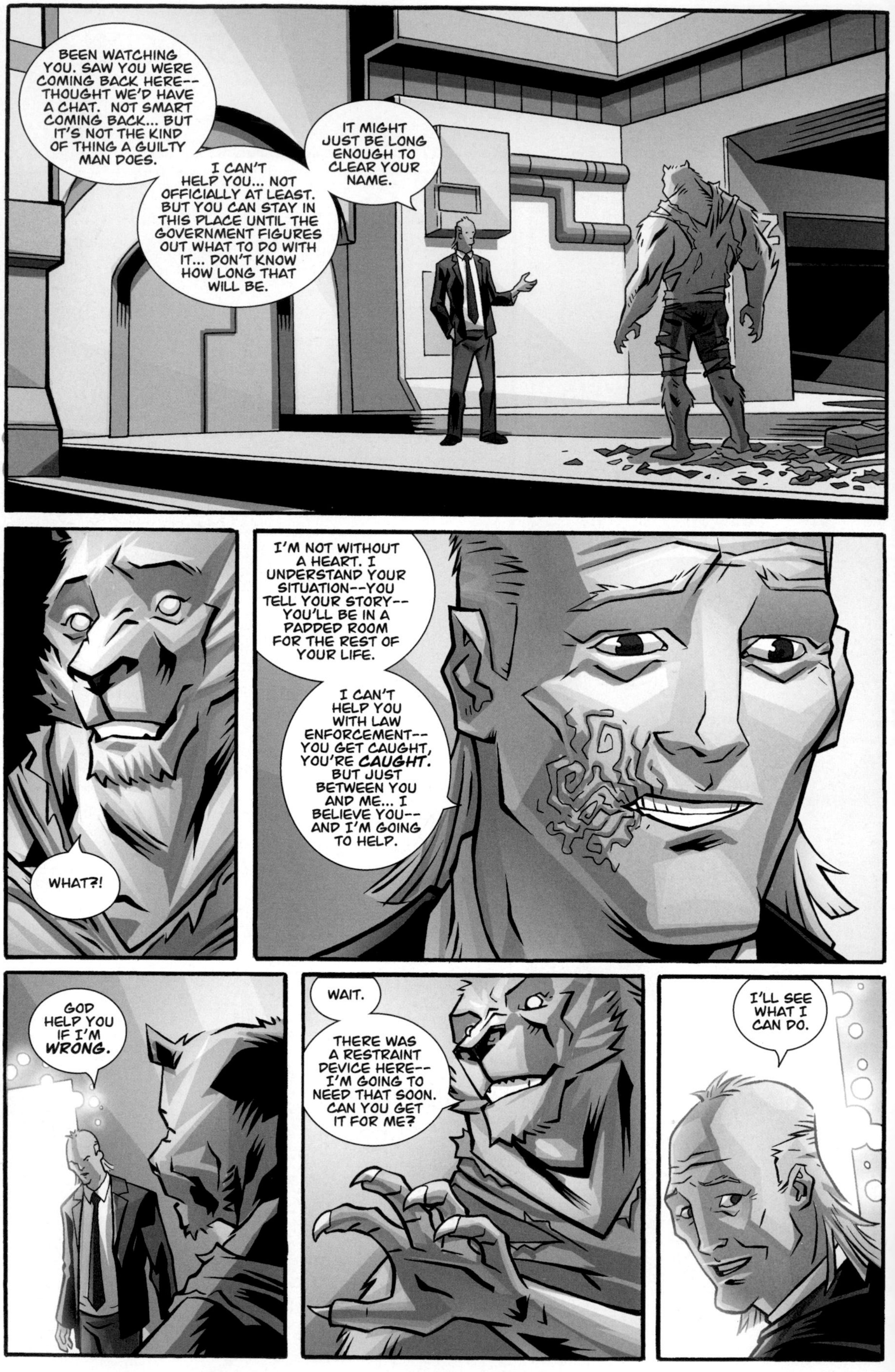
BEEN WATCHING YOU. SAW YOU WERE COMING BACK HERE--THOUGHT WE'D HAVE A CHAT. NOT SMART COMING BACK... BUT IT'S NOT THE KIND OF THING A GUILTY MAN DOES.
I CAN'T HELP YOU... NOT OFFICIALLY AT LEAST. BUT YOU CAN STAY IN THIS PLACE UNTIL THE GOVERNMENT FIGURES OUT WHAT TO DO WITH IT... DON'T KNOW HOW LONG THAT WILL BE.
IT MIGHT JUST BE LONG ENOUGH TO CLEAR YOUR NAME.
I'M NOT WITHOUT A HEART. I UNDERSTAND YOUR SITUATION--YOU TELL YOUR STORY--YOU'LL BE IN A PADDED ROOM FOR THE REST OF YOUR LIFE.
I CAN'T HELP YOU WITH LAW ENFORCEMENT--YOU GET CAUGHT, YOU'RE CAUGHT. BUT JUST BETWEEN YOU AND ME... I BELIEVE YOU--AND I'M GOING TO HELP.
WHAT?!
GOD HELP YOU IF I'M WRONG.
WAIT.
THERE WAS A RESTRAINT DEVICE HERE--I'M GOING TO NEED THAT SOON. CAN YOU GET IT FOR ME?
I'LL SEE WHAT I CAN DO.

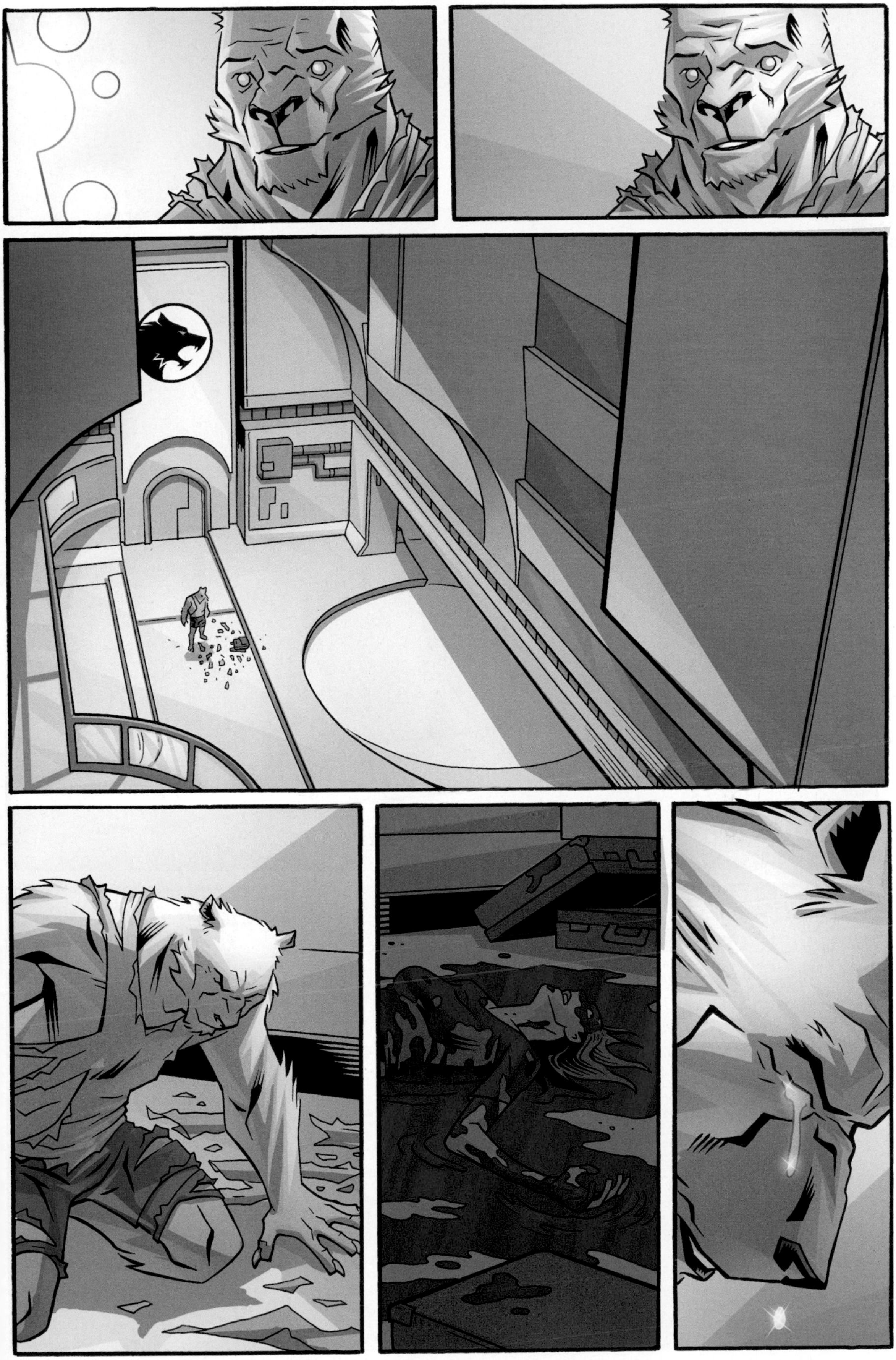

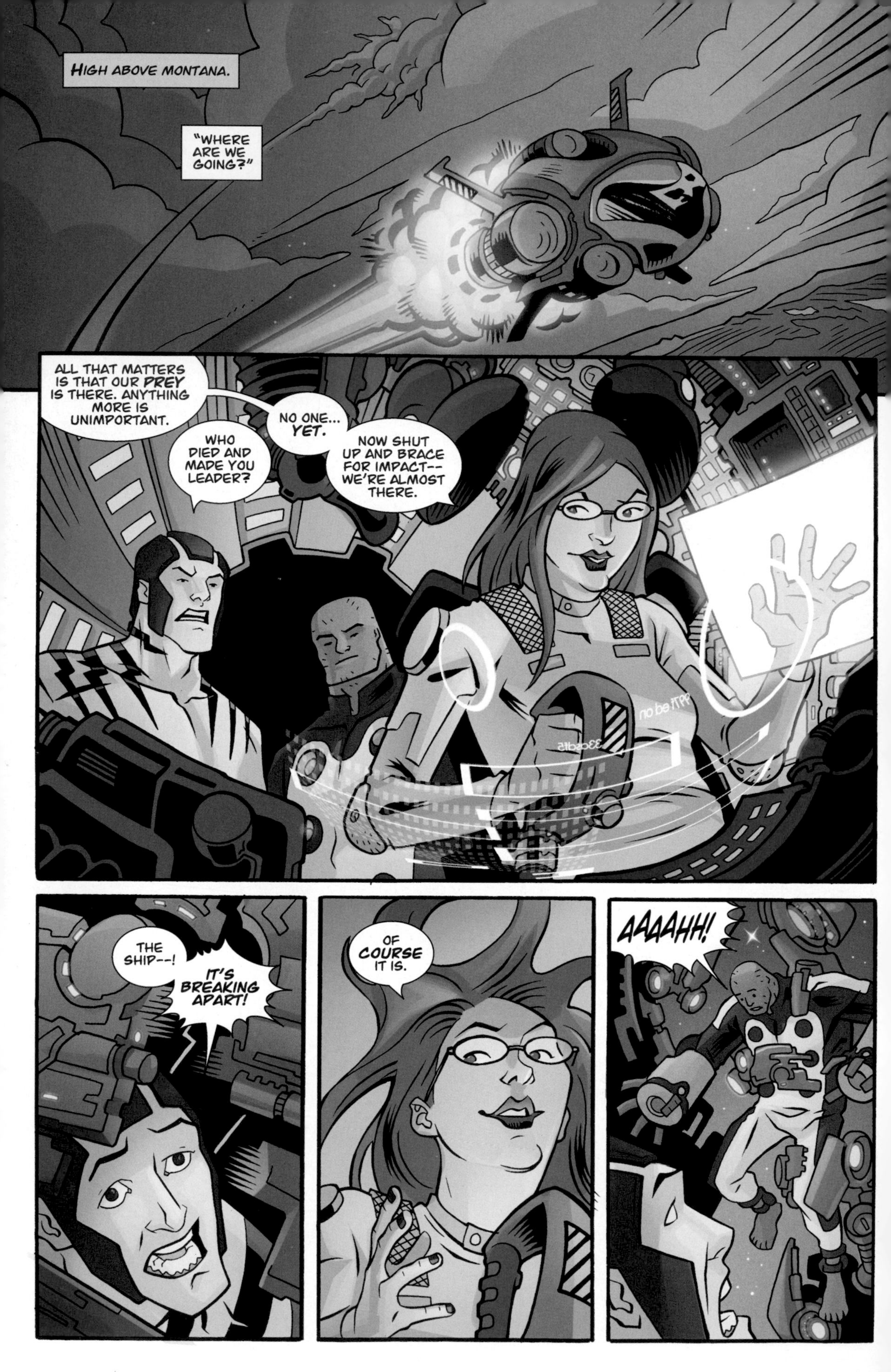

HIGH ABOVE MONTANA.
"WHERE ARE WE GOING?"
ALL THAT MATTERS IS THAT OUR PREY IS THERE. ANYTHING MORE IS UNIMPORTANT.
WHO DIED AND MADE YOU LEADER?
NO ONE... YET.
NOW SHUT UP AND BRACE FOR IMPACT-- WE'RE ALMOST THERE.
THE SHIP--!
IT'S BREAKING APART!
OF COURSE IT IS.
AAAAHH!

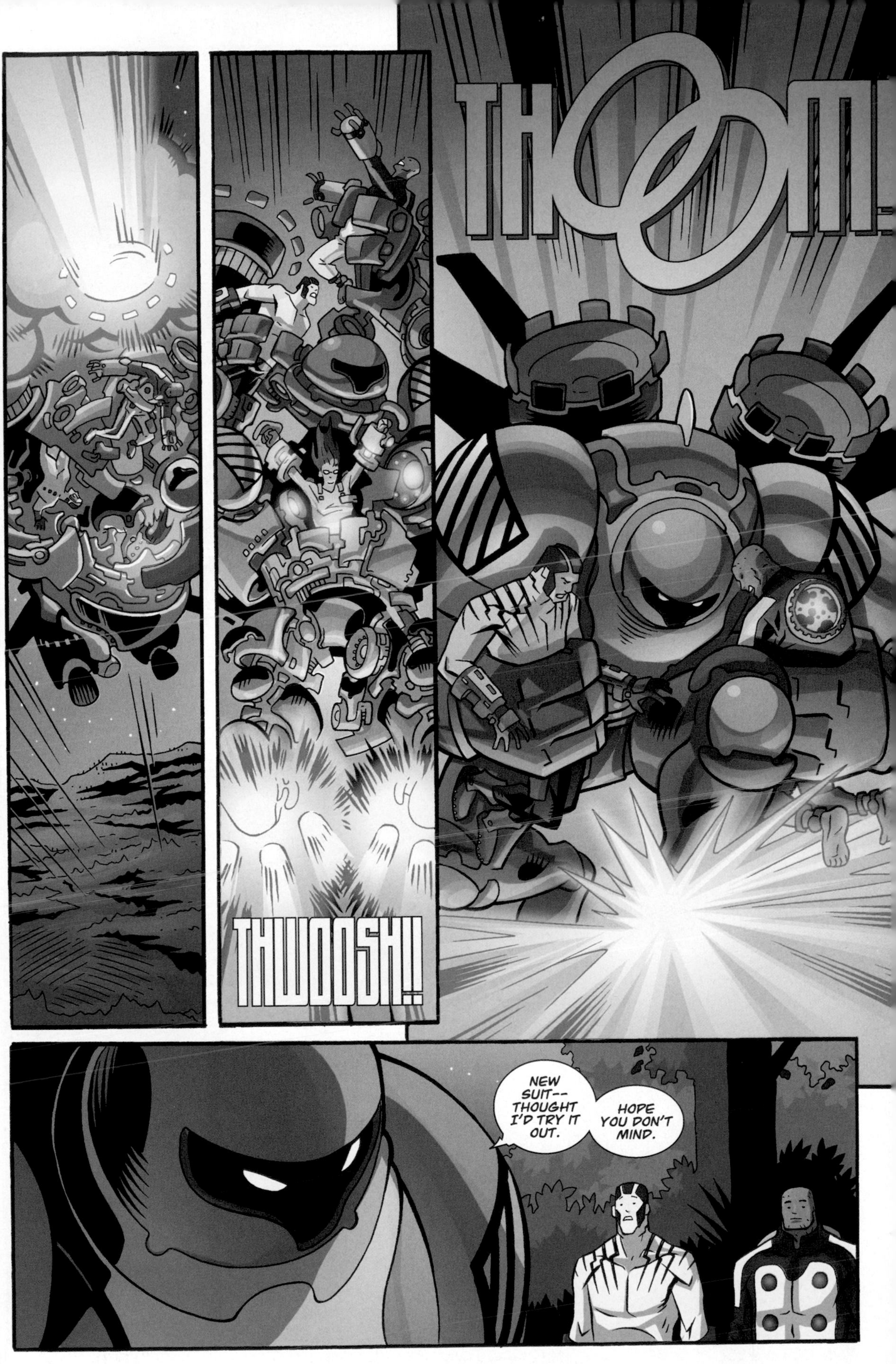
THWOOSH!!
THOOM!!
NEW SUIT--THOUGHT I'D TRY IT OUT.
HOPE YOU DON'T MIND.

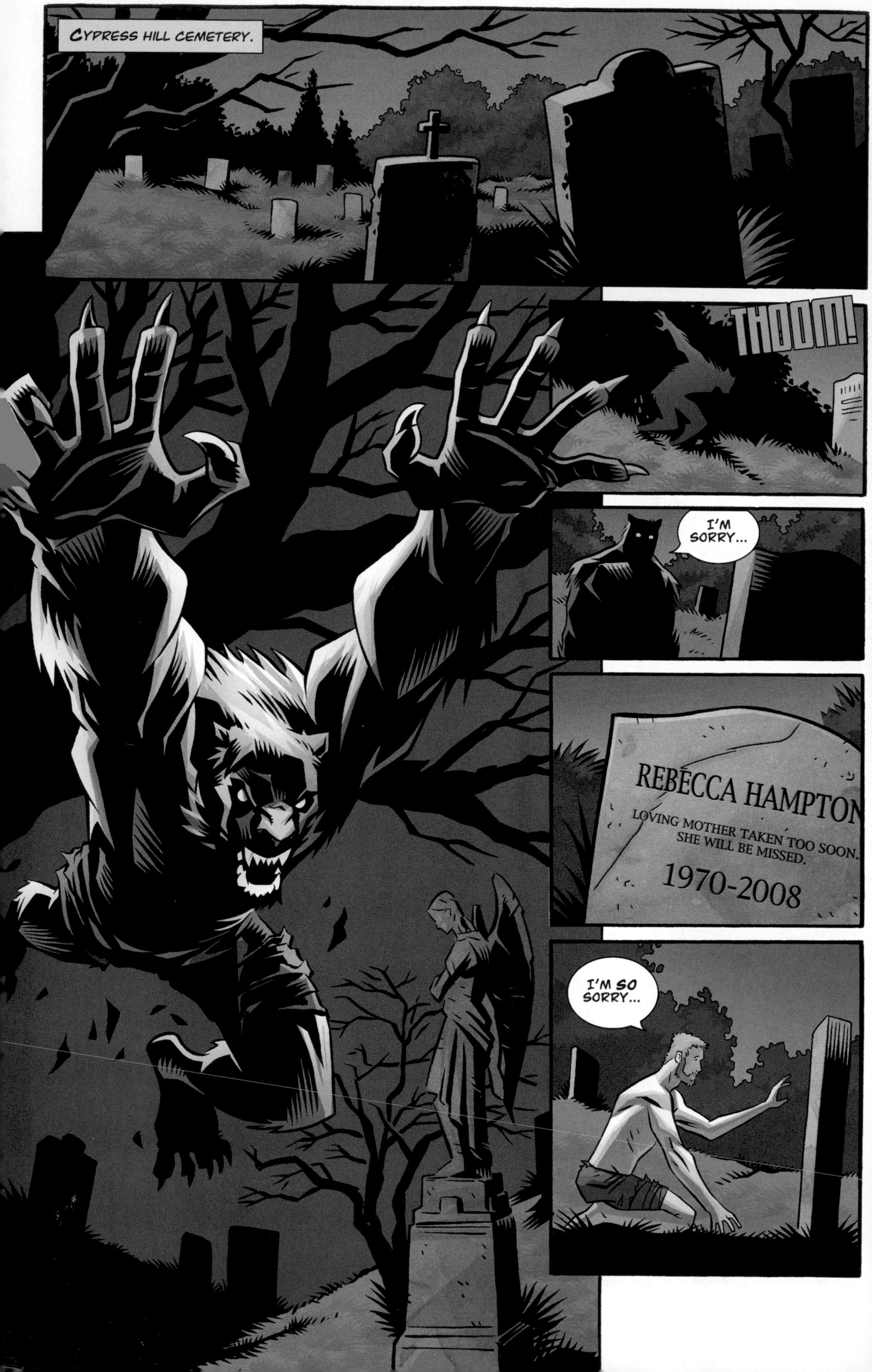
CYPRESS HILL CEMETERY.
THOOM!
I'M SORRY...
REBECCA HAMPTON
LOVING MOTHER TAKEN TOO SOON.
SHE WILL BE MISSED.
1970-2008
I'M SO SORRY...

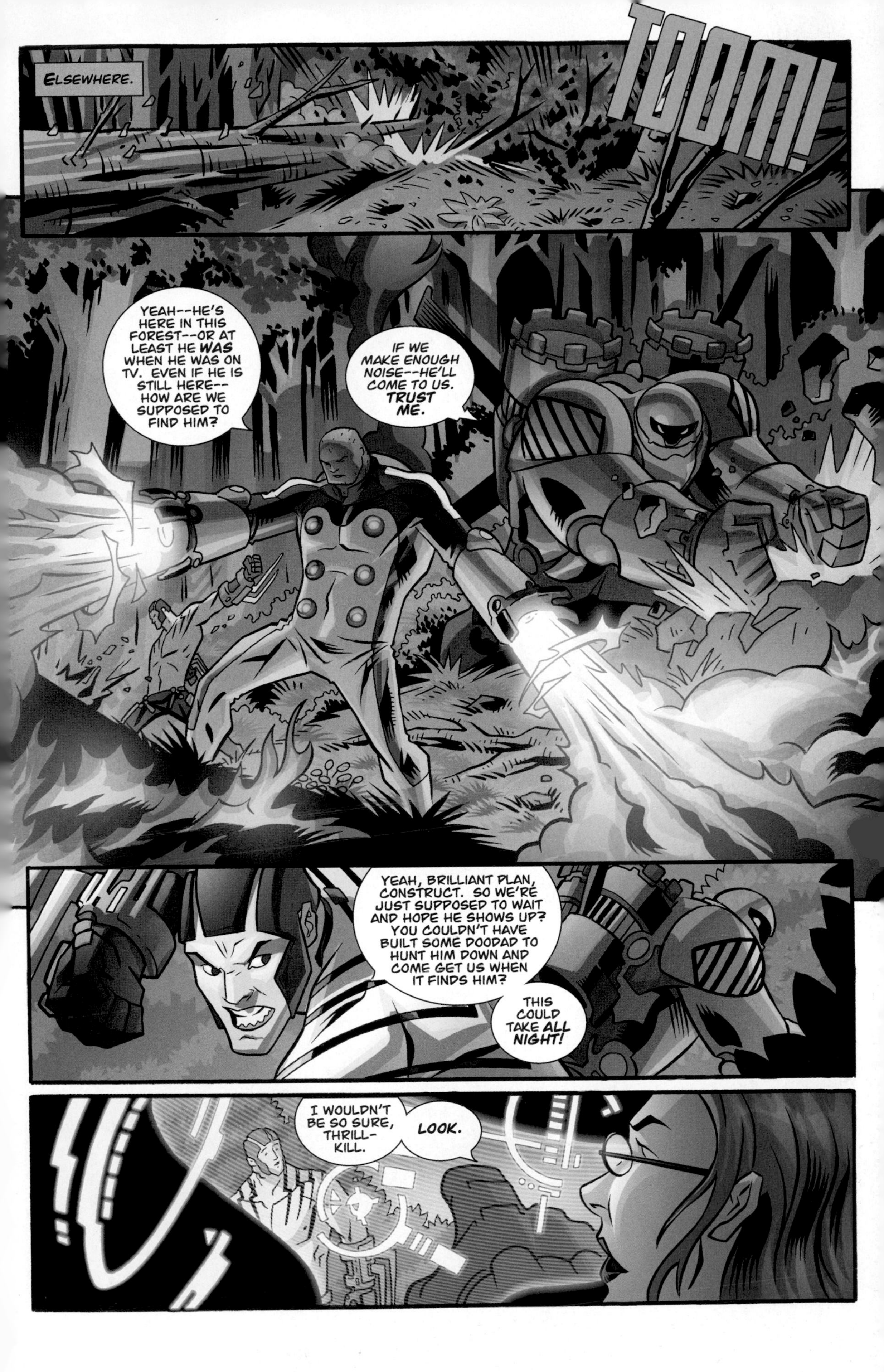
ELSEWHERE.
TOOM!
YEAH--HE'S HERE IN THIS FOREST--OR AT LEAST HE WAS WHEN HE WAS ON TV. EVEN IF HE IS STILL HERE--HOW ARE WE SUPPOSED TO FIND HIM?
IF WE MAKE ENOUGH NOISE--HE'LL COME TO US. TRUST ME.
YEAH, BRILLIANT PLAN, CONSTRUCT. SO WE'RE JUST SUPPOSED TO WAIT AND HOPE HE SHOWS UP? YOU COULDN'T HAVE BUILT SOME DOODAD TO HUNT HIM DOWN AND COME GET US WHEN IT FINDS HIM?
THIS COULD TAKE ALL NIGHT!
I WOULDN'T BE SO SURE, THRILL-KILL.
LOOK.

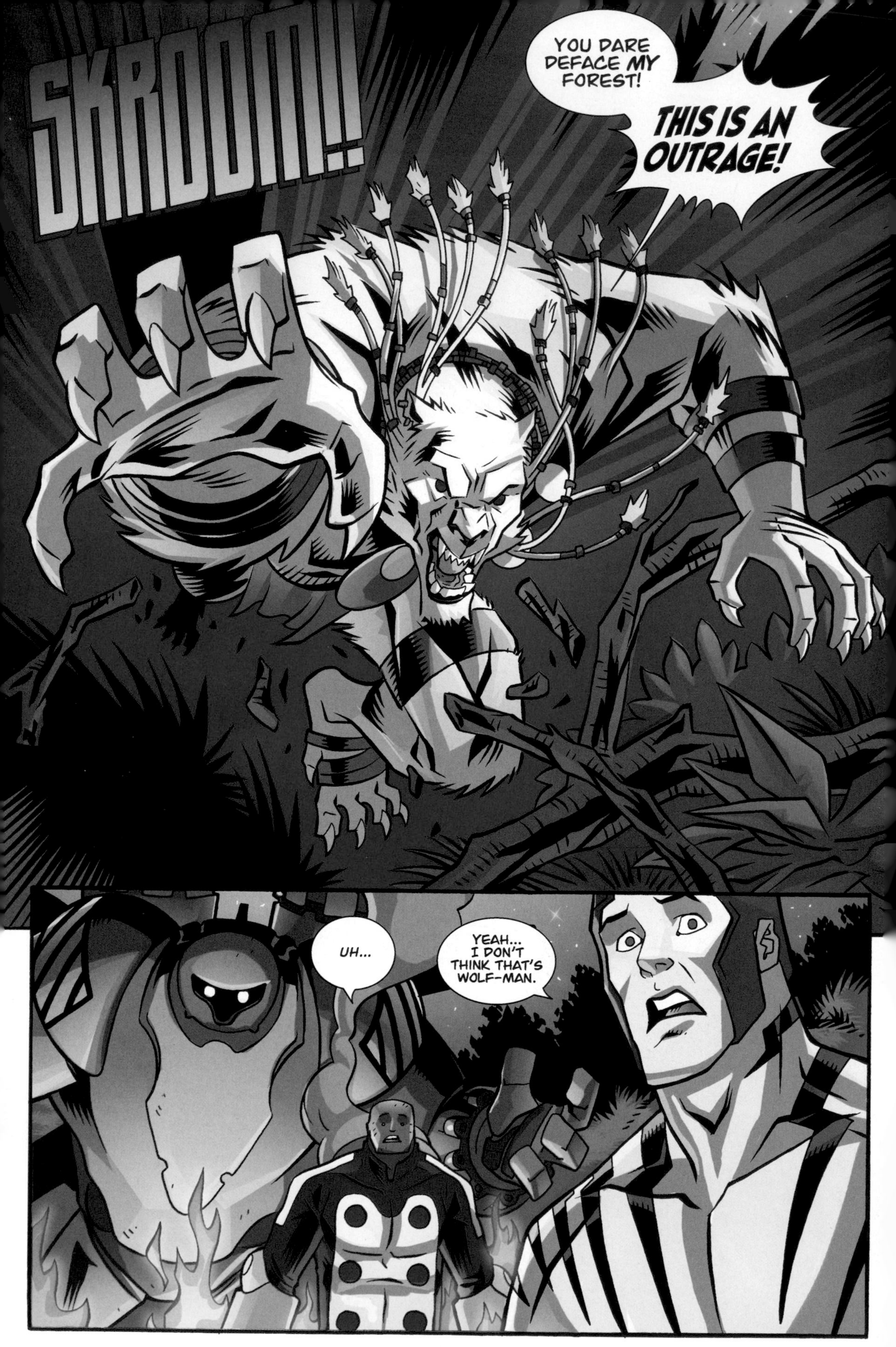
SKROOM!!
YOU DARE DEFACE MY FOREST!
THIS IS AN OUTRAGE!
UH...
YEAH... I DON'T THINK THAT'S WOLF-MAN.

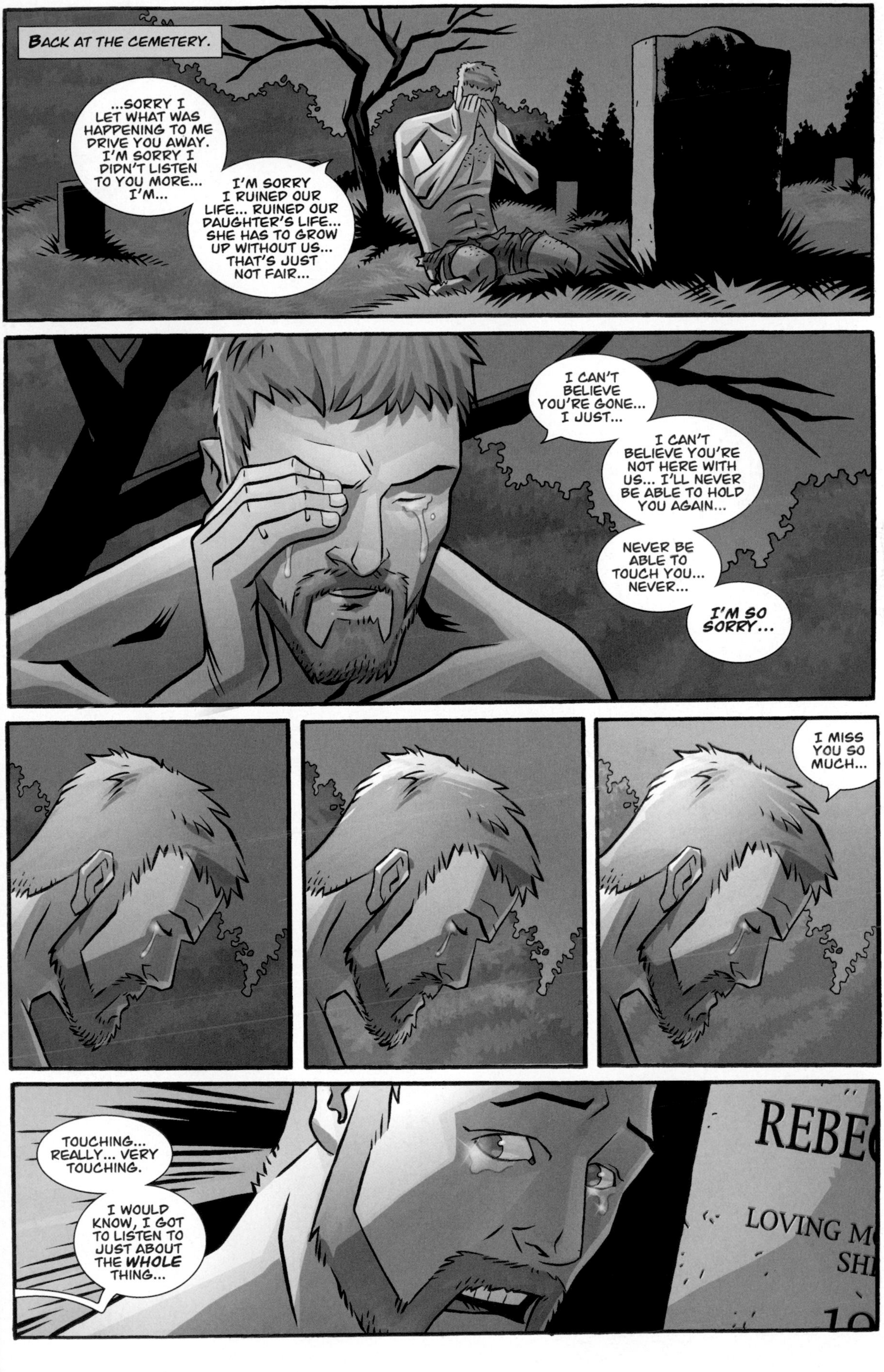

BACK AT THE CEMETERY.
...SORRY I LET WHAT WAS HAPPENING TO ME DRIVE YOU AWAY. I'M SORRY I DIDN'T LISTEN TO YOU MORE... I'M...
I'M SORRY I RUINED OUR LIFE... RUINED OUR DAUGHTER'S LIFE... SHE HAS TO GROW UP WITHOUT US... THAT'S JUST NOT FAIR...
I CAN'T BELIEVE YOU'RE GONE... I JUST...
I CAN'T BELIEVE YOU'RE NOT HERE WITH US... I'LL NEVER BE ABLE TO HOLD YOU AGAIN...
NEVER BE ABLE TO TOUCH YOU... NEVER...
I'M SO SORRY...
I MISS YOU SO MUCH...
TOUCHING... REALLY... VERY TOUCHING.
I WOULD KNOW, I GOT TO LISTEN TO JUST ABOUT THE WHOLE THING...
REBE
LOVING M
SH
19

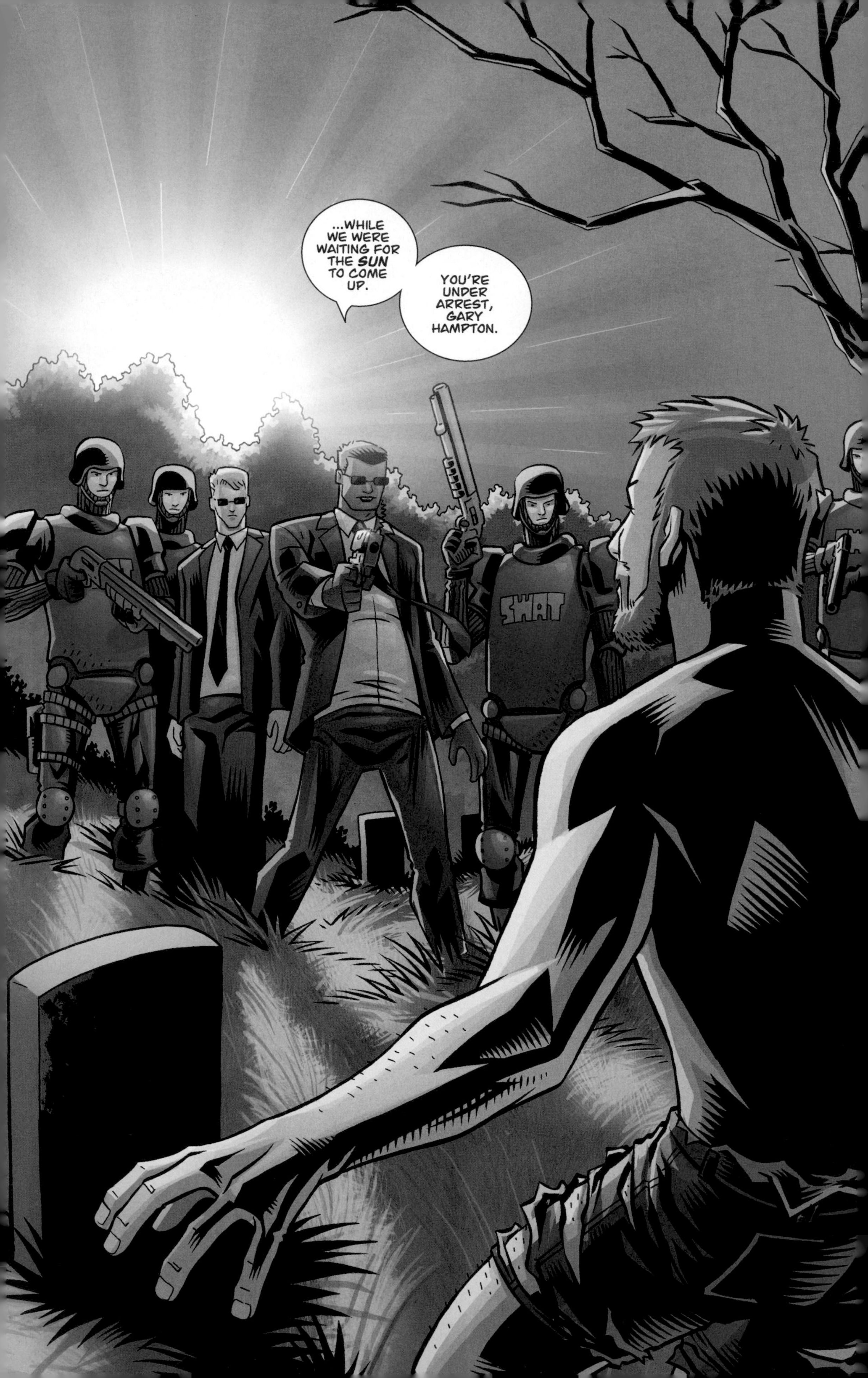
...WHILE WE WERE WAITING FOR THE SUN TO COME UP.
YOU'RE UNDER ARREST, GARY HAMPTON.
SWAT
SWAT

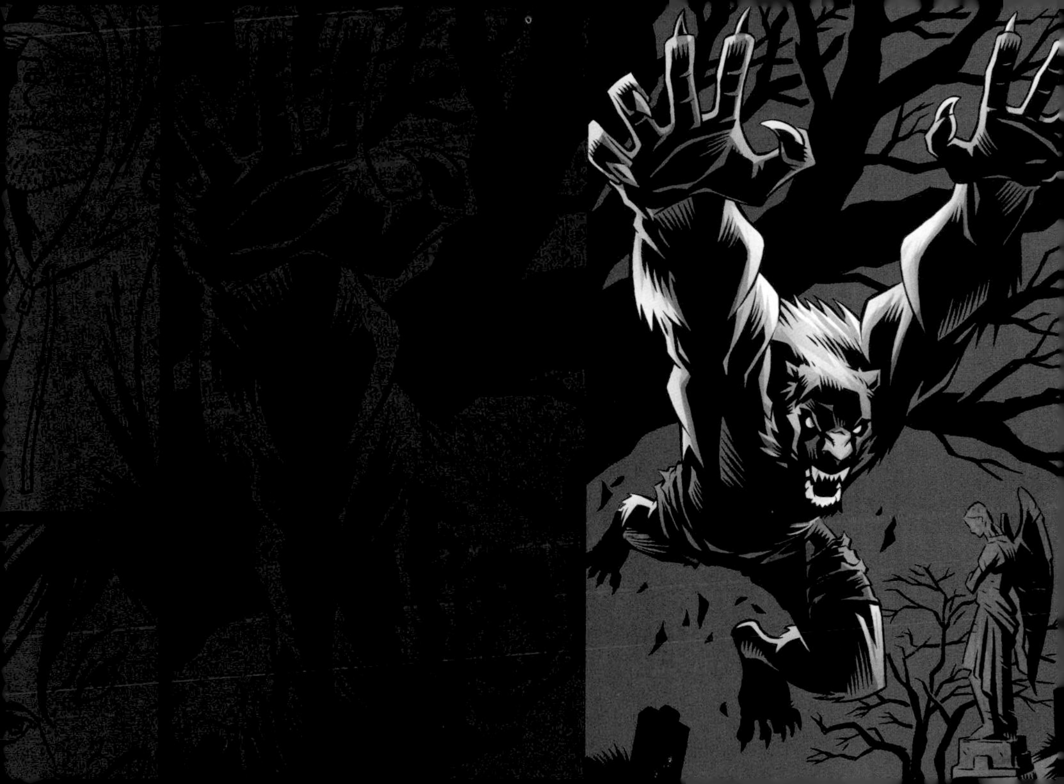

ROBERT KIRKMAN: Much like the trade paperbacks for my other series, INVINCIBLE, I wanted to have a uniform look to all our covers. As a consumer, I like it when a series of things matches... it makes me want to collect it that much more. And, theoretically, and Jason may disagree, it makes the covers easier to design. We just have to do something like the volume one cover... but different! Easy! Right Jason?

JASON HOWARD: Thats right, easy! Actually Robert has a good eye for design, and I totally agree about keeping a consistent theme in the trade paperback cover designs. But that enough of me being agreeable, from here on out I argue!

KIRKMAN: Bring it! Oh, and I should add, that I like this cover so much better than the one for volume one—it's damn sweet!

HOWARD: Thanks! I guess I won't be arguing with everything you say.

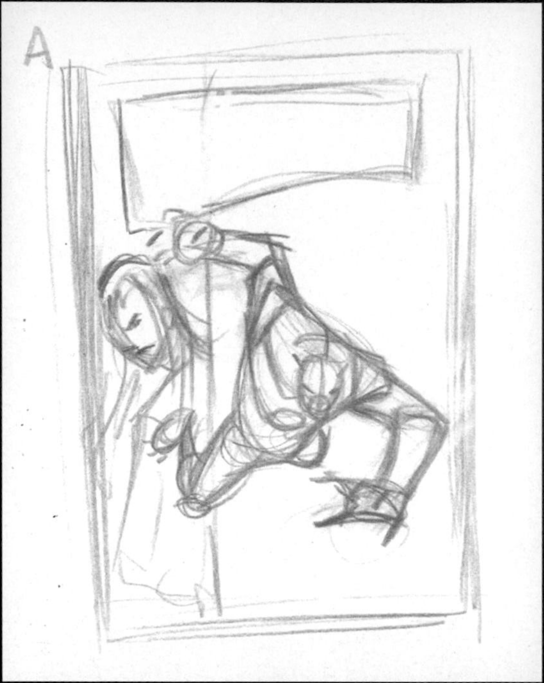
A

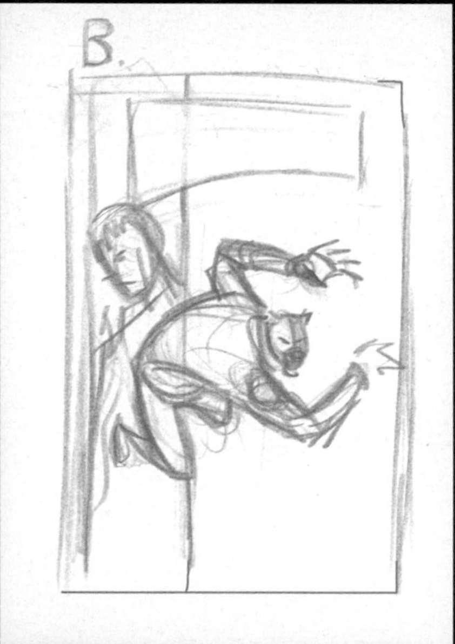
B.

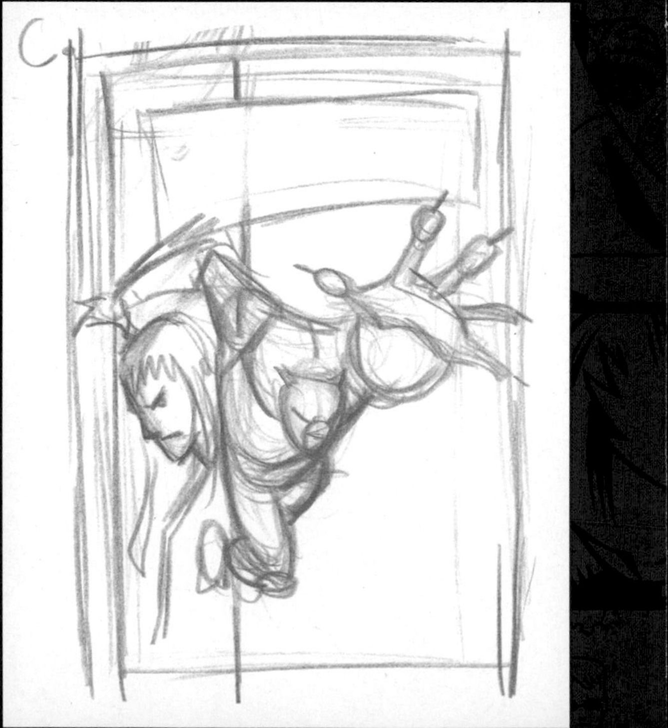
C

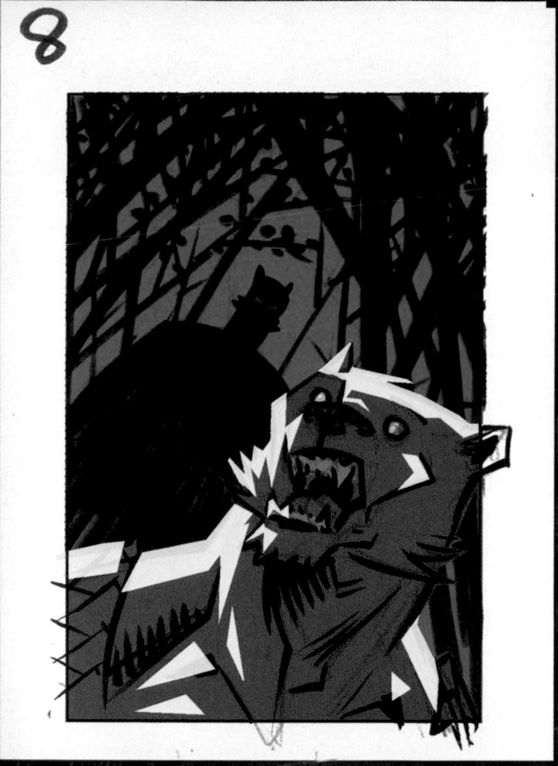
8

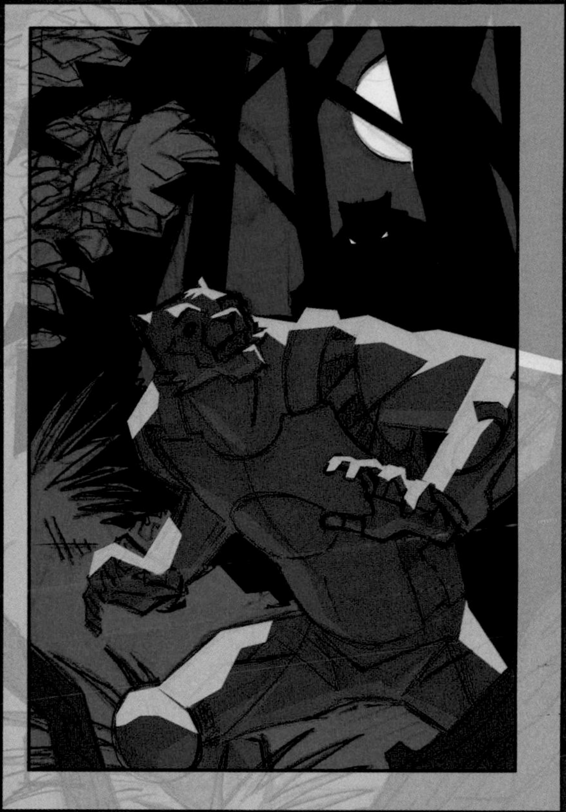

KIRKMAN: Jason does awesome color roughs for the covers from time to time... although, looking at these roughs for the cover to issue 8, it seems like he doesn't often use the color schemes from the roughs. I hope I didn't tell you to ditch the red on this cover—cause I dig it now.

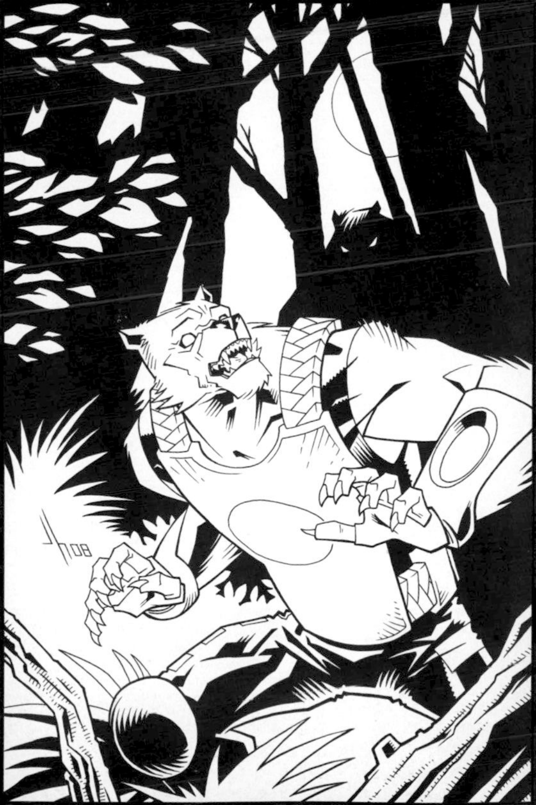

HOWARD: Nope, changing the color was my call, although I am not sure why as I also like the red from the rough. I probably thought that the blue and green scheme I used on the final cover felt more night time. Sometimes I am more daring with my color choices in the roughs, because I know it is preliminary and doesn't matter as much as the final. This is probably a case where I should have gone with my first instinct.

KIRKMAN: A mess of sketches for the cover to issue 9. This one was easy for me. I just said "let's do a wanted poster!" I'm pretty sure having the silver casings lying about was Jason's idea... I thought that was pretty cool. Jason is actually pretty awesome in that he comes from a graphic design background... so he can do all this design-oriented stuff on his own. It's awesome. I just sit back and wait for cool stuff to be turned in.

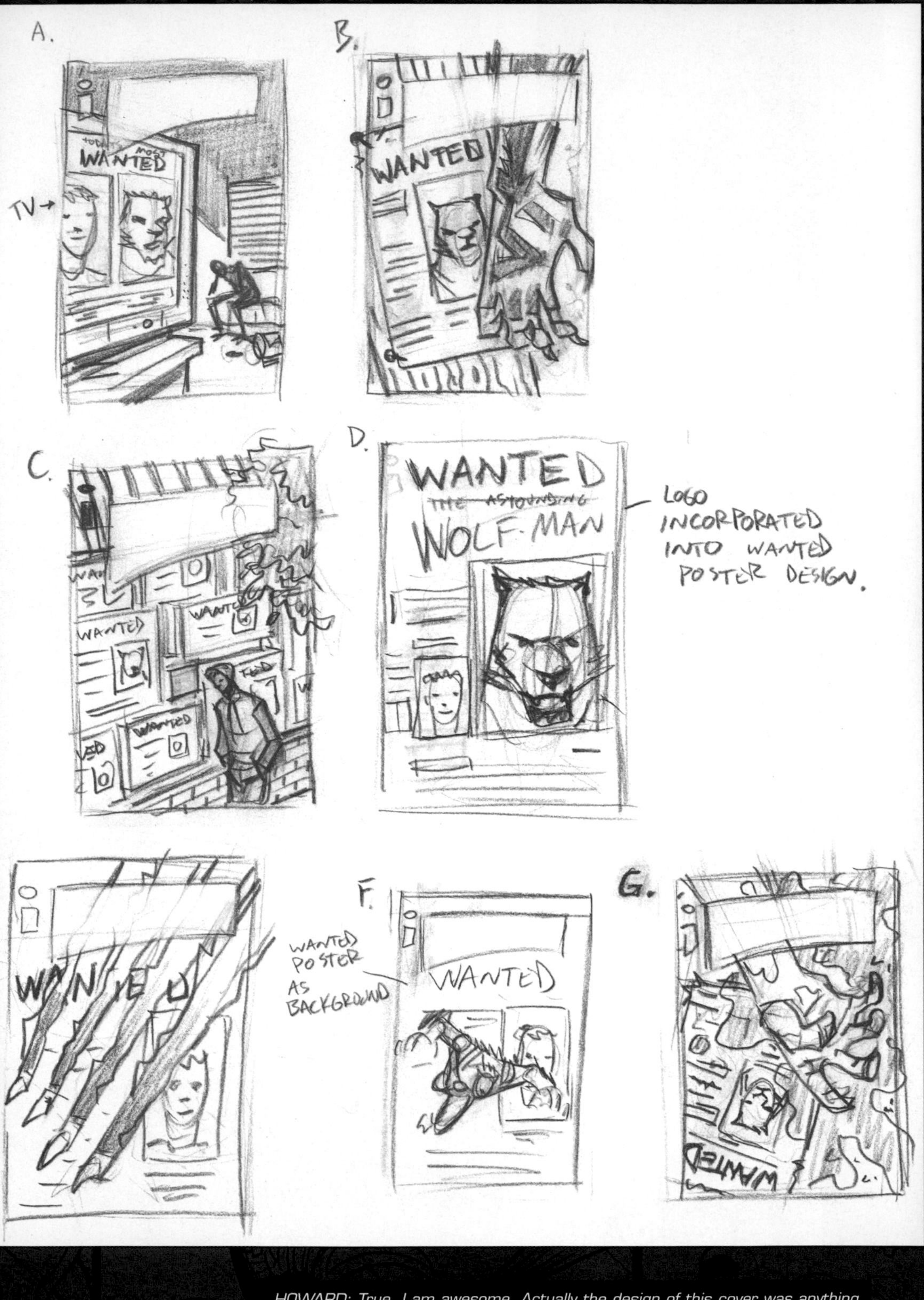
A.
TV →
WANTED
B.
WANTED
C.
WANTED
WANTED
WANTED
D.
WANTED
THE ASTOUNDING
WOLF-MAN
LOGO INCORPORATED INTO WANTED POSTER DESIGN.
F.
WANTED POSTER AS BACKGROUND
WANTED
G.

HOWARD: True, I am awesome. Actually the design of this cover was anything but easy for me. As you can see I tried a bunch of ideas trying to find something that looked a little more dynamic. I even thought about showing an Americas Most Wanted type of profile on the TV. Of the TV versions I think C could have been cool, but it still didn't feel right. Finally with version G I felt we had a workable design. Robert agreed and there you have it.

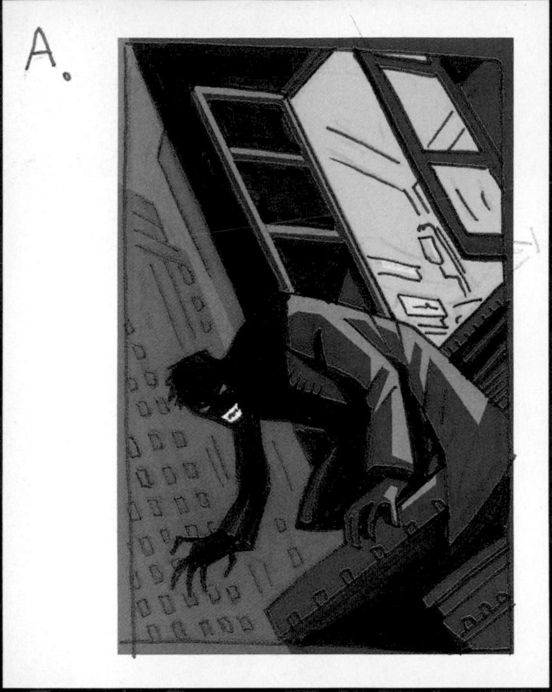
A.

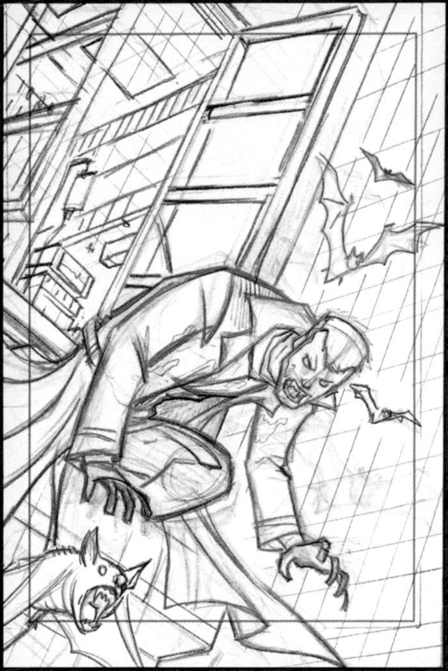

KIRKMAN: Sweet cover sketches for the cover to issue 10. He didn't use this color scheme, thank god. Nothing says "vampire" quite like hot pink!

HOWARD: Actually Robert, you may recall that my first pass at the colors for this cover I kept the hot pink. It was cool, maybe even groundbreaking. But SOMEONE made me change it. I actually like the red quite a bit, so it wasn't a bad suggestion, I guess.

KIRKMAN: Oh, boo hoo.

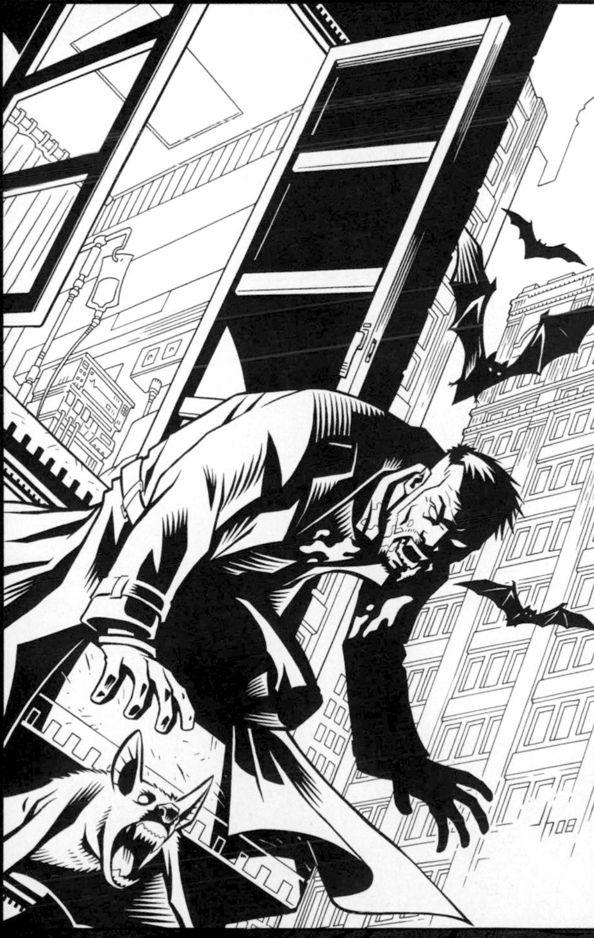

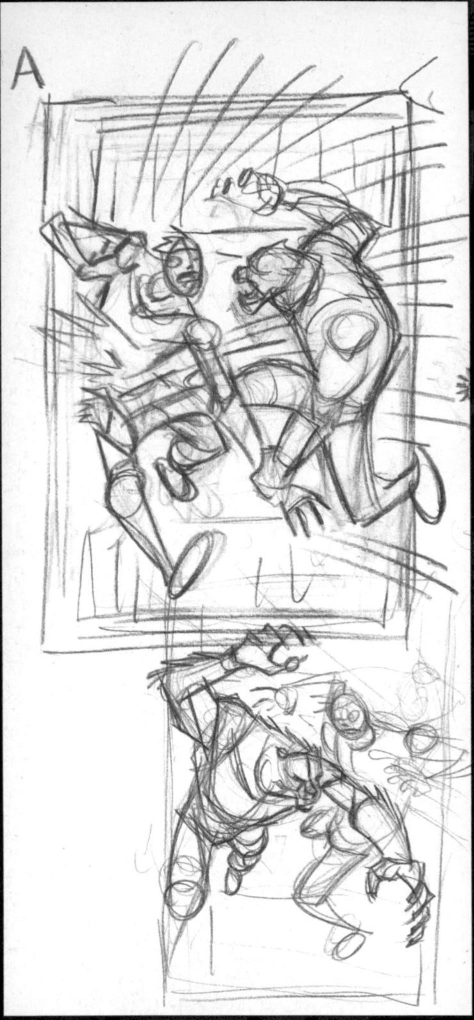
A

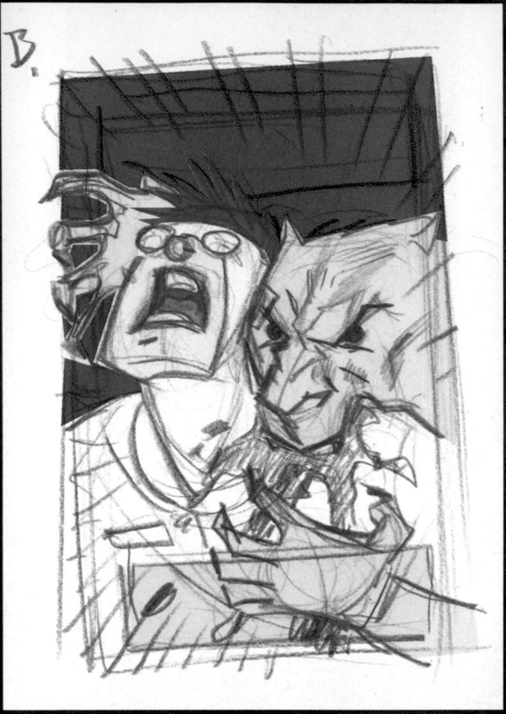
B.

KIRKMAN: For the big Invincible crossover, I went to Ryan and Jason and explained to them that I wanted to have both covers be the two characters fighting—with the logos for both books on the covers at full size. I thought it was a cool idea… and I like it even more because at no point does anything remotely like the two covers appear inside the books. That's always fun!

HOWARD: I fought hard to draw a cover where Wolf-Man was beating on Invincible. Its Wolf-Man's book, shouldn't he be winning? But Robert and Ryan ganged up on me and made me draw one where Invincible was winning. Sigh. I kinda liked version B, but Robert said it looked like they were making out. Really? Who makes out like that?

KIRKMAN: No comment

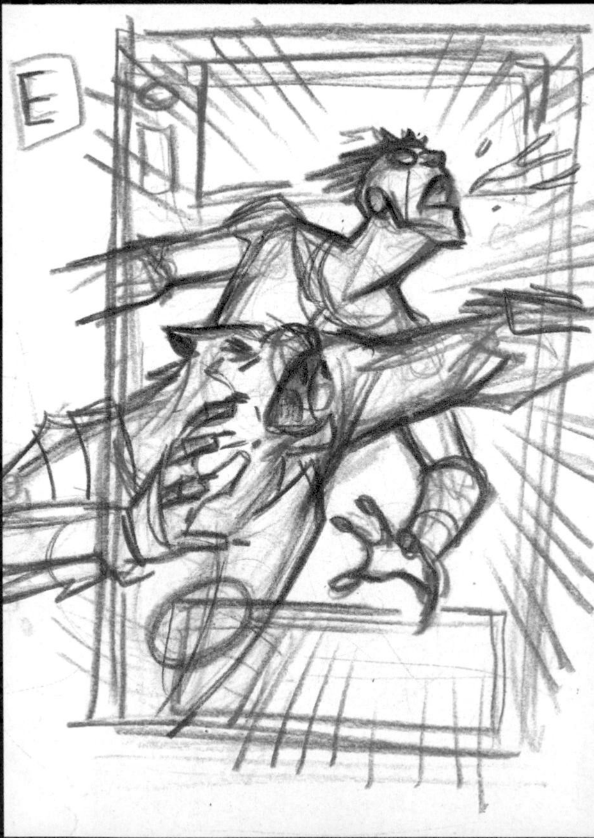
E

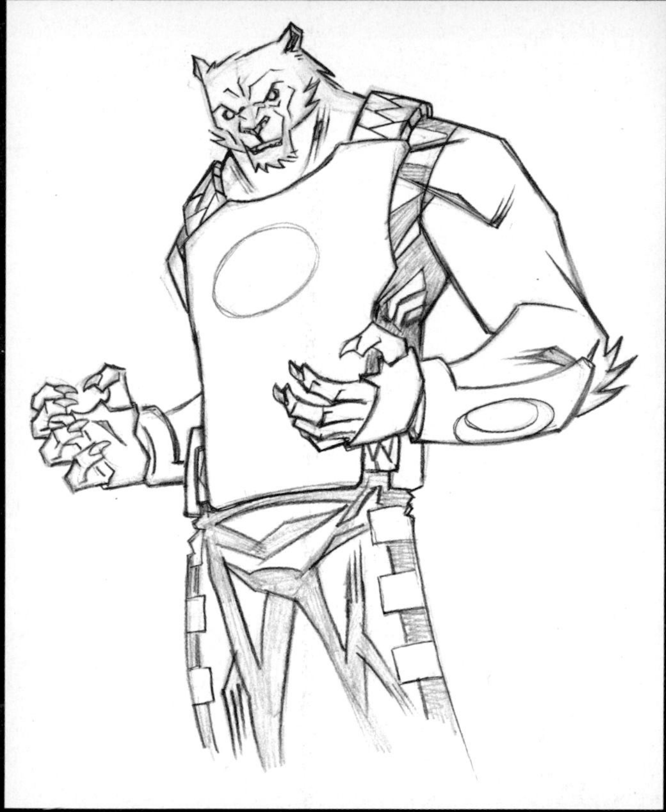

KIRKMAN: The first four pages of this TPB may appear to be from issue 8, but they're actually from a thing Image put out called MONSTER PILE-UP that spotlighted Image Comics' four monstery titles and featured four-page stories from the original creative teams. Our very own Jason Howard laid out and colored the cover.

HOWARD: Its true, I did those things. By all rights Andy (FrieBreather) Kuhn should have designed the cover, he is great at that stuff. But he lives the rock star life, so I tried to pick up the slack. Based on my layout each artist penciled their character and Riley (Proof) Rossmo composited them together and drew the background. This went off to Craig (Perhapanauts) Rousseau who inked the whole thing and then back to me for colors. I had a blast coloring it. This was one of the few times that I have colored something that was not my own drawing. Well I guess part of it was my drawing, but you know what I mean.

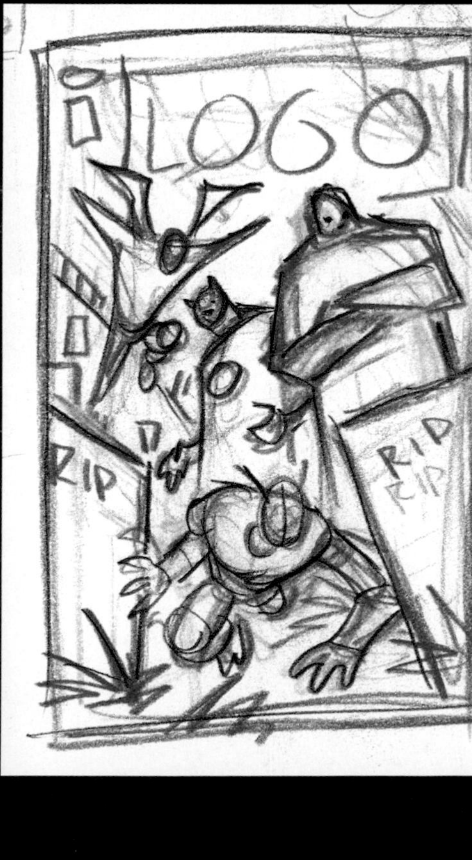
LOGO
RIP
RIP
RIP

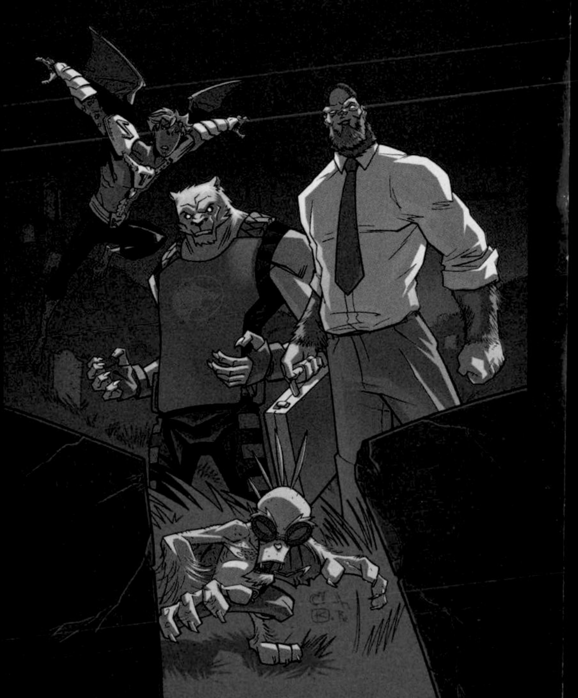

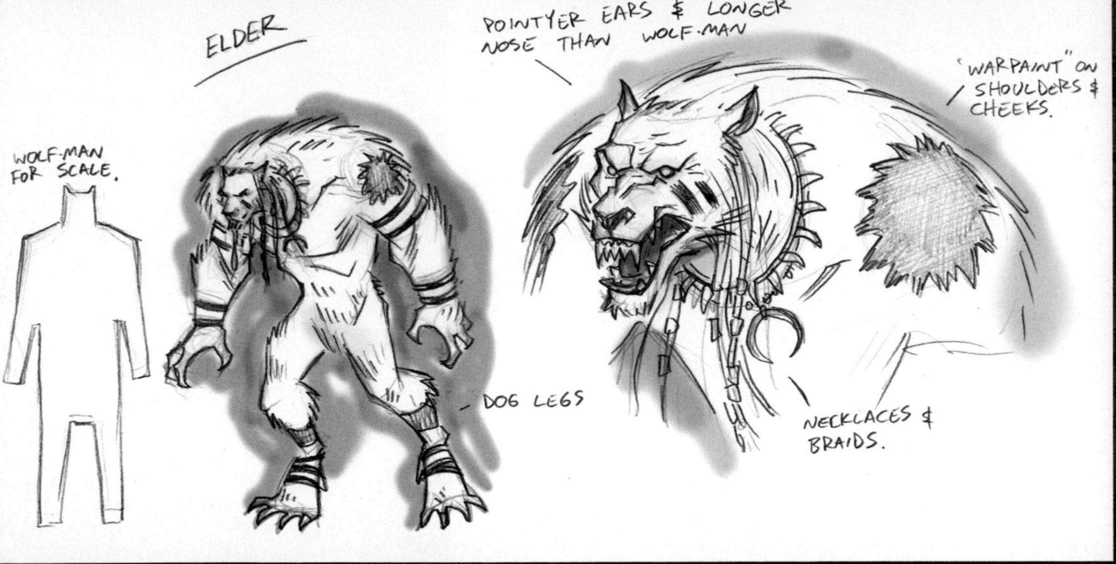
ELDER
WOLF-MAN FOR SCALE.
POINTYER EARS & LONGER NOSE THAN WOLF-MAN
"WARPAINT" ON SHOULDERS & CHEEKS.
DOG LEGS
NECKLACES & BRAIDS.

KIRKMAN: Early designs for the Elder. I knew I wanted a big hulking werewolf that would dwarf Wolf-Man and I wanted him to be more feral and always hunched over. Jason took it from there. Hey—explain the dark fur shoulder pads, you mad man!

HOWARD: Forget dark fur. Can you say "skull helmet"? That is legendary comic book design work, and it's now relegated to the sketchbook pages of a trade. If you asked Jack Kirby if he preferred "skull helmet" or "no skull helmet" I think we all know which

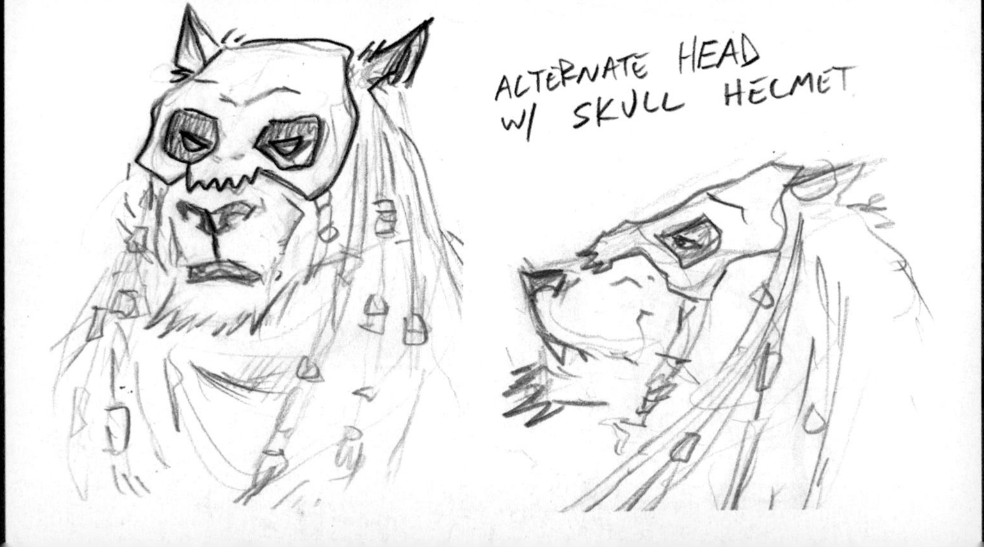
ALTERNATE HEAD W/ SKULL HELMET

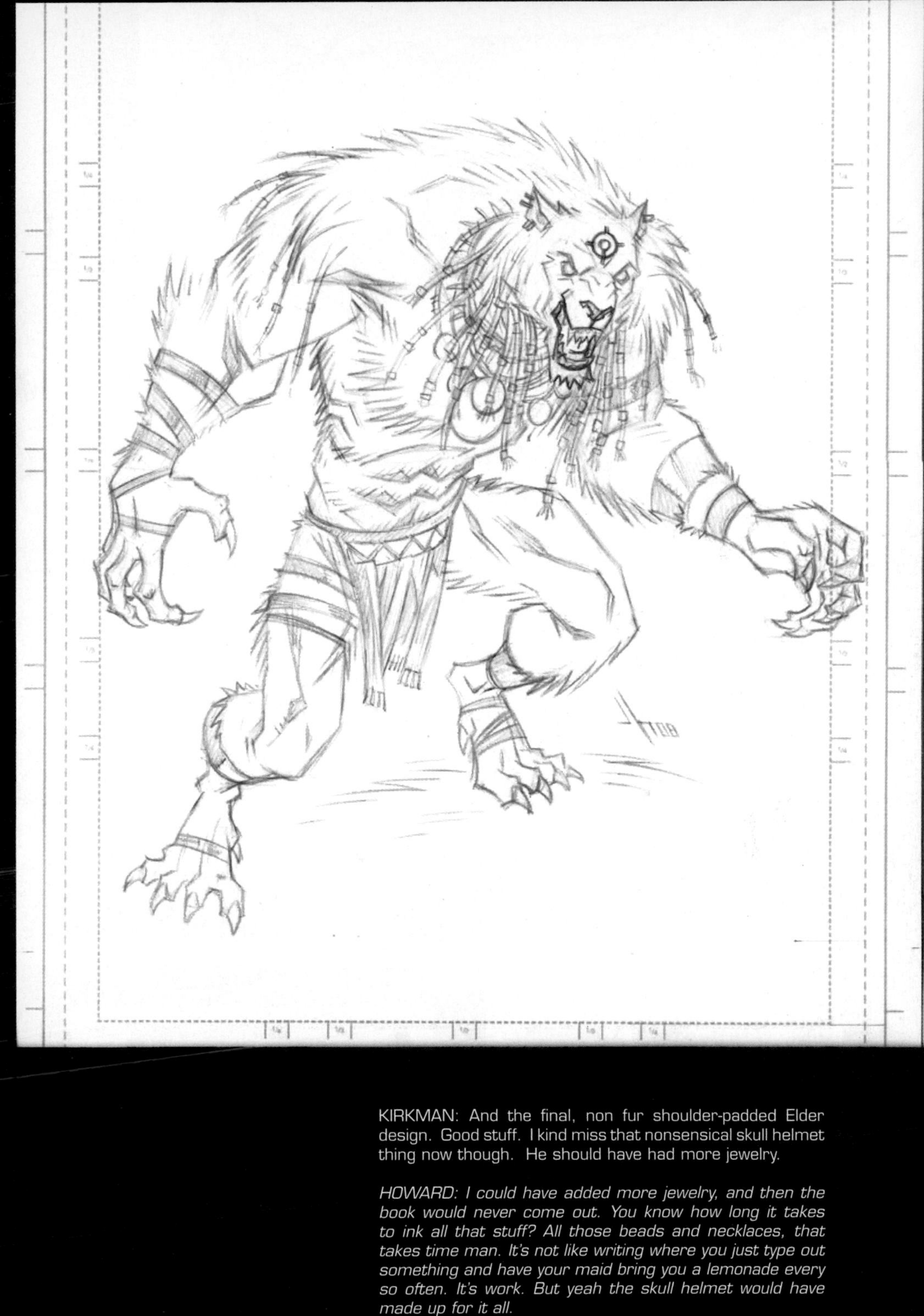

KIRKMAN: And the final, non fur shoulder-padded Elder design. Good stuff. I kind miss that nonsensical skull helmet thing now though. He should have had more jewelry.

HOWARD: I could have added more jewelry, and then the book would never come out. You know how long it takes to ink all that stuff? All those beads and necklaces, that takes time man. It's not like writing where you just type out something and have your maid bring you a lemonade every so often. It's work. But yeah the skull helmet would have made up for it all.

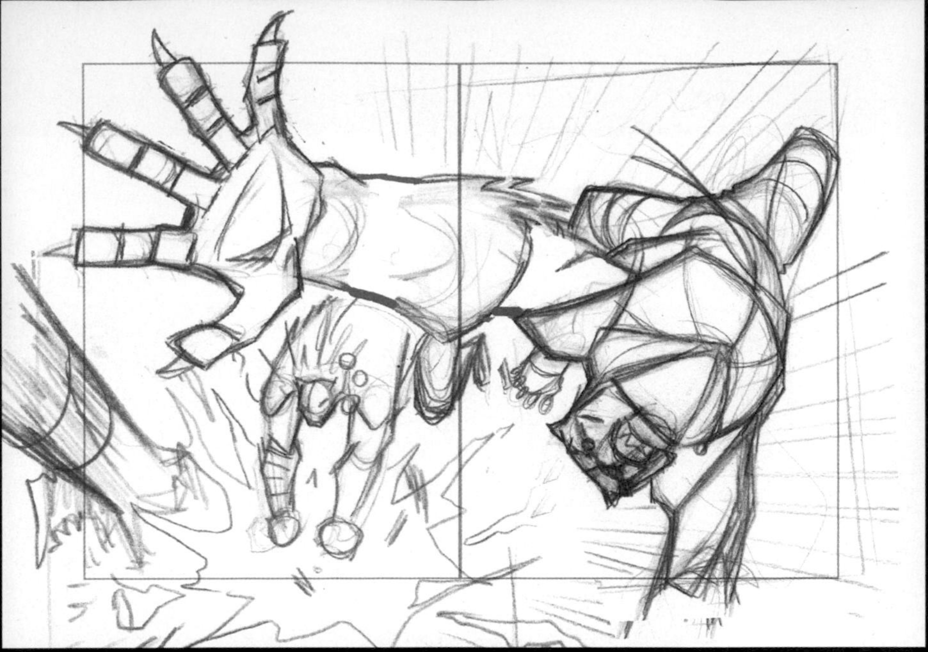

KIRKMAN: It's fun to get Jason's layouts because they're always awesome. Looking at all these files, it's also fun because he changed how he did them frequently during these issues. Jason?

HOWARD: The first few issues of the series I had a pretty consistent system for drawing a page. I would do layouts at about half of the printed size, then I would enlarge them and lightbox onto the final board where I would add detail and tighten up the drawing. Once that was done I would do the inks and then colors. Around issue #7 I began to experiment with different working methods. Sometimes I would still do layouts, but much of the time I just drew my rough right on the board, then I would lighten it with a kneaded eraser and tighten up the drawing in blue pencil a bit before inking it. There are things I like better about doing layouts and things I like better about drawing right on the board. But for better or worse about 80% of the pages in this trade were just pencilled directly to the board.

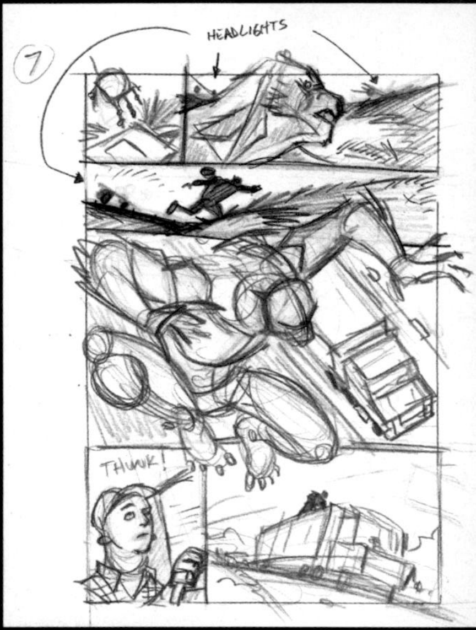
7
HEADLIGHTS

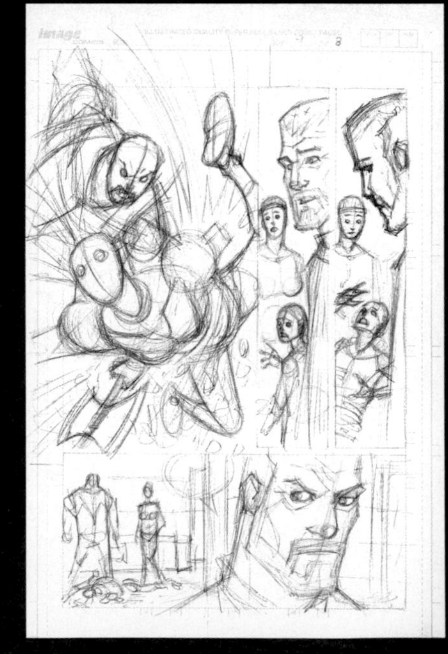

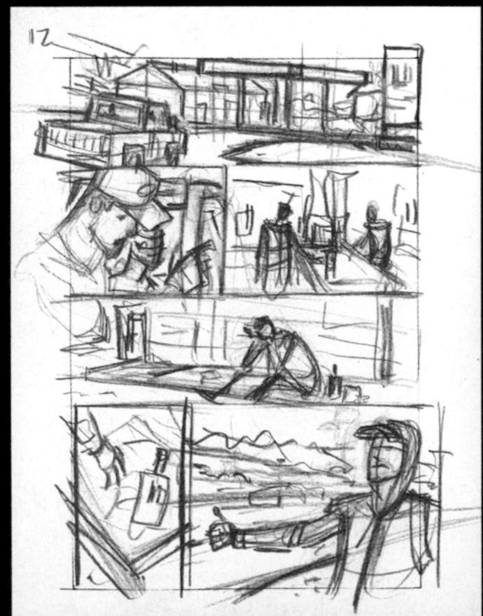
12

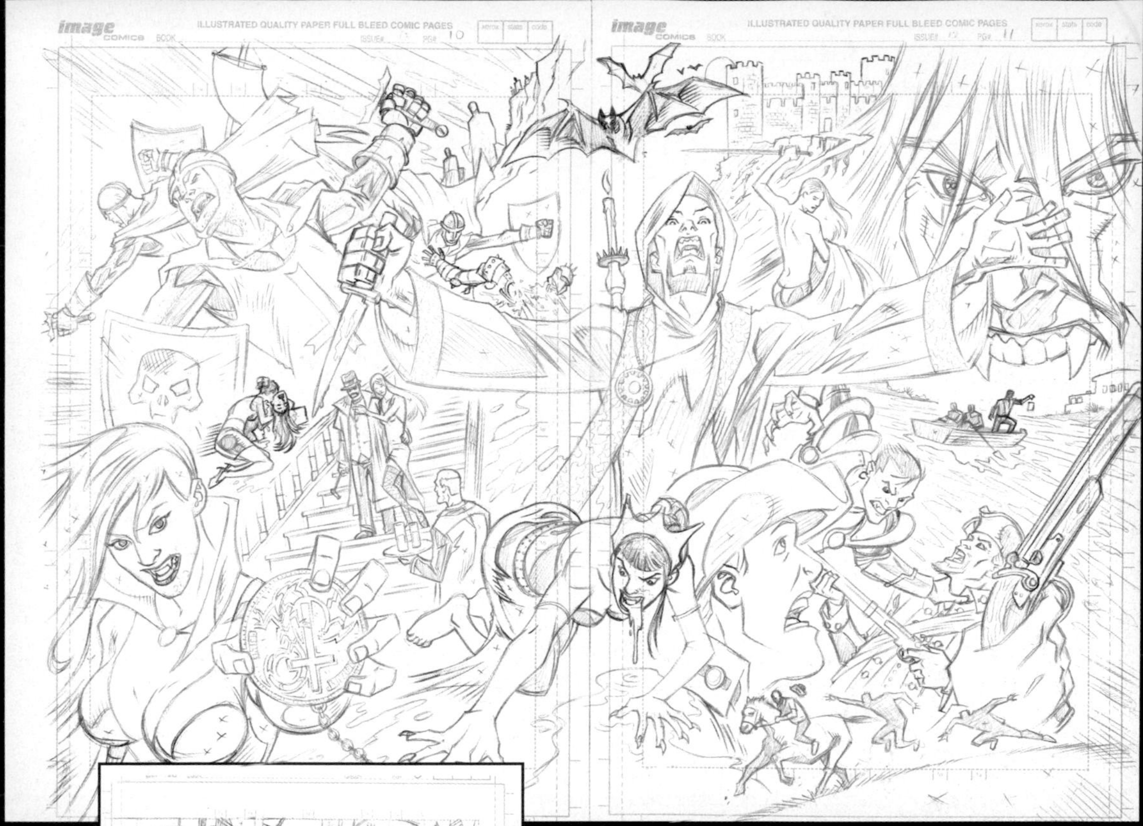

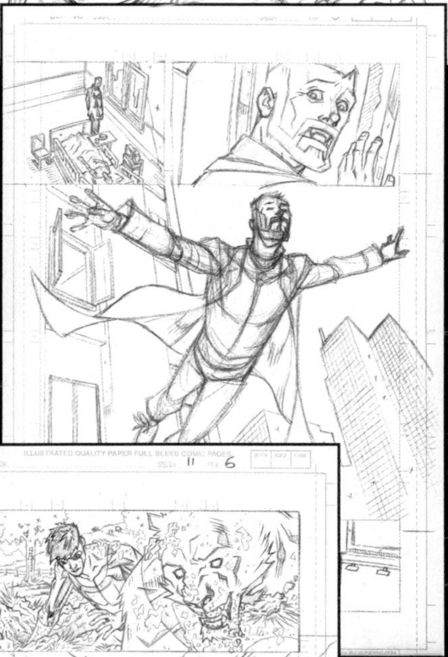

KIRKMAN: More layouts from issues 10 and 11 here. Basically just his pencils, as Jason was penciling directly on the boards during this time.

HOWARD: I tried to get a little tighter with the pencils for issue #11 as that issue was inked by the multi-talented Cliff Rathburn. This was the first time I had ever been inked by someone other than myself. It was fun to see the pages come back made all pretty by Cliff's slick lines. Issues 10 and 11 were some of the most fun for me to draw. Robert is really writing some cool stuff in this book

KIRKMAN: Aw, shucks.

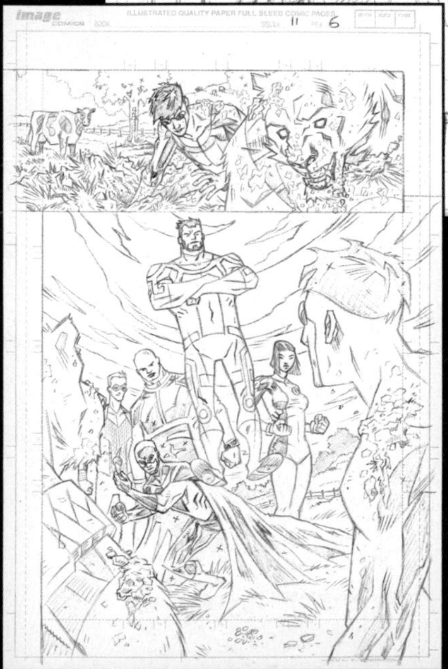

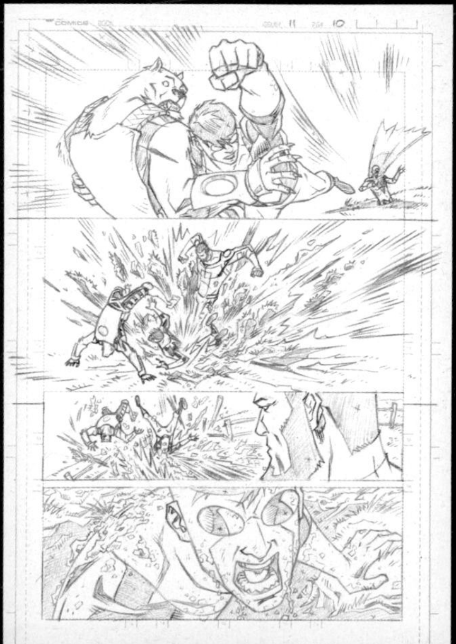

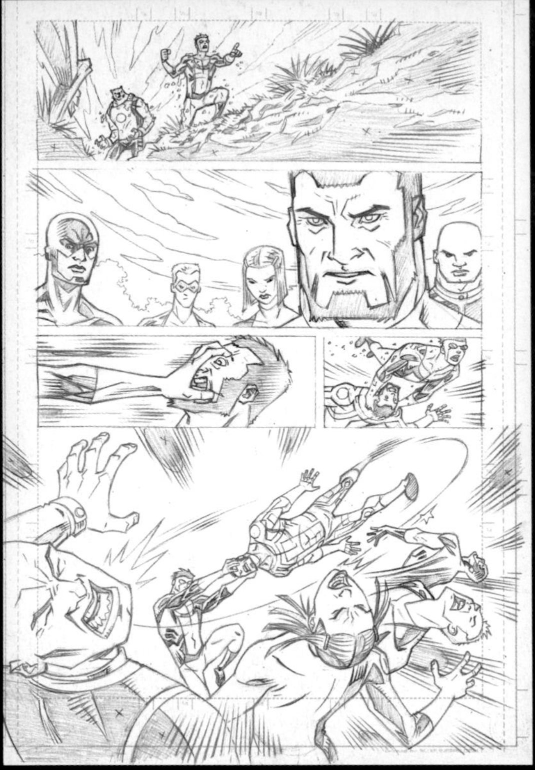

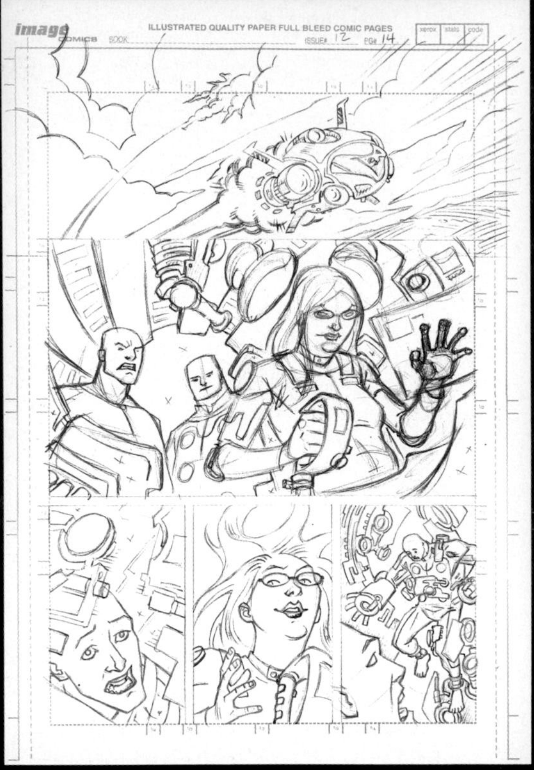
image COMICS
ILLUSTRATED QUALITY PAPER FULL BLEED COMIC PAGES
BOOK
ISSUE# 12 PG# 14
xerox stats code

KIRKMAN: Some penciled pages from 11 and 12 here. Any annoying corrections I gave you, Jason?

HOWARD: I don't think so... But I do recall an important discussion about whether Invincible should swing Immortal around by his head or by his feet in the last panel of page 11. I think head was clearly the right choice. Based on our ability to solve such key dilemmas as this, I think it is only a matter of time before Obama calls on us to tackle some of society's greater problems.

KIRKMAN: Oh, were you supposed to be on that call, too?

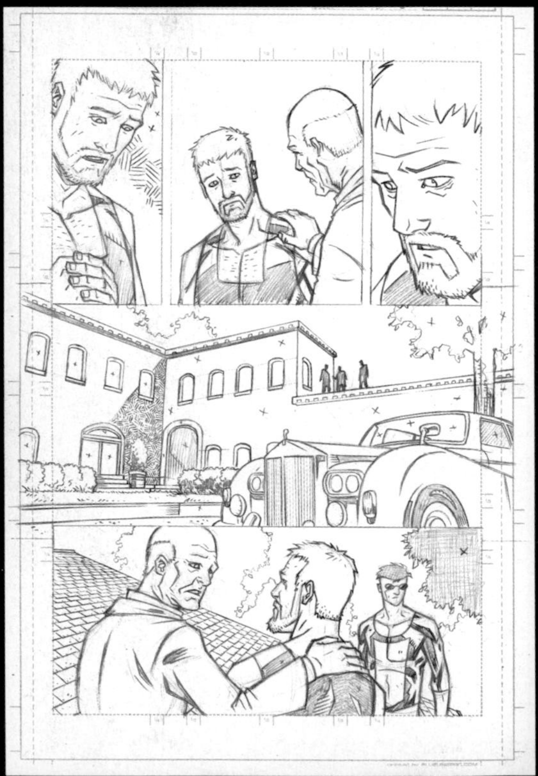

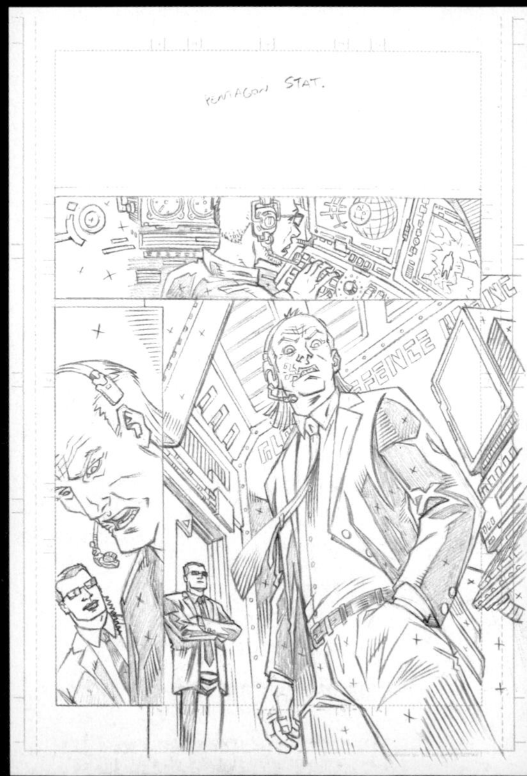
PENTAGON STAT.

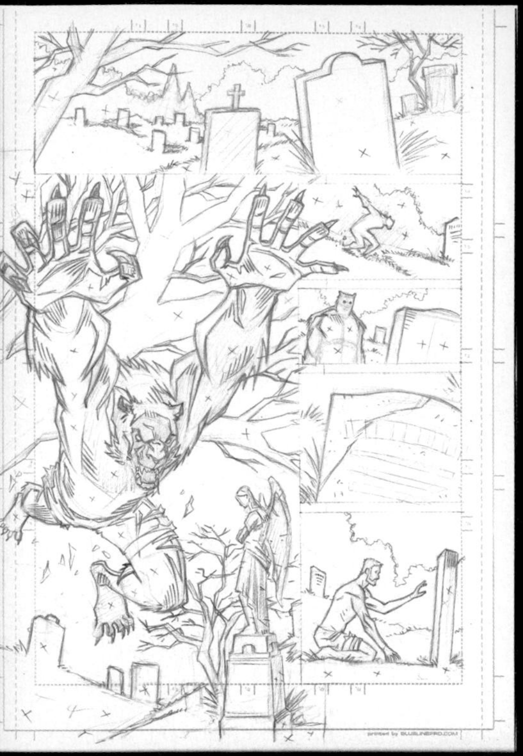

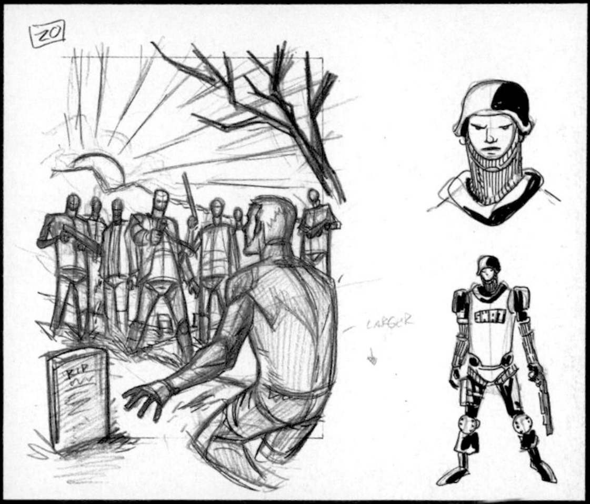

20
RIP
LARGER
SWAT

KIRKMAN: My favorite layouts are the ones with character designs in the margins. A couple from issue 12 here, along with some swat guy designs—and the first page from the Monster Pile-Up story. Hey! It looks like Hunter was originally supposed to be the other agent! When did we decide to make him the cool black guy?

HOWARD: I think he was always the cool black guy, the label is just sitting a little high. Or maybe we changed it, I can't remember.

KIRKMAN: Some help you are. And that's it from us, folks... we'll see you all back here for volume three!

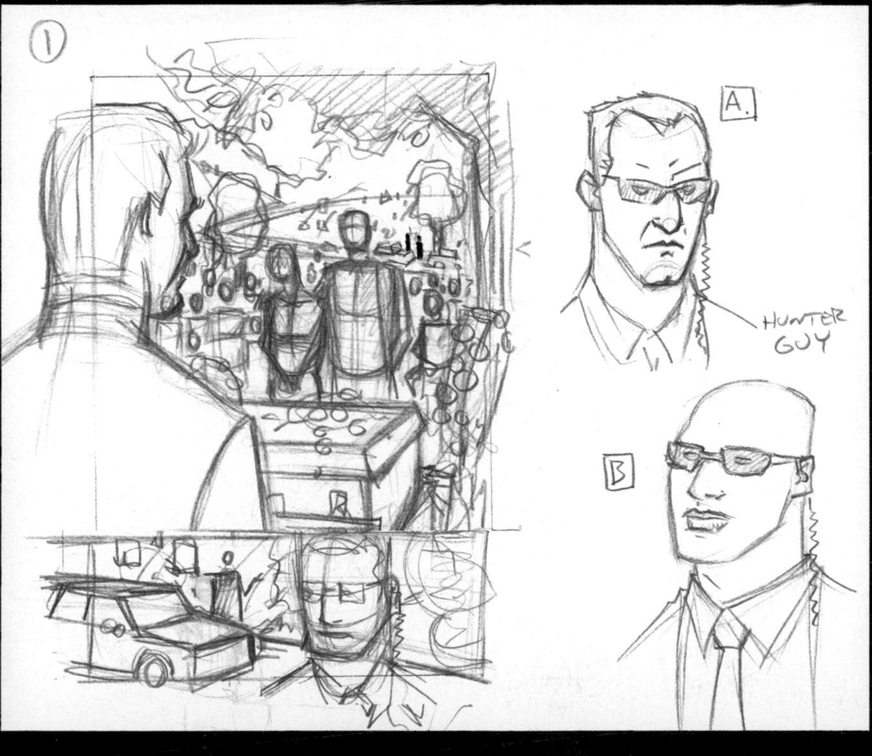

1
A.
HUNTER GUY
B

MORE GREAT BOOKS FROM
ROBERT KIRKMAN & IMAGE COMICS!

KIRKMAN · MOORE · RATHBURN · STAPLES
BRIT
VOLUME ONE: OLD SOLDIER

THE ASTOUNDING
WOLF-MAN
VOLUME ONE

THE WALKING
DEAD
HERE WE REMAIN

KIRKMAN · OTTLEY · CRABTREE
INVINCIBLE
VOLUME EIGHT
MY FAVORITE MARTIAN

KIRKMAN · MOORE · STAPLES
Battle
POPE
VOLUME FOUR
Wrath of God

THE ASTOUNDING WOLF-MAN
VOL. 1 TP
ISBN: 978-1-58240-862-0
$14.99
VOL. 2 TP
ISBN: 978-1-60706-007-9
$14.99

BATTLE POPE
VOL. 1: GENESIS TP
ISBN: 978-1-58240-572-8
$14.99
VOL. 2: MAYHEM TP
ISBN: 978-1-58240-529-2
$12.99
VOL. 3: PILLOW TALK TP
ISBN: 978-1-58240-677-0
$12.99
VOL. 4: WRATH OF GOD TP
ISBN: 978-1-58240-751-7
$9.99

BRIT
VOL. 1: OLD SOLDIER TP
ISBN: 978-1-58240-678-7
$14.99
VOL. 2: AWOL
ISBN: 978-1-58240-864-4
$14.99

CAPES
VOL. 1: PUNCHING THE CLOCK TP
ISBN: 978-1-58240-756-2
$17.99

CLOUDFALL
GRAPHIC NOVEL
$6.95

REAPER
GRAPHIC NOVEL
$6.95

TECH JACKET
VOL. 1: THE BOY FROM EARTH TP
ISBN: 978-1-58240-771-5
$14.99

TALES OF THE REALM
HARDCOVER
ISBN: 978-1-58240-426-0
$34.95
TRADE PAPERBACK
ISBN: 978-1-58240-394-6
$14.95

INVINCIBLE
VOL. 1: FAMILY MATTERS TP
ISBN: 978-1-58240-711-1
$12.99
VOL. 2: EIGHT IS ENOUGH TP
ISBN: 978-1-58240-347-2
$12.99
VOL. 3: PERFECT STRANGERS TP
ISBN: 978-1-58240-793-7
$12.99
VOL. 4: HEAD OF THE CLASS TP
ISBN: 978-1-58240-440-2
$14.95
VOL. 5: THE FACTS OF LIFE TP
ISBN: 978-1-58240-554-4
$14.99
VOL. 6: A DIFFERENT WORLD TP
ISBN: 978-1-58240-579-7
$14.99
VOL. 7: THREE'S COMPANY TP
ISBN: 978-1-58240-656-5
$14.99
VOL. 8: MY FAVORITE MARTIAN TP
ISBN: 978-1-58240-683-1
$14.99
VOL. 9: OUT OF THIS WORLD TP
ISBN: 978-1-58240-827-9
$14.99
VOL. 10: WHO'S THE BOSS TP
ISBN: 978-1-60706-013-0
$16.99
ULTIMATE COLLECTION, VOL. 1 HC
ISBN 978-1-58240-500-1
$34.95
ULTIMATE COLLECTION, VOL. 2 HC
ISBN: 978-1-58240-594-0
$34.99
ULTIMATE COLLECTION, VOL. 3 HC
ISBN: 978-1-58240-763-0
$34.99
ULTIMATE COLLECTION, VOL. 4 HC
ISBN: 978-1-58240-989-4
$34.99
THE OFFICIAL HANDBOOK OF THE INVINCIBLE UNIVERSE TP
ISBN: 978-1-58240-831-6
$12.99
THE COMPLETE INVINCIBLE LIBRARY, VOL. 1 HC
ISBN: 978-1-58240-718-0
$125.00

THE WALKING DEAD
VOL. 1: DAYS GONE BYE TP
ISBN: 978-1-58240-672-5
$9.99
VOL. 2: MILES BEHIND US TP
ISBN: 978-1-58240-413-4
$14.99
VOL. 3: SAFETY BEHIND BARS TP
ISBN: 978-1-58240-487-5
$14.99
VOL. 4: THE HEART'S DESIRE TP
ISBN: 978-1-58240-530-8
$14.99
VOL. 5: THE BEST DEFENSE TP
ISBN: 978-1-58240-612-1
$14.99
VOL. 6: THIS SORROWFUL LIFE TP
ISBN: 978-1-58240-684-8
$14.99
VOL. 7: THE CALM BEFORE TP
ISBN: 978-1-58240-828-6
$14.99
VOL. 8: MADE TO SUFFER TP
ISBN: 978-1-58240-883-5
$14.99
VOL. 9: HERE WE REMAIN TP
ISBN: 978-1-60706-022-2
$14.99
VOL. 10: THE ROAD AHEAD TP
ISBN: 978-1-60706-075-8
$14.99
BOOK ONE HC
ISBN: 978-1-58240-619-0
$29.99
BOOK TWO HC
ISBN: 978-1-58240-698-5
$29.99
BOOK THREE HC
ISBN: 978-1-58240-825-5
$29.99
BOOK FOUR HC
ISBN: 978-1-60706-000-0
$29.99
THE WALKDING DEAD DELUXE HARDCOVER, VOL. 2
SBN: 978-1-60706-029-7
$100.00

TO FIND YOUR NEAREST COMIC BOOK STORE, CALL: 1-888-COMIC-BOOK

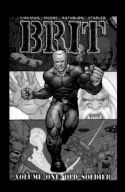

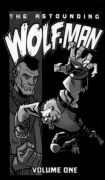

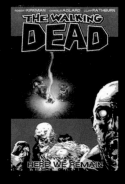

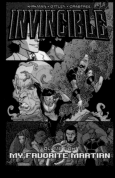

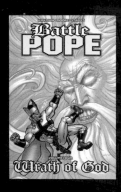